Framing Democracy

Framing Democracy

CIVIL SOCIETY AND
CIVIC MOVEMENTS IN
EASTERN EUROPE

John K. Glenn, III

Stanford University Press
Stanford, California
2001

Stanford University Press
Stanford, California
© 2001 by the Board of Trustees of the
Leland Stanford Junior University
Printed in the United States of America

Library of Congress Cataloging-in-Publication Data
Glenn, John K.
Framing democracy : civil society and civic movements in
Eastern Europe / John K. Glenn III.
    p.   cm.
Includes bibliographical references and index.
ISBN 0-8047-3861-0 (alk. paper)
    1. Democratization—Europe, Eastern.   2. Civil society—
Europe, Eastern.   3. Post-communism—Europe, Eastern.
4. Europe, Eastern—Politics and government—1989–.   I. Title.

JN96.A58 G58   2001
320.943—dc21   00-067034

This book is printed on acid-free, archival-quality paper.

Original printing 2001
Last figure below indicates year of this printing:
10   09   08   07   06   05   04   03   02   01

Designed and typeset by John Feneron in 10/13 Sabon

FOR MY PARENTS
John and Constance

Acknowledgments

This book represents the culmination of many years of travel, work, and research in Eastern Europe since my first visit to Prague in August 1989, weeks before the events that would become the "velvet revolution." Throughout, I have been enormously fortunate to have an appreciative and critical intellectual community of scholars that have supported me along the way. In its initial form, the manuscript was guided by my dissertation committee at Harvard University, chaired by Andrew G. Walder with Theda Skocpol and William A. Gamson. The material in the manuscript has benefited from the repeated feedback of many, including Michael Biggs, John L. Campbell, Grzegorz Ekiert, Benjamin Frommer, Andreas Glaeser, Jack Goldstone, Doug McAdam, Mitchell Orenstein, William Sewell, Jr., Miklos Sukosd, Roman Szporluk, Sidney Tarrow, Charles Tilly, and two anonymous readers at the Stanford University Press. Many in Poland and Czechoslovakia have offered me essential assistance, support, and guidance during my fieldwork, including Władysław Findeisen, Ivan Havel, Zuzana Jindrová and members of the Theater Institute in Prague, Juraj Kohutiar, Katrzyna Krajewska, Tomáš Kubeš, Čestmír Kubik, Władysław Kucner and members of the Archives of the Polish Senate, Milan Otáhal, Martin Palouš, Andrzej Rychard, Piotr Sztompka, and Jaroslav Veis. I am grateful to Laura Comay at Stanford University Press for her encouragement and to John Feneron for his assistance in the publication process. Special thanks go to my colleague and friend, Francesco Duina, for his tireless eye and support.

Portions of the book have also been presented at and benefited from feedback at the American Sociological Association's 1995 and 1996 annual conferences, the 1995 Eastern Sociological Association's annual conference, the 1995 European Sociological Association's annual conference, the Workshop on East European Politics at the Center for European Studies and Sawyer seminar on the performance of democracies at the Center for International Affairs at Harvard University, the Watson Seminar on Political Party Development at Brown University, and the contentious politics seminars sponsored by the Mellon Foundation and the Center for Advanced Study of Behavioral Sciences at Stanford University.

The research for this book was conducted with the assistance of funding from the Center for European Studies, Center for International Affairs and Russian Research Center at Harvard University, the Harvard Graduate Society, Kasa Josefa Mianowskiego in Warsaw, the Institute for World Politics, and the United States Department of Education. Revisions were written while I was a postdoctoral fellow at the Institute for Human Sciences in Vienna, Austria, the Institute of War and Peace Studies at Columbia University, the European University Institute in Florence, Italy, and the Vernon Center for International Affairs, New York University.

Above all, a note of grace and thanks for the support of my family and friends, without whom none of this would have been possible.

Contents

Tables and Maps

Abbreviations

CHAPTER ONE

Introduction

A T T H E C L O S E O F the twentieth century, democracy appeared to have overcome the Cold War partition of the world,
as countries across the globe deposed autocratic regimes and held
free elections. Nowhere was that dramatized more brightly than in
Eastern Europe in 1989 and the startling speed by which newly
formed civic movements replaced long-standing Leninist regimes
with democratic governments.[1] Yet today it is clear that the "waves"
of democracy that might have initially appeared to be similar have
led to different outcomes. Some countries in Eastern Europe have
been invited to join NATO and the European Union, while others
have been excluded. Whereas the democratic opposition of the
1980s has survived as a small party in countries like Poland, it has
virtually vanished from the political scene in others such as the
Czech Republic and Slovakia. Former communists were elected to
power in postcommunist Poland and Hungary, but they have been
largely absent in the Czech Republic and transformed into populists
in Slovakia. These differences compel us to re-examine how similar

---

[1] A few words on my use of terms at the outset. In this book, I use several
terms including "communism" and "Leninist regimes" interchangeably to refer to the state socialist regimes based upon the Soviet model. When speaking
of "Eastern Europe" I refer to the countries that were part of the sphere of
state socialist regimes during the Cold War era. Finally, I will refer throughout
the book to Czechoslovakia when referring to the federal state that existed until 1992 rather than the Czech and Slovak Socialist Republic or the Czech and
Slovak Federal Republic, and to the Czech Republic and Slovakia when referring to the two autonomous states formed in 1993.

the Leninist regimes and their demise actually were and raise the question, How did the way communism fell affect the founding of democratic states in Eastern Europe?

In retrospect, it is not surprising that the fall of communism was initially seen by Western observers as part of a common "wave" of democratization that had begun in the early 1970s, while Eastern European scholars emphasized the unique nature of the events in each country.[2] In the rhetoric of the Cold War, "democracy" was typically defined in opposition to "communism" and vice versa. Unlike the dictatorships of the old regimes in Latin America and Southern Europe that formed the basis for earlier theories of democratization, Leninist regimes made ideological claims that they represented a common universal model, which also helped to obscure significant differences between them. At the same time, the fascination with the unprecedented and novel nature of the fall of communism shifted attention away from analytic comparison of the processes by which communist parties across the region lost control over their governments in the face of democratic movements inspired by human rights language from earlier struggles.

This book offers a critique and reformulation of existing theories of democratization, as well as earlier understandings of the fall of communism. By contrasting the negotiated pact in Poland with the collapse of the regime in Czechoslovakia, it provides a theoretical framework to explain the impact of paths of democratization on prospects for sustainable democracy. It goes beyond a "Gorbachev" effect determining events in the late 1980s, contrasting the contingent processes of struggle by which movements contested Leninist regimes and negotiated democratic institutions. It highlights competition among challengers, reconceptualizing the notion of "civil society" as a master frame with which movements sought to mobilize

---

[2] The concept of "waves" was developed most prominently by Huntington, 1991 (see also Diamond and Plattner, 1993; Diamond et al., 1997). While the crowded field of single-country case studies in Eastern Europe is too broad for me to be exhaustive, examples include Connor et al., 1992; Gomułka and Polansky, 1990; Sanford, 1992; Szomolányi and Meseznikov, 1994; Taras, 1995; Wolchik, 1991.

popular support. It emphasizes the transformation of networks associated with the birth of the nation, such as the Catholic Church in Poland and the striking theaters in Czechoslovakia. Finally, it analyzes how paths of change structured political competition in new democracies in the short and medium term.

Before delving into the debates on democratization, it is necessary to reconstruct the uncertainty surrounding Eastern Europe in the late 1980s. Despite Gorbachev's declarations of glasnost and perestroika, few believed that communist leaders would permit change that would threaten the foundations of their authority. At best, most observers hoped for gradual reform that might someday lead to real democratic change. Although it may seem inevitable in hindsight, the paths that events would take remained uncertain. Brief sketches of the rebirth of Solidarity and the emergence of Civic Forum warn against the retrospective illusion that the fall of the Leninist regimes in Eastern Europe took place as part of an unavoidable, single burst of democratization. Even with the shift in international alliances after Gorbachev's rise to power in 1985, failed attempts at emergence by the democratic opposition in the late 1980s reveal Leninist regimes that had not lost control over the means of repression, while differences in outcomes highlight different political processes at work.

Eastern Europe in the Late 1980s

In February 1988, nearly seven years after the imposition of martial law in Poland, consumer prices were raised by as much as 40 percent, and on April 24, 1988, the workers began to strike. Strikes in Bydgoszcz were followed by strikes at the Lenin Steel Mill in Nowa Huta. On May 1, independent demonstrations were held throughout Poland, in Lodz, Cracow, Plock, Warsaw, Gdańsk, Wrocław, Bialsko-Biała, and Dabrów Gornicza. On May 2, the workers at the Gdańsk Shipyard—home of the birth of Solidarity in 1980—joined the strike, demanding an increase in salary, the indexation of wages and prices, and the reinstatement of the jobs of

Solidarity members. These strikes drew upon the repertoire of Solidarity: rather than leaving the shipyard, they occupied it and formed an interfactory strike committee. Once again the authorities surrounded the shipyard with riot police, whose movements around the shipyard were followed tensely from within. Negotiations began between the strike committee and the management, with each side shifting positions late into the night and consulting its supporters behind the scenes. The Polish Episcopate called for dialogue to solve the "crisis" facing Poland. Despite their apparent similarity to Solidarity in 1980, however, these strikes were neither organized nor fully supported by the familiar leaders of the first Solidarity. In Gdańsk, Lech Wałęsa declared, "I am not on strike, although I am not against it."[3] They were organized by a younger generation of workers, many of whom had not actually participated in the movement in 1980-81.

Even with the apparently successful mobilization for the strike, the outcome was resolved not by the strikers' demands but by use of force by the Leninist regime. On May 5, the militia entered the steel mill and broke up the workers' strike in Nowa Huta, and a strike by bus drivers in Szczeciń was similarly ended. On May 8, a group of intellectuals published a declaration that there could be no fulfillment of national aspirations without Solidarity. That night, however, the leader of the strike committee in Gdańsk announced that "neither the demands for increases in wages nor the restoration of Solidarity will be met" (Giełżyński, 1988: 3). Despite the National Coordinating Council of Solidarity's "calling upon all of Poland to come out in massive protests," the workers' chief negotiator, Siła-Nowicki, announced that all the strikers' demands had been rejected, that all they could hope for was to leave the shipyard without violence or arrest by the riot police (Giełżyński, 1988: 5). The strike had failed. At 8:08 P.M., the gates of the shipyard opened and the workers, linking arms and led by Wałęsa with Siła-Nowicki and Solidarity advisor Tadeusz Mazowiecki on either side of him, began a procession out of the shipyard. The symbols of Solidarity were

---

[3] Quoted in Stokes, 1993: 121.

everywhere. As one account illustrated:

> A cross made of planks heads the procession; behind it, the red and white of the Polish flag; the blue and white of the shipyard banner protrude from the sides; and a third flag becomes visible: *Solidarność*. . . . The final turn, and the procession stops in front of St. Brygida's Church. Throngs have gathered about the church, but a path to the door remains clear. Bells boom directly overhead. Flowers rain down. Then the doors of the church open. The bishop, His Excellence Tadeusz Goclɔwski, is there; at his side stands Father Jankowski, protector and friend of the shipyard workers. The procession fills the central nave, and the rest of the church is soon packed with the people of Gdańsk. (Giełżyński, 1988: 6)

This failure led Solidarity to announce that summer that the strikes "have also exposed the weakness of NSZZ Solidarity, weakness of its organization and of its programme."[4] Solidarity leader Wiktor Kulerski declared that the strikes, having occurred beyond the control of the union, "had completed the destruction of the myth of Solidarity as a mass movement."[5]

Only three months later, however, in August 1988, strikes broke out again in Poland. This time the workers would not be forced to leave the shipyard without an agreement. On August 15, miners in Jastrzębie went on strike and were joined on August 18 by an interfactory strike committee in Szczeciń. On August 22, the workers at the Gdańsk Shipyard declared themselves again on strike. This time, the main demand of most strike committees was for the restoration of Solidarity. Contact between the striking workers and politburo secretary Josef Czyrek was initiated, mediated by the head of the Warsaw Club of Catholic Intelligentsia, Andrzej Stelmachowski. After a series of late-night phone calls and meetings, on August 25, Stelmachowski traveled to the Gdańsk Shipyard with an offer to negotiate with the party. Declaring the situation to be "abundantly dangerous," Wałęsa suggested that a roundtable could be the first step in resolving the crisis as "a means of realizing civic principles of

---

[4] *Uncensored Poland News Bulletin*, no. 15/88 (Aug. 18, 1988): 5.
[5] Quoted in Stokes, 1993: 121.

shared responsibility for the development of the country" (Tabako, 1992: 248–49). The Catholic Church, "whose authority and role in the public life of Poland is universally recognized," would serve as an observer and guarantee the good conduct of both parties. On August 31, the shipyard gates opened and Lech Wałęsa marched out, arm in arm with Mazowiecki and Bishop Goclowski. He announced (on the eighth anniversary of the Gdańsk Accords that marked the birth of Solidarity in 1980) that Interior Minister Kiszczak had agreed to negotiations with the opposition to be held in February 1989, without preconditions concerning the issues or participants. The time had come, Wałęsa declared, for a "compromise, provided it is not a cheap deception trick but covers all aspects of real life and puts everything in good balance."[6] In the roundtable accords, the opposition agreed to participate in partially free elections by which they would run for a fixed 35 percent of seats of the Polish lower house of parliament and all the seats of a new upper house, while the government agreed to the relegalization of the Solidarity trade union. Rather than run as the Solidarity trade union, however, the opposition created a new electoral network called the Citizens' Committees of Lech Wałęsa Solidarity, most of which began their existence in Catholic Church parishes. To the surprise of participants and observers alike, Solidarity candidates won all but one of the seats for which they ran, and even more unexpectedly, the former-satellite parties defected from the government, enabling Solidarity to form its own "grand coalition" government. Consistent with the compromise agreement at the roundtable, General Jaruzelski was nominated president, and on August 20, 1989, Tadeusz Mazowiecki was named the first noncommunist prime minister in Eastern Europe since the early 1950s.

In Czechoslovakia, years of repression also suddenly gave way to mobilization and negotiation. August 21, 1989, was the twenty-first anniversary of the Warsaw Pact's invasion of Czechoslovakia. As noted, the day before, the leaders of the Solidarity movement in Poland had announced the formation of a new government led by a

[6] In *Uncensored Poland News Bulletin*, no. 20/88 (Oct. 31, 1988): 8.

noncommunist prime minister. In Prague, however, the Polish events appeared to have little effect upon the willingness of the state to repress protest. The authorities had announced that they would tolerate no observation of the anniversary and lined the streets of Prague with members of the police and workers' militia to underscore their resolve. Dissidents such as Václav Havel continued their habit of leaving Prague on major anniversaries to avoid being detained. As dusk fell, a group of around fifteen hundred demonstrators gathered in Wenceslaus Square, where they were promptly met and dispersed by the police in their riot gear. The official Prague radio reported laconically that "a group of hooligans met today in the centre of Prague and used the pretext of the anniversary for demonstrations. Police appealed for them to disperse and then restored order" (Traynor, 1989: 9).

Twelve weeks later, on November 17, the police and workers' militia once again dispersed a demonstration in Prague, this time by students commemorating the fiftieth anniversary of the murder of a student by the Nazi government in 1939. Unlike before, however, the city did not lapse back into its quiet state. The students went on strike, followed in an unusual twist by the Czech theater community, which halted its performances and opened the theaters to public discussions. Students and actors fanned out across the country calling for a general strike to be held on November 27. A new movement that called itself Civic Forum was founded on November 19, 1989, when its proclamation was read by Václav Havel in the Drama Club theater in Prague. Havel declared that the new movement "should represent a basis for all people . . . whose sole purpose is to unite people, to create . . . an atmosphere of effective pressure upon the existing government so that the government create sufficient space for a pluralistic society."[7] Civic Forum made four demands, which centered upon punishing those responsible for the repressive actions taken against the students. Eight days after this proclamation was read to the audience in this

[7] Unpublished transcript of Civic Forum press conference, November 23, 1989.

small theater, an estimated three-fourths of the country participated in a two-hour general strike. When Prime Minister Adamec
proposed a reform government on December 3, 1989, in which
members of the Communist Party maintained a majority, Civic Forum rejected it and again threatened to strike. On December 7, the
government capitulated and Adamec resigned. After two days of
hurried negotiations between the civic movements and representatives of the Leninist regime, President Gustav Husák announced
the formation of a Government of National Understanding in
which members of Civic Forum had a majority, and then he himself resigned. With the nomination of Civic Forum spokesperson
Václav Havel as president on December 30, 1989, the rapid demise of the political monopoly of the Communist Party in Czechoslovakia was completed.

The key puzzle of the events in these brief sketches is not what
triggered the rise of the civic movements. In hindsight, it is clear that
structural changes created powerful incentives to challenge vulnerable states: loss of international support from a powerful military
ally, fiscal crises, and eroding legitimacy of the old regime. Rather,
why did the fall of communism take different forms in different
countries, including pacts between states and democratic movements leading to elections in Poland (and Hungary), and mass protests leading to capitulation in Czechoslovakia (and East Germany)? In the late 1980s the Leninist regimes in Eastern Europe
controlled the military and police until the moment of their demise,
and the oppositions seemed unable to organize popular mobilization. After the Warsaw Pact's 1968 invasion of Czechoslovakia and
the imposition of martial law in Poland in 1981, the communist
parties in both those countries appeared to have underlined their
commitment to protect their authority, regardless of disapproba-
tion from the West. How was such rapid, unexpected change possible in countries where the regimes had so recently seemed so secure?

By now it is commonplace to observe that the revolutions caught
the Western political establishment by surprise (Kuran, 1991; Przeworski, 1991; Tarrow, 1991; Walder, 1994). Yet across Eastern

Europe, leaders of the civic movements, such as Wałęsa and Havel, and representatives of the old regimes, such as Jaruzelski and Adamec, were equally surprised by the speed and extent to which they found themselves negotiating the end of the monopoly over political power by the communist parties. In some ways it appeared paradoxical: in Poland, where Solidarity had nearly shaken the core of the system only eight years before, General Jaruzelski was nominated president and the Communist Party kept its presence in parliament, while in Czechoslovakia, a country infamous for its repressive regime, recently imprisoned dissidents vaulted into the government seats of their former oppressors.

How did the democratic movements—apparently unable to mobilize popular support only months before—succeed in mobilizing overwhelming support under either constrained conditions or, worse, facing the risk of repression? In light of the long-established willingness of the communist parties to defend their authority with force, why were these transformations peaceful? One of the most striking features of these events was the prominence of cultural institutions such as the Catholic Church in Poland and the theaters in Czechoslovakia. Why did the Solidarity movement organize its so-called Citizens' Committees in churches? Why would a movement ostensibly of workers rely so heavily upon religious symbols and imagery, from Lech Wałęsa's omnipresent Black Madonna lapel pin to the crucified anchors that compose the monument at the Lenin Shipyard in Gdańsk? Why would Civic Forum take for its headquarters the Magic Lantern Theater in Prague? Why choose actors and singers to speak to the crowds in Wenceslaus Square? All this raises a broader question: Under what conditions do churches and theaters serve to facilitate political dissent and mobilization against repressive states?

Finally, popular protest and mobilization alone cannot account for the actual form of reconstruction of states. Across Eastern Europe, representatives of the old regimes and the civic movements convened roundtable negotiations in which the path by which political power would be relinquished by the communist parties was agreed upon. The negotiations were extraconstitutional and un-precedented. How did both sides agree upon the terms for negotia-tion? What did it mean for the Leninist regimes, defined by their monopoly over political power, to accept as a legitimate bargaining partner an entity that challenged their claim to represent the work-ing class and the nation? How would the resulting agreements influ-ence the creation of new democratic institutions?

Paths of Democratization and
Forms of State Reconstruction

One of the central arguments of this book is that scholars must turn from comparing "transitions to democracy" to comparing dif-ferent paths of democratization that may lead to different forms of state reconstruction. That is, we should not be studying "democra-cy" as a dichotomous variable (either present or absent) but rather democratization as a continuous variable (as processes by which the relationship between the state and its citizens changes through the holding of free elections, the creation of accountable political insti-tutions, and the guaranteeing of freedom of association and the pro-tection of civil rights).[8] This book challenges the assumption that similar regimes fell in similar ways, and asks, How did the way communism fell affect the founding of democratic states in Eastern Europe?

This question must be justified. One could simply argue that there are no consequences, that the fall of communism created a blank slate or an equal starting point from which to construct de-mocracy and market capitalism. For example, Przeworski declares that although it "is true that transitions to democracy often leave institutional traces . . . these traces can be gradually wiped away" (1995: 48). If all paths lead to the same end, it doesn't matter how you get there so long as you do. Indeed, similar arguments seemed

---

[8] The debates in democratic theory are too extensive to do them all justice, but for works seeking to conceptualize democracy as a set of processes see Beetham, 1994; Dahl, 1989; Sorenson, 1993; Tilly, 1996.

to inspire the early intentions of many postcommunist advisors and actors (see Stark, 1992, for a critique of "designer capitalism"). Yet there are compelling empirical and theoretical reasons to argue otherwise. Scholars of Eastern Europe call attention to persistent differences deriving from varying legacies of the interwar period, as well as differences in "really existing socialism" (Bunce, 1999; Ekiert, 1996; Jowitt, 1998; Verdery, 1996). Further, despite the relative brevity of revolutionary moments, decisions made during revolutionary moments about future institutions can structure political competition in the short to medium term by defining who is permitted to participate in the polity and on what terms. Elster et al. argue that:

> actions and decisions which in the situation of a political revolution would be ephemeral and negligible . . . may acquire a thoroughly disproportionate relevance and exercise lopsided influence on the evolution of the new order simply because there are no forces or structures which would assign them their relative weight(lessness). (1998: 50)

Finally, the years since the fall of communism have in fact shown that there is no straightforward means by which to become a democracy, nor even a single model to imitate. Rather there are various forms of democracies, liberal and illiberal, fragile and sustainable (Collier and Levitsky, 1997; Zakaria, 1997). As others have argued, the fall of communism in Eastern Europe did not differ across countries in degree but in kind, and the path of change was consequential for the development of democracy (Stark and Bruszt, 1998; see also Linz and Stepan, 1992; Snyder and Vachudova, 1997).

I believe that scholars of Eastern Europe and of contentious politics have much to learn from each other. There is no shortage of writings about the demise of Leninist regimes in Eastern Europe, detailing a broad array of relevant factors: the loss of legitimacy of the communist parties, the increasing inability of central economies to produce basic consumer goods, the rise of international norms of human rights, leadership succession in the Soviet Union, and the rise of spaces of civic and political activity beyond the political sphere.[9] While all of these factors were doubtless important, many of the analyses lack theoretical parsimony, begin with the postcommunist period, and suffer from the attempt to generalize from single-country case studies.[10] On the other hand, the questions highlighted in the brief description of events in Poland and Czechoslovakia are familiar to scholars of comparative politics and political sociology. They are questions about how international factors influence domestic politics, how movements emerge and make challenges to states, how bargaining can create binding agreements for new institutions, and why authoritarian regimes become vulnerable to democratic challengers. Yet much of the literature on contentious politics remains limited by the assumptions of the Western parliamentary systems in which its theories were developed, such as the respect for rights of association, guarantee of civil liberties, electoral responsiveness of political representatives, and the role of the mass media as an independent watchdog upon governments.

A theoretically driven comparative analysis of paths of democratization is needed for the events in Eastern Europe not to remain the province of "area studies," and for theories of democratization and contentious politics to broaden their implicit biases toward Western parliamentary systems.[11] This book is driven therefore by two concerns. The first is to analyze in a comparative framework the consequences of the way communism fell for the founding of democratic states in Eastern Europe. I specify and compare two

[9]On the end of communism, see Banac, 1992; Brown, 1991; Chirot, 1990; Ekiert, 1996; Kubik, 1994; Kuran, 1991; Staniszkis, 1991.

[10]Reasons for this may include the initial need for descriptive information, the lack of prior training, historical understanding and language skills with which many Western social scientists came to the region in the early 1990s, as well as divisions within the earlier area studies among scholars of particular regions and countries (see Elster et al., 1996, and Bunce, 1999). Regrettably, even research designed to be comparative may rely upon parallel presentations of countries (such as Dawisha and Parrott, 1997) without elaborating theoretical insights across cases.

[11]Examples of recent theoretically driven work include Bunce, 1999; Elster et al., 1998.

mechanisms—bargaining and mobilization—by which paths of democratization are influenced under conditions of uncertainty. The second is to discuss the implications of the fall of communism for scholars of social movements, democratization, and globalization. In my analysis of the democratic challengers in Eastern Europe, I highlight the impact of political opportunity structures in creating incentives for insurgency, the transformation of pre-existing networks into resources for organizationally weak challengers, and the elaboration of framing strategies seeking to garner public support for particular paths of change.

This book makes three contributions, each of which I consider at length below in light of the existing scholarly literature. First, by comparing the responses of Leninist regimes to changes in the international arena in the late 1980s, the book goes beyond the simple explanations for the fall of communism in terms of the "Gorbachev" effect. Second, it specifies the mechanisms of mobilization and bargaining by which collective actors influence paths of democratization. And third, it redefines the notion of "civil society" as a successful framing strategy to explain how the civic movements (and not other real and potential challengers) were able to mobilize pre-existing networks on their behalf under uncertain circumstances.

BEYOND THE "GORBACHEV" EFFECT

By comparing the responses of the Leninist regimes to changes in the international arena in the 1980s, this book goes beyond an explanation for the democratic reconstruction of the state as the necessary outcome of the Soviet Union's policies of nonintervention in the domestic politics of Eastern Europe. These policies became clear on October 25, 1989, when Soviet spokesperson Gerasimov announced the replacement of the Brezhnev doctrine with the so-called Sinatra doctrine based on the song lyric, as he misquoted it: "I had it my way" (Ash, 1990b: 140). This explanation can be found from East to West. Hanak and Veis argue that the explanation for the fall of communism is simple: "The Communist regime was a regime imported and imposed. The importer was the Soviet Union. . . .

In the moment when the Bolshevik regime began to collapse in Russia, by law the empire too began to collapse" (1994: 1). Former Czech prime minister Petr Pithart would later declare: "After the Poles, the Hungarians, and the East Germans opened the gates to freedom and smashed the wall and the new power constellation was established in Moscow, it simply could not fail to be our turn. . . . Even without a riot on Národni Street on the 17th of November, the establishment would have collapsed" (1993: 756–57). Among Western social scientists, Valerie Bunce asserted: "The structure of the bloc, geographical proximity and the considerable similarities among these states in terms of regime structure, regime assets, and regime liabilities together guaranteed that every state would respond in a similar fashion to the opportunities of change provided by Gorbachev" (1992: 39–40). More hopefully, Adam Przeworski declared, "There is no place in Europe for nondemocratic politics" (1991: 190).

Comparison across countries however suggests that, while the removal of the Soviet threat was a necessary precondition, it is far from sufficient to explain the forms of democratization that took place (especially in Poland and Hungary, where the communist parties had lost their monopoly before the announcement on October 20, 1989). By analogy, to say that the French monarchy had been fatally weakened in 1789 is not to explain the outcome of the French revolution. Even when the fall of the Berlin Wall on November 9 made it clear that the Soviet Union would not intervene, it was far from clear that the Czechoslovak state that controlled the military and extensive administrative bureaucracy would surrender power peacefully. These facts highlight the need to distinguish between the domestic political opportunity structure (which did not show any signs of weakness, as the state never lost control over its military or administrative apparatus) and international polity (since the state became vulnerable in the context of increasing international isolation). Finally, as Koopmans and Statham note, shifting external opportunities cannot explain why particular movements succeed and others do not (1996). Such an approach suffers from being "contentless" in that it applies to all movements, regardless of their goals, ideologies, and discourse.

By analyzing different responses to changes in the international arena, I avoid the overgeneralized notions of "waves of democracy" (Huntington, 1991). I present detailed case studies that argue that differences across countries in Eastern Europe had consequences for the founding of democratic states that are otherwise obscured, most notably differences in the patterns of negotiation and mobilization that led to the creation of new political institutions. "Reconstruction of the state" is a concept used by scholars of revolutions (Goldstone, 1991; Skocpol, 1979) that I have chosen to define as my aim of inquiry rather than the more currently fashionable but conceptually ambiguous notions of "transition," which, as Przeworski notes, "suggests that the outcome is predetermined" (1991: 37f.; see also O'Donnell and Schmitter, 1986; Karl and Schmitter, 1991). At the same time, the literature on revolutions often fails to distinguish between the "state" (or the institutions that control the coercive monopoly within a bounded territory) and the "regime" (the actual organization of political power within the state). Thus, I distinguish between regime collapse and the reconstruction of the state, comparing forms of reconstruction as the process by which collective control over the state is transferred to new actors, involving a period of openly contested sovereignty (McAdam et al., 1996; Tilly, 1993). The concept allows for differences in the forms of reconstruction within Eastern Europe, as well as between Eastern Europe and other instances such as the demise of authoritarian states in Latin America and Southern Europe in the 1970s. [12]

The temporal clustering of the fall of communism in the late 1980s, however, rightly draws attention to the influence of changes in the international arena that affected all the countries in Eastern Europe. The earlier sketch of failed attempts at insurgency in the late 1980s demonstrate that the civic movements could not have survived repression. In my analysis of the reconstruction of the

---

[12] See the lively debates about the limits of generalizability in *Slavic Review* among Terry, 1993; Karl and Schmitter, 1991; and Bunce, 1995.

state, I draw upon the concept of *political opportunity structures*, emphasizing that movements do not emerge solely on the basis of their own efforts but are limited by the constraints of the political environment, especially by the institutions of the state (McAdam, 1982; Tarrow, 1998; Tilly, 1978). This insight has been the core contribution of structural theories of revolution (Goldstone, 1991; Skocpol, 1979, 1994). Rather than a single variable, political opportunity structures are better conceptualized as a cluster of variables that "provide incentives for collective action by affecting people's expectations for success or failure" (Tarrow, 1998: 76–77). Despite the lack of consensus in the literature, the concept has been broadly understood to refer to four features of the political environment: (1) openness or closure of the institutionalized polity; (2) stability or instability of the broad set of political alignments that typically undergird a polity; (3) presence or absence of elite allies; and (4) the state's capacity and propensity for repression (McAdam, 1996a). For comparative analysis, the causal nature of the concept must be clarified to avoid analytic ambiguity in which it becomes a variable for all external conditions that facilitate insurgency. Political opportunity structures have largely been conceptualized in two ways: as an independent variable that varies over time within countries (Jenkins and Perrow, 1977; McAdam, 1982) and as an intervening variable referring to stable features of states that vary across countries (Kitschelt, 1986; Koopmans and Duyvendak, 1995).

Further, the notion of political opportunities must be modified to explain the emergence of challengers in Leninist regimes. What is needed is a framework that distinguishes between international and domestic opportunities and between the capacity and the willingness to repress protest in nondemocratic contexts. Thus, although this book is premised on the argument that paths of democratization were consequential for the creation of democratic institutions, it does not ignore nor assume the legacy of the Leninist regimes. Rather it analyzes both similarities in Leninist regimes and variations across countries that created opportunities for change in the late 1980s. First, the concept of expanding political opportunities has tended to emphasize national state structures without accounting for the influence of international alliances that can reinforce weak or subordinate states. The authority of the Leninist regimes in East Central Europe rested upon an international political, economic, and military alliance of states sharing common political and economic structures (Misztal and Jenkins, 1995). For example, while the Czechoslovak state did not open, divide, or lose control over the repressive apparatus as the current conception of expanding opportunities might lead us to expect, it became vulnerable in light of Gorbachev's policies in the Soviet Union and the fall of the neighboring Leninist regimes, especially after the fall of the Berlin Wall in the former East Germany.

Second, attention to repression in Leninist regimes is essential, since it limited the capacity of potential challengers to create formal organizations, of the sort emphasized by social movement theory, that could offer selective incentives for participation and monitor and sanction the behavior of participants (Oberschall, 1994, 1996). By the mid-1980s, the formerly ten-million-strong Solidarity trade union could no longer mobilize its supporters for strikes in Poland. The activity of the democratic opposition in Czechoslovakia had focused on signing petitions, not organizing political movements. In a nation of fifteen million people, Charter 77 had fewer than two thousand signatories, and another petition in 1989, called "Several Sentences," had no movement or organization to organize its forty thousand signatories. Its leader, Václav Havel, was far better known in international circles than to most Czechoslovak citizens, whose primary source of information about him had been the constant defamation in the party press since 1977.

Yet we need to distinguish the state's *capacity* for repression from its *willingness* to repress protest in nondemocratic states. The current conceptualization of political opportunities assumes a Western democratic polity in which actors within and outside the polity compete to influence political decisions. An "opening" of political opportunities would therefore entail a combination of acceptance and benefits within the system (Gamson, 1990), not a fundamental breakdown of the system. In sum, political opportunity theorists rarely conceive of successful challengers actually threatening the basic institutions of a polity. By contrast, Leninist regimes are defined by the monopoly over the polity maintained by the Communist Party through a variety of mechanisms including international military pressure, state repression, and social contracts in exchange for compliance (Jowitt, 1992). Although divisions among elites may create opportunities for reformers to mobilize public support against hard-liners (as in the Prague Spring in 1968), all political claims by actors beyond the control of the Communist Party are illegal. Declining repression of independent claims upon the regime is therefore a sign of regime breakdown, rather than of expanding opportunities within the polity. Finally, the attempt to distinguish political opportunities is complicated in Leninist regimes where the polity and economy are both controlled by the Communist Party. Economic difficulties can become politicized and create incentives to challenge the state as much as realignments within the polity (Walder, 1994). In Poland and Hungary, economic crisis would play a key role in spurring negotiations that would begin the processes of change in East Central Europe.

In my analysis of the reconstruction of the state in Eastern Europe in the 1980s, I analyze changes in the structure of political opportunities over time within countries by distinguishing changes in the international arena from domestic economic crisis and the state's capacity and willingness to repress protest. The distinction between international and domestic opportunities explains how repression can deter protest at some times but make it more likely at others. Thus, while the Leninist regime never lost control over the police and military in Czechoslovakia, it was not declining but *continued* repression in a changing international context that provoked the emergence of Civic Forum and Public Against Violence.

COMPARING MECHANISMS OF CHANGE: ELITE
BARGAINING AND COLLECTIVE PROTEST

Having argued against the notion of a single Gorbachev effect in each country, I contrast paths of democratization in Eastern Europe by distinguishing two mechanisms of change: bargaining and mobilization. Since the 1980s, the democratization literature has been elaborated as a model of the process by which elites negotiate and craft democratic institutions.[13] Criticism of the emphasis on elites in this approach has taken two forms: (1) questioning the model's assumption of elite preferences; and (2) challenging the epiphenomenal role that collective actors are assigned in the process. The round-table negotiations in Eastern Europe took place in conditions that were, in the words of Jon Elster, "unique, novel and urgent" and entailed complex, strategic interaction with state authorities (1989a: 35). In such situations, Elster argues, both costs and benefits of action are uncertain, and "rational choice theory or game theory has little prescriptive or predictive power" (1996: 8). Haggard and Kaufman argue that since "these models are disconnected from economic conditions and social forces, they miss important determinants of bargaining power as well as substantive concerns that drive parties to seek or oppose democratization in the first place" (1997: 263). As Jowitt (1991) notes, the exclusive focus on elites suffers from excessive voluntarism. With the possible exception of Poland, the challengers in Eastern Europe had emerged too recently and were too underdeveloped to fit into the model's two-by-two categorization of negotiators as hard-liners and soft-liners within the regime, moderates and radicals among the challengers. Kitschelt observes that "the conventional game-theoretical approach, without sophisticated assumptions about actors' belief systems, is insufficient to arrive at substantive predictions of outcomes" (1993: 420).

Criticism of the assumption of elite preferences highlights the

[13]See Casper and Taylor, 1996; DiPalma, 1990; Karl and Schmitter, 1991; Przeworski, 1991; Welsh, 1994.

epiphenomenal role to which collective actors have been assigned. For instance, while O'Donnell and Schmitter are not inattentive to what they refer to as the "resurrection of civil society," they argue that "regardless of its intensity and of the background from which it emerges . . . popular upsurge is always ephemeral" (1986: 55). Similarly, while Linz and Stepan observe that the transition to democracy in Spain took place in a "context of heightened societal pressure for, and expectations of, change," their framework lacks the analytic tools to explain the influence of collective actors upon the elite negotiations at the center of their analysis (1992: 6). What is needed is to situate elite negotiations within the constraints created by their need to secure the conditional support of the collective actors they claim to represent. Although mass protest rarely defines new political institutions, the impact of collective action may be long-lasting when actors are admitted to the political arena as a result of protest, and new demands are articulated that shape the range of outcomes considered in negotiations. Many scholars have argued for the influence of particular collective actors upon democratization. For example, Rueschemeyer et al. insist that the possibilities for democracy rest upon "the structure of class coalitions as well as the relative power of different classes" (1992: 6). Collier and Mahoney observe that labor unions in South America and Southern Europe were "not limited to an indirect role, in which protest around workplace demands was answered through cooptive inclusion in the electoral arena. Rather, the labor movement was one of the major actors in the political opposition, explicitly demanding a democratic regime" (1997: 286). Further, Bermeo (1990) argues that transitions to democracy must include the influence of political parties responsive to the voting public.

Despite the above criticisms, however, the mechanism by which collective actors influence democratization remains unspecified. In this book I argue that demands by collective actors mobilizing public support can introduce new issues and limit the range of outcomes considered in elite negotiations. I contrast the impact of collective actors across two ideal paths varying in terms of the impetus for change: in cases of democratization "from above," when elites initiate political reforms without widespread public mobilization, the agenda for change can be limited by their need to secure the conditional support of groups they represent. Second, in cases of democratization "from below," revolutionary movements mobilizing mass support are emboldened to challenge the agenda of elites by introducing new demands. These categories are not exhaustive, but a survey of the literature on democratization reveals no consensus surrounding criteria and categories of change. For example, Huntington (1991) describes transplacement, replacement, and intervention, while Karl and Schmitter (1994) refer to pact, imposition, reform, and revolution. The two paths of democratization compared in this book are perhaps most similar to the contrast between *reforma* and *ruptura* in Linz and Stepan (1996).

This argument directs attention to agenda setting, or "the process by which demands of various groups in the population are translated into items vying for the serious attention of public officials" (Cobb et al., 1976: 126). Bachrach and Baratz (1962) argue that the ability of a group to place an issue on a government's agenda (or keep it off) is an often overlooked form of power. Current scholarship on agenda-setting in the mass media argues that it is a theory about the salience of objects and of their attributes. Thus, agenda-setting tells us more than what to think about; it tells us "how to think about it" (McCombs and Shaw, 1993: 62). As Kosicki argues, the media "do not merely keep watch over information, shuffling it here and there. Instead, they engage in active construction of the messages, emphasizing certain aspects of an issue and not others. This creates a situation in which the media add distinctive elements of public discourse, instead of merely mirroring the priorities set out by the various parties or candidates" (1993: 113). Similarly, agendas for democratization cannot be simply derived from elite interests but reflect interactions among elites seeking support from collective actors making demands on behalf of particular paths of change.

By suggesting that either the need to secure the support of collective actors or demands made by collective actors themselves can influence agendas for democratization, I am not arguing that outcomes simply reflect the symbolic content of appeals for support, but that these appeals filter the perception of choices considered in negotiations. Mobilization by collective actors can generate uncertainty and alter elite behavior in at least three ways: (1) by demonstrating that new political actors exist whose future actions might affect elite interests (by participating in future elections or by publicizing human rights abuses in the international arena, for example); (2) by threatening attacks upon elite resources or alliances that undergird previously stable patterns of elite authority (such as strikes at state enterprises, withholding of taxes, or appeals to the military for support); and (3) by threatening direct attacks on elites themselves (such as terrorist attacks or hostage-taking).[14] Mobilization strengthens the ability of collective actors to make claims upon states, yet also constrains them by limiting the range of acceptable outcomes because of the conditional nature of popular support.[15] The authority of elites in turn rests in part upon their ability to secure support from the groups they represent, including the military, political parties, the working class, revolutionary movements, or the voting public.

Claims that elite negotiators are constrained by demands from collective actors or the conditional nature of their support cannot be simply accepted at face value. They must be examined in light of the frequency of such claims, the likelihood of threats being carried out, and the impact of such constraints upon the decisions taken. Agenda-setting effects are not equally probable in every situation, nor for every issue. Saideman (1994) argues that agenda-setting matters most when leaders do not have clearly defined preferences, when there are no clear ways to achieve a preferred outcome, and when popular opinion is not strongly mobilized on behalf of a par-

[14] Thanks to Charles Tilly for his recommendations surrounding this point on an earlier draft.

[15] For recent syntheses of the literature on mobilization and social movements, see McAdam et al., 1996; and Tarrow, 1998.

ticular issue. This directs attention to the congruency between appeals to supporters and demands at the bargaining table, as well as to mechanisms by which actors can be held accountable to their members and broader constituencies. Even if direct public involvement in negotiations is low, elite choices may be constrained by future public attention to their actions.

By examining the influence of collective actors across paths of democratization, I explain variation in reconstruction of the state in terms of interactions between elite negotiators and collective actors in conditions of uncertainty and conditional public support. This argument could be falsified if it could be demonstrated that stable support for particular actors or paths of change preceded democratization or that elites imposed an agreement, such as by means of force. Further, agenda-setting would be less relevant if the same information or metaphors always arose around democratization, if there was a single, dominant attitude about paths of change, or if people's attitudes about it were integrated into a single measure. Such conditions seem unlikely given the uncertainty surrounding democratization when new actors may emerge to challenge nondemocratic states under extraconstitutional terms, nor are they likely to be the basis for generalizable theory.[16] Rather, variation in the popular support for elites, mobilization by collective actors, and consensus surrounding paths of change seem a more promising set of assumptions, which structure the arguments in the following chapters.

"CIVIL SOCIETY" AND COMPETING CHALLENGERS

By analyzing competing attempts to mobilize popular support in the wake of the weakening of Leninist regimes, I redefine the notion

[16] Prior sociological and political science research concerned with agenda-setting, primarily in the field of industrial relations and public policy, has limited application to democratization due to its assumption of interests and the institutional framework in which bargaining takes places. See, for example, Bacharach and Lawler, 1981; Kingdon, 1995.

of "civil society" as a successful framing strategy with which the democratic movements mobilized support in behalf of their aims. This departs from the widespread argument in the literature on Eastern Europe that "civil society played a key role in the overthrow of communist regimes in 1989" (Bernhard, 1996: 308). Bernhard defines civil society as composed of four critical components: a "public space . . . located between official public and private life," composed of a range of "autonomous organizations" that are "separated from the state by law" and guarantee those within civil society "personal and group liberties" that enable them to "pursue their broadly conceived interests" (1993: 309). Thus, Weigel and Butterfield argue that "expanding independent activism increasingly contradicted the legitimacy and power base of the single ruling party, leading to the end of Communist rule" (1992: 1–2). Drawing upon Habermas's conception of the public sphere, Cohen and Arato argue that the "groups, associations, and indeed movements outside the official institutions would have the primary task of pushing the reforms through" (1992: 64). Similarly Tismaneanu argues that these "nuclei of autonomous social and cultural initiative" in each country explain how "the breakthrough could result in a smooth, nonviolent change" in 1989 (1992: x, xiii).

Such explanations are limited by their monocausal logic and conceptual imprecision. They obscure the impact of the Leninist regimes as repressive agents and negotiating partners in the reconstruction of the states. These regimes were not simply overcome by political protest led by independent groups but shaped the patterns of reconstruction independently of the efforts of the movements. They cannot explain the reconstruction of the state because they lack a model to explain the interaction between states and movements that created the political institutions of postcommunist states. Further, these explanations fail to distinguish between a wide array of independent activities in Leninist regimes (from rock music to underground publishing to religious pilgrimages) with an oppositional strategy of self-organization adopted in Eastern Europe in the

1970s (Ekiert, 1991). They misunderstand the strategic nature of the discourse of civil society and the conditional nature of public support for the civic movements. For example, Cohen and Arato do not resolve Jadwiga Staniszkis's critique that the self-limiting strategy "was . . . always a purely defensive one and is not suited for real social change" (quoted in Cohen and Arato, 1992: 59).

Drawing upon the literature on contentious politics, I argue that the notion of "civil society" should be reconceptualized as a master frame with which civic movements across Eastern Europe sought to mobilize public support in light of changing political opportunities. Like Verdery, I analyze civil society and nation as "key symbolic operators, elements in ideological fields, rather than organizational realities" (1996: 105). This grounds the concept in its articulation by competing political actors seeking to influence paths of change and enables comparison of its impact across countries. To explain the success of the civic movements, I analyze competing attempts to mobilize public support by examining the congruency between claims of what should be done and potential networks of organizational resources. The focus on competing challengers highlights the limitations of the traditional case study of single movements (Giugni, 1998; Meyer and Staggenborg, 1996; Tarrow, 1998). Because outcomes can rarely be attributed to the actions of any single movement, I analyze competition among challengers by highlighting failed alternatives and counterfactuals representing other potential outcomes (Fearon, 1991). Although not all alternatives have an equal probability of success, comparison provides analytic leverage in explaining the contestation that shapes outcomes. By focusing on the claims challengers make, I do not make any assumptions that such claims represent comprehensive ideologies or rational blueprints for the future. Rather, I analyze how movements offer competing claims about injustice, identity, and agency in their attempt to mobilize networks of support.

Collective action frames are defined as strategically oriented interpretations of events by which movement activists seek to mobilize a previously quiescent group in pursuit of their aims (Snow and Benford, 1988; Snow and Benford, 1992; Snow et al., 1986). Master frames are broader models that specific movements draw upon in their struggle; they are to framing strategies as "paradigms are to finely tuned theories" (Snow and Benford, 1992: 138). They explain why and how movements frame their claims in particular ways, attempting to draw upon resonant symbols and the collective memory of previous struggle. By framing their challenge in particular ways, movement activists seek to motivate people to act by shaping what they perceive they are capable of doing and what they should do in particular circumstances. Framing strategies link participation to cognitive "schema," or shared, internalized patterns of thought and feeling that mediate between individual drives and the external environment in which those drives are pursued (D'Andrade and Strauss, 1992). Their influence, therefore, is partly informational, signaling changes in the potential for action, but also motivational, appealing for individuals to act in particular ways. Thus, framing by movement leaders operates within the latitude between their strategic aims and their moral commitments to principled beliefs as well as to those whose support they seek.

The challenge is to operationalize framing so that their claims can be compared against those of competing challengers and analyzed in light of their alignment with potential networks of support. I analyze competing framing strategies following Gamson (1992a) as three types of claims: injustice, identity, and agency. Injustice refers to moral indignation about a situation that is laden with emotion. Although Gamson acknowledges the criticisms of resource mobilization theorists that injustice may be seen as too widespread to account for collective action, he argues that the transformation of injustice into a shared grievance with a focused target of collective action cannot be taken for granted. The failure by movement activists to do so may explain the absence of movements even when structural conditions otherwise seem ripe (such as opportunities created by state breakdown). A sense of injustice must be combined with identity, which defines "us vs. them" and a sense of agency, or an awareness that change is possible and that individual action can be effective. It is this last claim, agency, that bears most directly upon the question of competing visions of what should be done.

Competing attempts to frame state breakdown, however, must be linked to the broader political environment and to organizational resources. Mobilization rarely succeeds without sufficient institutional resources that shape the ability of the movements both to deploy framing strategies and to form strategic alliances among social groups. The framing of the April strikes in Poland in 1988 or demonstrations on national anniversaries in Czechoslovakia in 1988 and 1989—no matter how resonant—could not mobilize national support when confronted with state repression. Although recent research has emphasized the influence of political opportunities upon successful framing (Diani, 1996; Gamson and Meyer, 1996; Koopmans and Duyvendak, 1995; Noonan, 1995; Oberschall, 1996; and Zuo and Benford, 1995), attention must be paid to the potential links between competing appeals for public support and networks that provide organizational advantages to challengers. This entails bargaining between social movement entrepreneurs and representatives of networks, beliefs about what is right and what is possible, and the need to maintain the conditional support of network members. Framing plays an essential role not merely by persuading individuals to join the movement under favorable opportunities but also by aligning the claims of challengers with the identities of pre-existing networks. As Friedman and McAdam note, framing typically does not create entirely new collective identities but rather "redefine[s] existing roles within established organizations as the basis of an emerging activist identity" (1992: 163). Such organizations may link previously isolated groups by fostering "the creation of social ties that encourage the recognition of commonalties on a scale considerably broader than could be expected on the basis of informal social networks alone" (Gould, 1995: 22). Thus, the mechanism by which framing links its claims to pre-existing networks is by making more likely the "attribution of similarity" between the identity of members of networks and mobilizing claims by challengers (Strang and Meyer, 1993).

Framing and agenda-setting effects are not equally probable for every person nor for every issue. Broadly speaking, Popkin argues that framing effects occur "whenever altering the formulation of a problem, or shifting the point of view of an observer, changes the information and ideas the observer will use when making a decision" (1994: 82). Thus, there are no framing effects if the same information or metaphors always arise around a given subject, if there is a single, dominant attitude about a subject, or if people's attitudes about a subject were integrated into a single measure.

By examining competing attempts to mobilize public support once the state has broken down, this book explains the outcomes of social movement challenges in light of multiple possible equilibria. These may include, among others, reform, revolution, and repression, as well as different forms of each of these outcomes. This is not an account of how revolutions result from the intentions of leaders armed with revolutionary ideologies nor a cultural explanation focusing on the elaboration of symbolic discourses by movement leaders. Rather, it is a *political* explanation for how competing challengers mobilize resources on behalf of particular visions of what should be done, given the constellation of political opportunities. By analyzing competing challengers, I stress that the eventual outcome will not be simply the result of intentional, purposive action by successful movements but of the interaction between multiple movements, the state, and the publics for whose support they compete.

This argument could be falsified if it could be demonstrated that a particular outcome was the only possible or likely outcome of state breakdown or if the outcome could be explained by features other than competition among challengers, such as external intervention. Because such conditions seem an unlikely basis for theories of contentious politics, this book highlights variation in the range of possible outcomes and in resources available to competing challengers.

Comparing Cases

By focusing on variation in the paths of democratization, this book is grounded in the comparative tradition (Goldstone, 1991; Ragin, 1987; Skocpol, 1984; Skocpol and Somers, 1980; Tilly, 1984, 1997; Weber, 1949). I compare my cases not in terms of universal laws but rather as historical concatenations of common causal processes, avoiding both overgeneralized models of change and an emphasis on the unique characteristics of particular cases. I emphasize the contingent nature of outcomes by which increasing political opportunities, patterns of mobilization, and processes of bargaining combined to lead to various forms of reconstruction of the state in Eastern Europe. In this way, I address both concerns of this book: to demonstrate the usefulness of my general theoretical framework and to illustrate how general processes vary across historical cases. The book combines, in other words, "parallel demonstrations of theory" with "contrasts of contexts" (Skocpol and Somers, 1980).

In the chapters that follow, I contrast the path of democratization from above in Poland with democratization from below in Czechoslovakia in 1989. These two countries represent cases that scholars have generally taken to represent the two major paths by which communism fell in Eastern Europe: negotiated pacts for elections in Poland and Hungary, and popular upsurge leading to the fall of the Leninist regimes in East Germany and Czechoslovakia.[17] For example, Linz and Stepan (1996) contrast the "pacted transition" in Poland with the "collapse" in Czechoslovakia (see also Bunce, 1999). Similarly, David Stark and Lazlo Bruszt (1998) analyze the paths of democratization in Poland as "compromise" and in Czechoslovakia as an instance of "capitulation."[18]

---

[17] For comparative purposes, I have excluded countries in which democratization could be said to be questionable, when the old regime maintained power through reform after 1989 (such as Bulgaria and the former Yugoslavia), as well as the violent struggle in Romania.

[18] Exceptions can be found in early analyses, which stressed presumed

In comparing two countries, I risk disappointing both quantitatively oriented scholars who might wish to see a larger sample size and historically minded scholars who might stress the unique features of countries that make comparison difficult. What such a comparison might give up in terms of hypothesis-testing or historical elaboration, I believe it gains in terms of the ability to develop and elaborate theoretical concepts to explain paths of democratization and their consequences for future developments. A purely structural comparison across countries would be problematic, since each successful attempt shaped the international opportunity structure for the later attempts in the remaining Leninist regimes. Yet while Poland may have set a precedent for the possibility of change, attention to variation in paths of democratization cautions against the idea that a Polish model was simply imitated across Eastern Europe. In the early 1980s both Poland and Czechoslovakia were Leninist regimes premised on the monopoly over the political sphere by the Communist Party and, to differing degrees, military force (imposed in Poland by its domestic forces in 1981 and in Czechoslovakia by international forces in 1968). In both cases, it appeared that the Leninist regimes were, if not permanent, unlikely to give up power without dramatic, perhaps violent, struggle. The rise of Gorbachev in the Soviet Union in 1985 created a common shift in the international political opportunity structure, yet the form of reconstruction of the state differed across countries. In Poland, Solidarity negotiated a pact with the government for partially free elections in which it won all but one of the seats it contested, enabling it to form a coalition government with the small parties formerly allied with the Communist Party; in Czechoslovakia, Civic Forum and Public Against Violence formed a Government of National Understanding after a national strike led to the capitulation of the Leninist regime.

---

similarities in outcomes to the fall of communism without attention to the different paths whereby change took place. See, for example, Huntington's categorization of both countries as instances of transplacement (1991: 276); and Karl's and Schmitter's discussion of them as cases of reform (1991).

Rather than examining only the civic movements that succeeded in forming the new governments, the appropriate units of analysis are the range of existing and potential competing challengers seeking to influence reconstruction of the state. Although I emphasize macro- and meso-level propositions, this explanation is consistent with micro-level assumptions about individual behavior of both potential participants and movement activists. I assume that movement participants are purposive individuals sensitive to the costs and benefits of collective action but expand the analysis of their decision-making to include the impact of their positions within institutions and cultural frames of meaning that argue for particular paths of action. Similarly, I examine movement activists as political entrepreneurs but examine how the construction of collective action frames, as well as the securing of material benefits, can mobilize others. In this work, these micro-level assumptions are not tested in themselves but remain assumptions from which I develop my argument.

First, I analyze the extent to which the civic movements were successful in mobilizing support in each country. Were the framing strategies of the civic movements' leaders adopted by others? Did the movements rely upon similar networks across the country? To answer these questions, I analyze the mobilizing strategies of movement leaders and their diffusion, as the process by which movements in capital cities rallied public support in the rest of the country. This process varied across countries, as movement leaders adopted different strategies in light of the opportunities they faced, the strength of pre-existing local networks, and the ethnic and social composition of the regions. Notably, local leaders rarely simply adopt the strategies of central branches, but typically adapt them to meet their needs. I explore whether the proclamations and speeches by regional and local actors correspond to the framing strategies of the center and whether they organized in a similar manner. Where possible I utilize available public opinion data. Data gathered under Leninist regimes and in dynamic times must be used with care and can be only suggestive of broad patterns or trends, as all information reported is liable to have been distorted for several reasons (CBOS, 1994; Mason, 1985; Vaněk, 1994). Individuals under Leninist regimes were unlikely to reveal their true attitudes to regime pollsters in light of fears of penalty and mistrust in the preservation of their anonymity. These regimes controlled the media and kept these polls secret, raising problems of the manipulation of information. Differences across countries must be noted as well: while documents from the Polish Central Committee (Perzkowski, 1994) suggest that the Polish regime undertook regular surveys and utilized this information in its debates, there is little indication that the Czechoslovak leadership was informed by or considered available public opinion data (Vaněk, 1994).

Second, did the framing strategies of the civic movements in Poland and Czechoslovakia exclude the efforts of plausible alternatives? Were there competing groups with different framing strategies that failed to mobilize others and influence the outcome? To answer these questions, I analyze the efforts of competing challengers to mobilize support, contrasting their claims concerning injustice, identity, and agency, as well as the potential networks available to them. I explain failed attempts in terms of their articulation with existing opportunities and, critically, the ability to link their claims to pre-existing networks. By contrasting the failed efforts of smaller groups with the successes of Solidarity in Poland and Civic Forum/Public Against Violence in Czechoslovakia, I demonstrate the mechanism by which challengers gain access to organizational resources under repressive and uncertain conditions by transforming pre-existing networks into local branches of the movement.

Third, I analyze the ability of competing groups to influence agenda-setting processes in negotiations between challengers and the state. How and why did the terms of negotiations change during the bargaining process? Were the Leninist regimes or challengers able to influence the agenda in negotiations so that the agreements in negotiations were more likely to be favorable to them? What were the constraints upon participants that shaped the definition of an acceptable agreement? To answer these questions, I analyze the transcripts and accounts of negotiations between the Leninist regimes and civic movements. I analyze the expectations of the participants at the outset of negotiations and explore whether the outcomes reflect these expectations. If not, I identify turning points in setting the agenda and ask why particular groups were able to make and support particular claims. In particular, I examine the constraints framing strategies in filtering the perception of choices considered that would maintain or risk conditional popular support. In the case studies of Poland and Czechoslovakia, I contrast variation in the aim of roundtable negotiations: whereas the roundtable negotiations in Poland initially focused on recognition of the democratic opposition in exchange for acceptance of the economic policies of the Leninist regime, the negotiations in Czechoslovakia primarily concerned personnel changes in state institutions, namely those associated with the policies of normalization after the Warsaw Pact invasion of 1968.

Finally, I extend the book's analysis into the early 1990s to demonstrate the consequences of the paths of democratization in each country for sustainable democracy. Although a complete account of postcommunist politics is beyond the scope of this book, I analyze the consequences of these patterns of bargaining and mobilization upon political competition within new democratic institutions. I highlight attempts by the new governments to maintain the unity of the civil society master frame that had been so important in mobilizing initial support and analyze the results of free and fair elections. I contrast the dissolution of Solidarity through political competition surrounding the legacy of the roundtable agreement in Poland with the stability in Czechoslovakia premised on an ambiguous relationship between the two republics that composed the federation. Analyzing the first fully free elections and breakup of the civic movements into parties suggests that not only was "civil society" not an empirical reality to be measured across countries when explaining the fall of communism but it was also not a political program for the future.

The materials for this book come from five principal sources: (1)

internal documents of the movements and states collected in archives; (2) interviews with participants in these events; (3) public proclamations and statements by competing movements and the Leninist regimes published in the media and primary literature; (4) national data on the economic, political, and social situation in each country, including public opinion polls; and (5) the existing secondary literature on the events in Eastern Europe. Although I rely heavily upon primary sources and original language materials gathered from field research between 1992 and 1997, I utilize sources translated into English wherever possible for the benefit of readers unfamiliar with the languages of the region.

Outline of the Book

The comparative strategy discussed above suggests the following outline for the rest of the book. In Chapter 2, I contrast changes in the international political opportunity structure with variation in domestic opportunities. I examine the differing responses by the Leninist regimes in Poland and Czechoslovakia to changes in the international political environment, in light of economic crisis, and to their willingness to maintain order through repression. I discuss and elaborate what I refer to as the "civil society" master frame across Eastern Europe. By demonstrating the way that international and national political opportunities constrained but did not determine the outcomes of challenges, I demonstrate the limitations of alternative explanations.

Chapters 3 through 6 are case studies of Poland and Czechoslovakia, explaining the mobilization of support and the agenda-setting influence of framing strategies. Chapter 3 analyzes the negotiations at the Polish roundtable, culminating in an agreement for partially free elections, while Chapter 4 examines the pacted resolution in Poland, concluding with the formation of the Solidarity-led coalition government. Chapter 5 discusses the mobilization of Civic Forum and Public Against Violence in Czechoslovakia, culminating in the general strike, while Chapter 6 examines the formation of the

Government of National Understanding and the nomination of Václav Havel as president.

In Chapter 7, I conclude by reviewing the puzzle that drives the book and presenting its major findings. I observe the implications of the civil society master frame for democratic political competition in free elections in each country. In Poland, I analyze the competition for the presidency in 1990; in Czechoslovakia, I focus on the plebiscite elections that gave Civic Forum and Public Against Violence democratic legitimacy. I conclude by discussing the implications of this work for theories of contentious politics and suggest lines of inquiry that could further elaborate the argument of the book. Finally, for readers less familiar with the history of Eastern Europe, the Appendix includes a chronology of major events from 1968 through 1991.

CHAPTER TWO

Political Opportunities and Master Frames

> In this situation, no attempt at revolt could ever hope to set up
> even a minimum of resonance in the rest of society.
>
> —Václav Havel in 1977[1]

THIS BOOK ARGUES that paths of democratization varied across countries in ways that were consequential for the founding of new political institutions. It does not, however, suppose that these processes emerged out of nothing, nor that the legacies of communism were irrelevant. On the contrary, it analyzes similarities that derive from the institutions of Leninist regimes and common positions in the international sphere, as well as differences in "really existing socialism" that shaped the paths of democratization. In short, the fall of the Leninist regimes across Eastern Europe was the result of "both short-term crises and long-term developments" (Bunce, 1999: 11). In Poland, the regime sought to take advantage of Gorbachev's policies of perestroika by reforming itself to escape from fiscal crisis; its attempts at limited reform and repression of strikes however led to political stalemate in which neither the regime nor the democratic opposition appeared capable of mobilizing support. In Czechoslovakia, the policy of repression of all independent activity begun after the Warsaw Pact invasion in 1968 continued, but the regime became vulnerable in light of its increasing isolation with the fall of neighboring Leninist regimes. In both countries, failed attempts at insurgency by the democratic opposi-

---

[1] Havel 1991: 183.

tion prove that the Leninist regimes maintained their capacity for repression while the democratic opposition remained unable to mobilize support unilaterally. In light of scholarship on Eastern Europe concerned with the democratic opposition, I redefine the notion of "civil society" as a master frame that emerged across Eastern Europe in the 1970s and shaped the claims made by the democratic opposition in the late 1980s. In so doing, I demonstrate that the breakdown of the Leninist regimes is a necessary but not sufficient condition to explain the founding of democratic states.

In contrast to the case studies, this chapter is explicitly comparative. Returning to the concept of political opportunity structures discussed in the first chapter, I distinguish changing international opportunities faced by Poland and Czechoslovakia from their differing domestic responses in light of state capacity and willingness for repression. I highlight the emergence of what I refer to as the "civil society" master frame and its use by different forms of democratic opposition in each country.

Changing International Opportunities
in the Late 1980s

Any observer of Eastern Europe in the 1980s must note the key change in the political opportunity structure across Eastern Europe: the policies of perestroika and nonintervention initiated by Mikhail Gorbachev after becoming general secretary of the Communist Party of the Soviet Union in 1985. Yet the existing literature has tended to define political opportunities in terms of the features of nation states without accounting for the influence of international alliances that can reinforce weak or subordinate regimes. The authority of the Leninist regimes in East Central Europe rested upon an international political, economic, and military alliance of states sharing common political and economic structures (Misztal and Jenkins, 1995). As Barrington Moore observed, the international environment plays a decisive role in the actions of small states, since they are in part dependent upon the support of their larger neighbors (1966: xii–xiii). Most prominently, in 1956 in Hungary and 1968 in Czechoslovakia, the Soviet Union had demonstrated its willingness to intervene in the domestic politics of Eastern Europe if the leaders of the Leninist regimes were unable or unwilling to adhere to Soviet policy.

Gorbachev, it must be stressed, did not see himself (in the language of political opportunities) as an external ally to the democratic opposition. On the contrary, he believed himself to be an ally of party reformers who would undertake perestroika-inspired reforms to strengthen socialism. Notably, Gorbachev identified his aim not as revolution but to "complete the creation of a socialist state based on the rule of law."[2] These policies were explicitly driven by a new pragmatism and awareness of economic problems facing the Soviet Union. Initially, his policy of glasnost was driven by the belief that "the people" should have an increased voice in how society is run through open discussion of the current problems, culminating with the release of Andrei Sakharov, the dissident scientist, from exile outside of Moscow in 1986. By 1988, Gorbachev had concluded that political reform was needed to bypass the state bureaucracy, which was blocking economic reform. To that end, he created a new Congress of People's Deputies, which was to be elected by secret ballot in open elections. On May 25, 1989, the elected members of this congress held its first session, which was televised nationally with dramatic fanfare.

The encouragement of country-specific reform within the Warsaw Pact—although aimed at promoting party-driven reform rather than the democratic opposition—seriously weakened the likelihood of repression by the Warsaw Pact armies and shifted the concern to whether national armies and militias would be deployed against domestic political protest. The policies of perestroika and glasnost were accompanied by declarations that the Soviet Union would not interfere in the processes of change in Eastern European countries. This culminated on October 25, 1989, with Soviet spokesperson Gennady Gerasimov's announcement of the replacement of the

[2] Quoted in Stokes, 1993: 73.

Brezhnev doctrine with the so-called Sinatra doctrine, based on the song lyric, as he misquoted it: "I had it my way" (Ash, 1990b: 140). Despite the boldness of Gorbachev's policies at the time, the latitude for permissible change remained unclear. Gail Stokes observed, "Ever since Khrushchev had apologized to Yugoslavia in 1955, Soviet and East European leaders alike, albeit in different contexts and with different meanings, had claimed that each socialist state was free to pursue socialism in its own way" (1993: 73). Even in the 1980s Gorbachev's pronouncements were often accompanied by statements about the harmonization of initiatives between the Soviet Union and Warsaw Pact countries. The limits of change appeared to be clear in his speech to the Polish parliament in 1986: "To threaten the socialist system . . . means to encroach not only on the will of the people, but on the entire postwar arrangement and, in the last analysis, peace."[3] Below, I examine differences in the impact of the policies of perestroika and nonintervention upon perceptions of the vulnerability of the Leninist regimes in Poland and Czechoslovakia.

Differing Domestic Opportunities

In Chapter 1, I argued that the influence of changes in international alliances should be distinguished from that of domestic political opportunity structures, including the capacity and propensity for repression and economic crisis since the Leninist regimes also managed their economies through central planning (Campbell, 1996; Walder, 1994). I analyze the impact of changing political opportunities in Poland and Czechoslovakia in the late 1980s upon the perception of vulnerability of the Leninist regimes.

THE POLITICAL STALEMATE IN POLAND

In the context of perestroika, the Polish regime sought to maintain the initiative on political and economic reform through a policy

[3] Quoted in ibid.

of "consultative democracy," based in the vague notion that the authorities should consult society in their political decision-making. As General Jaruzelski declared, "[P]erestroika . . . helps us in our work."[4] The first such attempt had been in 1982, with the creation of the Patriotic Front for National Revival (*Patriotyczny Ruch Odrodzenia Narodowego*, hereafter referred to by its Polish acronym, PRON). Upon the constitutional amendments of July 1983, it became the official organization "for uniting the patriotic forces of the nation . . . and for the cooperation of political parties, organizations, social associations, and citizens."[5] This organization was notably to be implemented within the organized framework of legal social structures by the authorities and representatives of the party, minor parties, trade unions, youth organizations, associations, and others. Participation by Solidarity was forbidden on the grounds that they represented those who did not accept the legal framework of the Polish People's Republic. The failure of PRON to gather social support was clear even to the government itself. A government poll in 1984 found that only 23.6 percent of respondents voiced trust in PRON, compared to 30.8 percent for the government, and 91.5 percent for the Church (CBOS, 1994: 108).

A second failed attempt at limited inclusion beyond the party structures emerged in 1986 with the proposal for a Social Consultative Council. This was to be, in language consistent with Gorbachev's policy of glasnost, "an open, unrestrained exchange of views on the most vital issues for the people and the state."[6] Despite the announcement of a general amnesty for political prisoners earlier in 1986, most Solidarity figures and intellectuals refused to participate, considering it too small a concession without broader change. Still, the council generated tremendous interest and concern among the opposition. Was this the opening they had been waiting for, or was it just another attempt by the regime to gain legitimacy without making any real change? To address this question, the Club

---

[4] Quoted in Perzkowski, 1994: 6.
[5] Quoted in Stokes, 1993: 110.
[6] *Uncensored Poland News Bulletin*, no. 23–24/86 (Dec. 25, 1986): 12.

of Catholic Intelligentsia in Warsaw held a meeting on how to respond to the offer and decided in favor of nonparticipation. Club chairman Święcicki decided to join as a private citizen, resigning his chairmanship, despite Adam Strzembosz's warning that "they do not need you either as a person or as a scientist, they want you only as our chairman."[7] Despite meetings whose published proceedings indicate discussion more open than had been previously permitted, the Consultative Council remained ineffective without the participation of Solidarity or agreement for political reform.

In the late 1980s it appeared that Gorbachev's policies would benefit the Polish regime by providing it with the opportunity to implement economic and political reforms and thereby secure its leading position in the face of continuing economic problems. The impact of economic sanctions imposed against Poland after martial law contributed to a failing economy that made it difficult for the regime to maintain its repressive rule. To demonstrate his commitment to economic reform, Jaruzelski appointed Zbigniew Messner as the new prime minister on November 6, 1985. Messner was intended to be a technocrat-politician who would implement economic reform rather than socialist ideology. The final economic program agreed upon in 1987 called for a shift of trade away from the Soviet Union, expanded the possibilities of joint ventures, and, for the first time, permitted the founding of private firms with a limited number of employees. Despite the government's claim to have attempted economic reform influenced by the Hungarian experience, economic performance reached crisis proportions in the late 1980s. After a government attempt to realign prices by administratively raising the price of energy and some food products, inflation, having remained at 20 percent until 1987, shot to 60 percent in 1988 and 150 percent in the first half of 1989 alone. External outstanding debt reached 55 percent of GDP, with interest owed on the debt at another 5 percent. Basic foodstuffs such as sugar and flour were scarce in the retail market, and the standard of living fell (World Bank, 1990: 1–9).

[7] In ibid.: 18.

Economic difficulties drove the regime to seek public support for its policies, but it proved unsuccessful. In 1987, the regime announced that it would hold a referendum on the planned Second Stage of Economic Reform, designed to create public support for its policies. The referendum asked if voters supported "radical economic reform" and favored "deep democratization." Although Solidarity naturally supported both and could hardly ask voters to vote against them, it eventually advised people simply to ignore the referendum. On November 30, the party surprised the country when it announced that although 68 percent of the electorate voted and almost two-thirds of them voted yes, the positive votes came to only 44 and 46 percent for the two questions, so that the government had lost, falling 5 percent short of approval by a majority of voters. This announcement, in contrast to the government's willingness to declare victory in earlier elections, shaped the perception that the government would no longer even pretend to have the support of the public for its economic policies

Even given changes in the international environment and fiscal crisis in Poland, the opportunities for insurgency were constrained by the regime's capacity and propensity for repression. In the late 1980s a political impasse emerged whereby neither the regime nor the opposition could mobilize public support unilaterally. Martial law had demonstrated the regime's ability to repress challengers and deny the opposition the opportunity to participate within the public political sphere: leaders of the opposition were arrested, independent meetings were forbidden, and the military and police were active in the surveillance of the population. Striking miners at the Wujek mine were shot. General Jaruzelski characterized himself as a Polish patriot, forestalling Soviet intervention, although the available information suggests that the Soviets had decided against such an invasion before martial law was imposed.[8] Even with

---

[8] With the end of the Cold War and the opening of formerly secret archives, new information has come to light surrounding Jaruzelski's decision and considerable debate about whether his interpretation is fair or accurate. Information and documents concerning this question can be found at the

changes in the international political opportunity structures in the late 1980s, the regime maintained its capacity and propensity for repression. In 1984, the repressive potential of the regime was made starkly clear when a popular priest associated with Solidarity, Father Jerzy Popiełuszko, was abducted and murdered. Although it is generally believed that his murder was part of a plot by hard-line elements within the regime (referred to as the Concretes) to discredit the top leadership, it demonstrated the apparent willingness of some conservative parts of the regime to defend their interests against reform efforts. Demonstrations on the anniversary of martial law in Gdańsk and Cracow were broken up by the militia in 1987, as were demonstrations commemorating the March 1968 events in 1988. By 1987 the historian of Solidarity, Jerzy Holzer, commented: "Seven years on from August . . . [in] Poland the cards are held by General Jaruzelski and his team. Ever since violence became the decisive factor, the opposition has been unable to put forward any detailed programme or indeed respond to the authorities in any other way than by pressuring them towards slight modifications in their decisions" (1987: 4).

After martial law, on the principle of decentralized activity, an Interim Coordinating Committee (*Tymczasowa Komisja Koordynacyjna*, hereafter referred to by its Polish acronym, TKK) was founded by members of Solidarity who had escaped capture, led by Zbigniew Bujak. Facing the repressive policies of the regime, the TKK was notably unable to coordinate the activities of the workers it claimed to represent. Prior to a strike planned for October 10, 1982, the TKK announced its postponement on the basis of public opinion polls in industrial enterprises that "suggested that there was absolutely no question of a general strike in response to the dissolution of Solidarity."[9] The inability of the TKK to control the country became clear when Gdańsk went on strike anyway and was

---

Document Library of the Cold War International History Project at the Woodrow Wilson International Center for Scholars, available on the Internet at http: //cwihp.si.edu.

[9] Quoted in Łopiński et al., 1990: 176.

crushed. In Bujak's words, this showed that the leadership wasn't "equal to the task, and this led to the demobilization of the broader population."[10]

The Soviet Union's policies of nonintervention were ambiguous in their influence on the perception of the vulnerability of the regime in Poland, whose roundtable negotiations preceded the announcement of the Sinatra doctrine. Solidarity advisor Michnik insisted, "All the changes taking place are designed to maintain or modernize its empire. Gorbachev is not a man fighting for freedom. He instead wishes to make the Soviet Union more powerful" (1988: 24). Similarly, General Jaruzelski declared, "[T]he presence of Gorbachev makes our situation easier, because it underlines the correctness of our path of reform."[11] By 1988, Lawrence Weschler argued that "the regime became convinced that, for all intents and purposes, it had won, that after over six years of sometimes withering repression, it had outlasted Solidarity and achieved a sullen acceptance on the part of the body politic, or at least it had succeeded in enforcing an apathetic resignation."[12] This seemed to be confirmed in April 1988, when strikes burst out but failed to lead to wider mobilization (as observed in Chapter 1). These strikes were neither organized nor led by the Solidarity figures of 1980–81, but independently by younger, so-called radical workers in the factories. On May 5, 1988, the riot police broke up the strike in the Lenin Steel Mill in Nowa Huta. Despite the Solidarity National Coordinating Council's call for "all of Poland to come out in massive protests," the strike in the Gdańsk Shipyard ended on May 10 without agreement from the authorities (Giełżyński, 1988: 5). The statement on the ending of the strike in Gdańsk declared:

> The country is steeped in crisis. The economy is dying. The Polish masses cannot see any life opportunities in their own country. The

[10] Quoted in ibid.: 179.

[11] Quoted in "After the elections," in *Uncensored Poland News Bulletin*, no. 10/11 (June 1989): 21.

[12] Quoted in Łopiński et al., 1990: 259.

state continues to be treated by those who rule as their own property. If this state of affairs is allowed to continue it will lead to a national catastrophe. . . . The ending of the strike without agreements is witness to the fact that Poland's political, social and economic paralysis continues, that the crisis is going to get worse and the solution to it still lies ahead of us.[13]

In a statement by the Leadership of the Mazowsze (Warsaw) Region to Members of Solidarity, the leaders argued that the failure of the strikes "exposed the weakness of NSZZ Solidarity, weakness of its organization and of its programme."[14]

CZECHOSLOVAKIA: CONTINUED REPRESSION
IN LIGHT OF INTERNATIONAL VULNERABILITY

In contrast to the new initiatives by the regime in Poland, the Leninist regime in Czechoslovakia maintained its policy known as "normalization," begun after the Warsaw Pact invasion in 1968, which entailed a two-pronged policy of repression of public dissent and of buying off the population with material benefits without modifying the command economy or the party's dominant position (Otáhal et al., 1993; Šimečka, 1984). The repression of public dissent began with the party purges following 1968, which were estimated to involve 10 percent of the entire population (Ash, 1990b: 63). Consistent with perestroika, there were changes in the Czechoslovak leadership of the state and party in the 1980s, but the new leaders were as conservative as their predecessors. General Secretary Milos Jakeš declared to the Western press on the twentieth anniversary of the 1968 Warsaw Pact invasion that the party "must retain control over developments" (1988: 42). Václav Havel declared: "While Gorbachev is certainly a more enlightened ruler than his predecessors, and Jakeš is doing his best to verbally imitate Gor-

---

[13] In "Statement on the Ending of the Strike at the Lenin Shipyard in Gdansk, 10 May 1988," *Uncensored Poland News Bulletin,* no. 9/88 (May 16, 1988): 19.
[14] Quoted in ibid., no. 15/88 (Aug. 18, 1988): 5.

bachev, talking about would-be restructuring and democratization for his country as well, these two men have, in fact, changed our lives very little" (1988a: 27).

In return for political obedience, the government provided a relative degree of economic comfort and security for its citizens, described by some as a socialist consumer society. Unlike other East European countries, Czechoslovakia did not suffer from drastic food shortages, nor build up a Western debt. Timothy Garton Ash has described this "deal" as if the government were saying to its people:

> Forget 1968. Forget your democratic traditions. Forget that you were once citizens with rights and duties. Forget politics. In return we will give you a comfortable, safe life. There'll be plenty of food in the shops and cheap beer in the pubs. You may afford a car and even a little country cottage—and you won't have to work competitively. We don't ask you to believe in us or our fatuous ideology. By all means listen to the Voice of America and watch Austrian television (*sotto voce*: So do we). All we ask is that you will outwardly and publicly conform: join in the ritual "elections," vote the prescribed way in the "trade union" meetings, enroll your children in the "socialist" youth organization. Keep your mind to yourself. (1990b: 62)

The ability of the regime to buy off the population rested on the absence of fiscal crisis. Inflation averaged less than 2 percent from 1980 to 1989, hard currency debt was only 15 percent of GDP in 1989 (taking into account reserves and claims on developing countries, the net position was close to zero), and basic consumer goods remained available and affordable (OECD, 1991: 28). Relative to the economic crises of their Polish and Hungarian neighbors, Czechs and Slovaks could reasonably view themselves as luckier. Even in Czechoslovakia, however, economic difficulties persisted into the 1980s, and national income showed a constant downward trend after 1969 (Turek, 1995: 17).

In the absence of fiscal crisis, there was little change in the political opportunity structure in Czechoslovakia. Havel's essay "The Power of the Powerless" explains the difficulties of political resistance in a system that provided powerful economic incentives for its maintenance. He describes the average citizen as someone who is not outside the system but divided within by his loyalties to the system and his personal feelings about what the system demands from him. In this situation, as noted in Chapter 1, Havel argued that

> no attempt at revolt could ever hope to set up even a minimum of resonance in the rest of society. . . . It would interpret the revolt as an attack upon itself and, rather than supporting the revolt, it would very probably react by intensifying its bias toward the system, since, in its view, the system can at least guarantee a certain quasi-legality. (1991: 183)

In this way, Czechs and Slovaks had a strong interest in maintaining the system, which appeared to continue to provide for their basic needs. As late as June 1989, a former Charter 77 spokesperson wrote that "the time is not ripe for a slowly awakening society to respond more forcefully to the current situation in an attempt to change it" (Ruml, 1989: 38).

Gorbachev's policies appeared to have little to no impact upon the Czechoslovak regime's determination to repress all independent petitions and new political movements. Demonstrators in Prague expressing their support for Gorbachev were greeted with force by the security forces and, in the process, Gorbachev's portrait was demolished (Wheaton and Kavan, 1992: 28). The policies of repression are best illustrated by the immediate and harsh response to Charter 77, accompanied by arrests and interrogations at random of its signatories. The reaction in *Rude Pravo*, the communist daily newspaper, which described Charter 77 as "a group of people from the class of the bankrupt Czechoslovak reactionary bourgeoisie and also from the class of bankrupt organizers of the 1968 counterrevolution delivered to Western agents as instructed by anti-Communist and Zionist headquarters," is remarkable for its vitriol:

> It is a case of antigovernmental, antisocialist, antipopulist, and demagogic libel, which coarsely and deceitfully slanders the Czechoslovak Socialist Republic and the revolutionary achievement of the people. Its authors fault our society because life here does not suit their bourgeois and elitist ideas.

These pretenders who despise the people, the people's interests, and the people's chosen representative bodies arrogate to themselves the right to represent our people. They ask for "dialogue with the political and state authorities," and even want to play the role of some kind of "mediator in various conflict situations." The pamphlet mentions the existence of socialism in only one instance—in the name of the republic. It comes out of a cosmopolitan position, out of the class position of the overthrown reactionary bourgeoisie, and rejects socialism as a social system. . . . They are concerned with certain "rights and freedoms" that would enable them once again to freely organize antistate and antiparty activities, propagate anti-Sovietism, and try again to destroy the power of the socialist state. . . . This time the bourgeois agents have been indiscreet, and they refer to several names with which the reactionary pamphlet is connected. In a political sense, it is a jolly ragbag of human and political castaways. Among them are V. Havel, a man from a family of millionaires and a confirmed anti-socialist. . . . Socialism, however, is not frightened by atomic blackmail and is surely no coward before the scribblers of reactionary pamphlets.[15]

The regime indicated its willingness to use force, and the philosopher Jan Patočka died after one series of interrogations. Its emergence even led the regime to publish that same year a so-called anti-charter whose signature was used by the regime as evidence of loyalty. Charter 77's signatories (subject to arrest and persecution by the authorities) remained a very small minority of the population until November 1989, with only 1,886 signatures (out of a nation of fifteen million) (Skilling, 1989).

In the late 1980s new petitions and demonstrations appeared in Czechoslovakia, but they were greeted with silence at best and repression at worst. Protests by comparatively small numbers of people began to take place on historical anniversaries in Czechoslovak history: August 21, the anniversary of the Warsaw Pact invasion in 1968, and October 28, the anniversary of the founding of the Czechoslovak state. Table 1 lists the demonstrations and number of participants.

[15] Quoted in Kriseová, 1993: 122–24.

TABLE I

Demonstrations in Prague in 1988–89

Date	Number of participants	
	Czechoslovak media	Radio Free Europe
1988		
August 21	4,000	10,000
September 24	100	several hundred
October 28	2,000	5,000
1989		
January 15	300	5,000
January 18	1,000	5,000
August 21	2,000	5,000–10,000
October 28	3,000	10,000–20,000

SOURCE: Tuma, 1994: 27.

As the table indicates, participation remained small, and, with the exception of December 10, 1988, repression by the regime continued. Debates emerged within the opposition about whether it should organize protests, with Havel refusing to endorse calls for protest on behalf of Charter 77. These protests included the events referred to as Palach Week, which took place from January 15 through 19, 1989, in Prague. Timed to coincide with the Vienna Conference on Security and Cooperation in Europe, all but one of these demonstrations were dispersed by police units in riot gear using police dogs and water cannons and led to the virtual closing down of the center of Prague. Some 1,920 people were temporarily detained and imprisoned, including Václav Havel, who was sentenced to nine months in prison (Vladislav and Prečan, 1990). In Slovakia, the numbers attending religious pilgrimages in the summers began to grow, and a petition of Thirty-One Demands written by a group of Moravian Catholics gathered nearly 600,000 signatures by the summer of 1988. This and letters by Cardinal Tomášek were dismissed by the head of the national office for religious affairs as a pretext for "[providing] the Western press with new motives for attacking the CSSR" (Ramet, 1991: 390). Despite the publication of more conciliatory statements about religion by party leaders and an offer by Cardinal Tomášek to mediate between the opposition and the regime, as in Poland, these efforts had little impact upon broader mobilization.

The "Civil Society" Master Frame

In Chapter 1, I argued that "civil society" should not be understood as an empirical reality whose strength or weakness can be compared across countries, but rather as a "master frame" that emerged across Eastern Europe in the 1970s. In spite of differences in "really existing socialism" across countries that I have characterized as political opportunities, similarities in the structure of Leninist regimes led the democratic oppositions in Poland and Czechoslovakia to develop a broadly similar interpretation of the aims of political opposition in terms of the concept of civil society. Master frames, I suggested, are broader models for mobilizing support that movements draw upon. They are not unified cultural systems, nor universally accepted, but are contested, emerging through struggle with adversaries and within movements. The civil society master frame made three interrelated claims that can be described as follows: because the Leninist regimes were violating human rights held in common by citizens across classes, one should support nonviolent action designed to pressure the regime to reform itself by legal means. The claims served to create meaning out of particular events surrounding the Leninist regimes, to link individuals and collective identities as embodied in networks outside the regime, and to provide a blueprint for action drawn on by efforts to mobilize support. Because framing cannot be studied solely in symbolic terms, it must be linked to institutions that enable movements to deploy framing strategies and form alliances across groups.

Framing strategies can be characterized as claims about injustice, identity, and agency. The civil society master frame defined the claim of injustice as the persecution of human rights that were protected by international agreements and national constitutions. This claim, although not new in history, was given international legitimation with the signing of the Helsinki Accords in 1975 by thirty-five governments of Europe (including all the governments of Eastern Europe but Albania) after two years of negotiations concerning peace and security in Europe. These accords, also containing the first formal recognition of East Germany by West Germany, lay the groundwork for the rise of human rights as a sphere of political protest. All signatories, in a provision contained in what was known as "basket three," committed themselves to respect "civil, economic, social, cultural, and other rights and freedoms, all of which derive from the inherent dignity of the human person."[16]

The notion of human rights was embodied in the collective identity of "citizens." In the context of Eastern Europe the notion of citizens stood in opposition to that of membership in particular classes, nations, or political parties whose voice the regime claimed to represent. As Tony Judt points out, the language of human rights provided the opposition with a way of confronting the regime on the basis of its own stated intentions (forcing it to reveal its own illegality), but it goes beyond these strategic considerations (1988: 192–95). The notion of rights "detotalizes," as rights are inherent to all individuals and cannot be superseded by a totalitarian state. Finally, the language of rights recalled earlier, democratic periods that preceded socialism in Eastern Europe.

Finally, the agency claim was legal, nonviolent protest seeking to pressure the regime to reform itself, rather than attempting to gain political power. This entailed the "identification of social participation, rather than any revisions *within* the party-state apparatus, as the key to fundamental reform" (Ash, 1983: 43, italics in original). As Adam Michnik argued in an influential essay entitled "The New Evolutionism":

> To believe in overthrowing the dictatorship of the party by revolution and to consciously organize actions in pursuit of this goal is both unrealistic and dangerous. . . . In my opinion, an unceasing struggle for reform and evolution that seeks an expansion of civil liberties and human rights is the only course East European dissidents can take. (1985: 142–43)

[16] Quoted in Stokes, 1993: 24.

As a master frame, the notion of civil society took different forms within particular countries, even within movements. While it made certain claims, it also "contained several possible meanings, and excluded many significant questions from its conceptualization" (Kennedy, 1992: 29). Below, I analyze the symbolic features of the civil society master frame and its emergence within the democratic oppositions in Poland and Czechoslovakia. As Solidarity leader Zbigniew Bujak famously commented:

> Reading [Havel's essay "The Power of the Powerless"] gave us the theoretical underpinnings for our activity. It maintained our spirits; we did not give up, and a year later—in August, 1980—it became clear that the party apparatus and the factory management were afraid of us. . . . When I look at the victories of Solidarity and Charter 77, I see in them an astonishing fulfillment of the prophecies and knowledge contained in Havel's essay.[17]

It is beyond the scope of this chapter and this book to analyze the history of the democratic oppositions in both countries prior to 1989, about which so much has been written.[18] Yet for the purpose of explaining the legacies of democratic opposition upon the democratic challengers in the late 1980s, I analyze the legacy of the "civil society" master frame upon the claims made by democratic challengers in the late 1980s and upon the ties to pre-existing networks that could be mobilized on their behalf. I contrast the legacy of the Committee for the Defense of Workers and Solidarity in Poland, which sought to mobilize workers and intellectuals with the support of the Catholic Church, and with that of Charter 77 activists in Czechoslovakia, who limited their activity to petitions in light of the repressive regime.

SOLIDARITY AND THE CATHOLIC CHURCH

In the 1980s, the term "civil society" became so pervasive in Poland that a party official once mocked Solidarity's program by re-

[17] Quoted in Havel, 1991: 126.
[18] A necessarily limited review of works on Solidarity and Charter 77 includes Ash, 1983; Bernhard, 1993, 1996; Kennedy, 1991, 1992; Kubik, 1994; Ost, 1990; Skilling, 1981; Staniszkis, 1991.

ferring to "His Excellency, Civil Society" (Ost, 1990: 19). The roots of this master frame can be traced to the 1970s after the repression of protesting intellectuals in 1968 and of striking workers in 1970. Its earliest embodiment was in the Committee for the Defense of Workers (or KOR, as it is known by its Polish acronym), in which intellectuals sought to provide technical and practical assistance to workers and their families who had been punished for striking (see Bernhard, 1993; Lipski, 1985; Ost, 1990). The civil society master frame was further elaborated by Solidarity in August 1980, which relied upon a framing strategy that called for the creation of free trade unions on the basis of an alliance among workers, intellectuals, and the Church in the environment of Gdańsk (Karabel, 1993). Let me be clear that I am not suggesting that Solidarity can be understood simply in terms of the civil society master frame. Solidarity was a mass movement with nearly ten million members at its peak based on multiple identities and alliances. As Touraine et al. (1983) observe, it was a trade-union movement that struggled to realize democracy and national self-determination. Even so, although Solidarity "varied by region, occupation, gender, organizational level and local culture . . . the discourse around these three points helped construct the movement's aims and form" (Kennedy, 1991: 114).

The influence of the civil society master frame is evident in Solidarity's history, from its initial demands in August 1980 to its various statements during its fifteen-month legal period. For example, rather than economic grievances concerning prices or wages, the element of injustice in Solidarity's demands was focused on the broader context that gave rise to the economic crisis. Notably, the fourth demand of the Lenin Shipyard in August 1980 called for the restoration of former "rights" to those dismissed from work after striking in 1970 and 1976 and to students expelled from universities, for the release of political prisoners, and for the prohibition of reprisals on the basis of beliefs. In a statement of general principles prepared in February and March 1981, Solidarity declared that the economic crisis had "political-social causes": "The disappearance of democratic institutions and the resulting profound division between society and the apparatus of power within the present system of public life are at the bottom of that crisis" (Raina, 1985a: 175).

Consistent with the civil society master frame, the identity claim of Solidarity sought to unite "citizens" against the regime. As one analyst observed, "Among the most admirable of Solidarity's achievements was its ability to attract members of two 'Marxist' classes—workers and peasants—and engage them in the struggle against oppression not as mere workers and peasants, but as *citizens*" (Król, 1994: 87, italics in original). Survey data collected in the 1980s showed that support for Solidarity was not divided by traditional class variables but rather was polarized into those for and those against the regime (see Adamski et al., 1981, 1982, 1986). That is, one could find members of each social class, group, and social category at both ends of the spectrum. Thus, Kubik defines Solidarity as a "cultural-political class in statu nascendi" made up of "all those who subscribed to a system of principles and values, usually referred to as counterhegemonic, unofficial, independent, or alternative—who visualized the social structure as strongly polarized between 'us' ('society,' 'the people,' etc.) and 'them' ('the authorities,' 'Communists,' etc.)" (1994: 236; see also Kennedy, 1991). The identification as citizens drew upon a construction of the Polish nation that emphasized its civic, rather than ethnic, qualities and that identified itself with the history of the Catholic Church. Ash argues that the prominence of human rights discourse during the strike at the Lenin Shipyard in 1980 was an "astonishing" development resulting from the "consistent propagation by the Polish Catholic Church, since the late 1960s, of the idea that every human being is endowed with certain fundamental, inalienable rights" (1983: 61). Especially with the nomination of Pope John Paul II in 1978 and his subsequent pilgrimages to Poland, the Catholic Church provided a language consistent in many ways with the civil society master frame. To give but one example, in a speech in Gdynia during his third pilgrimage in 1987, the Pope proclaimed rhythmically, "[W]hat does solidarity mean? Solidarity means a way of living in the human community, for example of the nation, in unity, in respect for all differences, all dissimilarities which arise between people, and more unity in the community, and more pluralism, in all towns in the idea of solidarity."[19] The notion of "society" should not be understood somehow as the actual uniting of Polish society due to a conversion of beliefs, but as a strategic framing strategy that sought to build public support for Solidarity. Kowalski argues that Solidarity activists sought to define communism as evil and foreign in opposition to a vision of Poland united by religious and national values because "it seemed capable of providing the foundations for an absolute rejection of the Communist system" (1993: 233).

Finally, rather than challenging the Communist Party through armed insurrection, Solidarity emphasized the need for independent trade unions outside of the political sphere, as guaranteed by international agreements signed by the regime. The first of the twenty-one demands at the Lenin Shipyard observed that free trade unions were in accordance with Convention 87 of the International Labor Organization convention concerning trade union freedom that had been ratified by the Polish People's Republic. The notion of self-governing trade unions outside of the political sphere drew upon a strategic repertoire of political action developed in the workers' protests in 1970–71, which Laba argues is "a popular tradition specific to industrial workers of the Coast" (Laba, 1991: 112, 113). It can be understood as an extension of the principle of self-organization of civil society, although admittedly workers' self-management could hardly be fully independent of a regime that controlled a centralized economy (Szacki, 1994: 100). The demand for free and independent trade unions necessitated a reframing of this concept so as to be within the sphere of the politically possible by not threatening the leading role of the party nor the geopolitical constraints of membership in the Warsaw Pact. August 28th's Solidarity bulletin proclaimed:

[19] Jan Pawel II, 1987: 125. See Ash, 1983; Ost, 1990; and Kubik, 1994 for the impact of the pope's first pilgrimage in 1979.

> Our demands are intended neither to threaten the foundations of the so-
> cialist regime in our country nor its position in international relations,
> and we would not support anyone who wanted to exploit the present
> circumstances to that end; on the contrary, we would oppose them.[20]

The vision of an independent trade union that did not challenge the
monopoly of the Communist Party was set out in the agreements
signed by the authorities and Solidarity in Gdańsk on August 31,
1980, and in Szczeciń on August 30, 1980. The Gdańsk agreement
stated: "Establishing new, independent, self-governing labor unions, the MKS [Inter-factory Strike Committee] states that they will
abide by the principles stated in the PPR [Polish People's Republic]
Constitution. The new unions will defend both the social and the
material interests of the workers and have no intention of playing
the role of a political party."[21] Similarly, the Szczeciń agreements refer to "[s]elf-governing labor unions, which will be socialist in character, in keeping with the Constitution of the Polish People's Republic."[22]

After martial law was imposed in 1981, the civil society master
frame guided the strategy of Solidarity leaders in the underground.
Kulerski wrote that Solidarity need not choose between revolution
or compromise:

> Instead of organizing ourselves as an underground state, we should be
> organizing ourselves as an underground society. Not into a movement
> directed by a central headquarters requiring absolute discipline, but
> into a loosely structured, decentralized movement composed of mutu-
> ally independent groups, committees, etc., each of which would be
> largely autonomous and self-directed. . . . Such a movement should
> strive for a situation in which the government will control empty
> shops but not the market, employment but not the means to liveli-
> hood, the state press but not the flow of information, printing houses
> but not the publishing movement, telephones and the postal service
> but not communication, schools but not education.[23]

[20] Quoted in Ash, 1983: 62.
[21] Quoted in Robinson, 1980: 423.
[22] Quoted in Robinson, 1980: 416.
[23] Quoted in Stokes, 1993: 106.

Similarly Bujak wrote, "Local groups and social circles in the community should organize . . . to build a system of social structures independent of the state."[24] This master frame existed, however, not simply in the proclamations of strike committees but as it built ties to the Polish Catholic Church.

WHY THE CHURCH?

Because frames must be linked to networks, the link between the civil society master frame and the Polish Catholic Church deserves elaboration. To explain why an alliance was possible between the Church and the democratic opposition in Poland in the 1970s and 1980s, I analyze the impact of national tradition as well as the institutional legacy of the Leninist regime in Poland. The alliance between Solidarity and the Church completed a three-part symbolic association of Church-nation-society that drew upon traditions of resistance in Polish history, most notably the role of the Church as the symbolic bearer of national identity during the partitions of the eighteenth and nineteenth centuries, when the Polish state was absorbed into its larger neighbors, Russia, Germany, and Austria.[25] In such times the Church was identified by some as the "inter-rex" or the legitimate representative of Polish sovereignty between coronations. In the words of Bishop Dąbrowski, "[T]he Catholic Church in Poland was and is always with the nation and the nation with the Church. In the many times in which there have been conflicts between the ruling government and Polish society, the Church has always stood for the protection of society" (Raina, 1995: 468). The values and discourse of the Church were understood by some of its hierarchy as an explicit antidote to Marxism under state socialism. Father Wojciech Giertych explained:

> [D]uring all these years [of Communism], Christian values were present. The church always said, "This is not the ultimate world, this is not the ultimate answer that we are receiving from the Party. We have

[24] Quoted in ibid.
[25] See Morawska, 1984; and Walaszek, 1986 for arguments about the role of the Church resting upon national tradition and history.

to view this world in light of objective moral standards. Remember, we have two thousand years of Christianity behind us." (Hedberg, 1992: 111)

As others have observed, the Church "thought of itself, in keeping with a long tradition, as the depository of national values, the supreme public authority, the representative of a nation deprived of sovereign representation" (Smolar, 1994: 79).

Yet although national tradition may make certain kinds of alliances more or less possible, it alone cannot explain the role of the Church because traditions are complex, multivocal, and constantly constructed in the present by political actors. It must be combined with attention to the institutional structure of the Church and changing political opportunities for opposition under communism. During World War II, the Polish Catholic Church was decimated by the invading German forces, leading to the development of "an informal network of communications and support for the Polish underground . . . that included much of the clergy" (Osa, 1989: 287). This included secret schools, underground seminaries, aid to the Polish army, and the operation of hospitals, orphanages, and other social services. Following World War II, the Polish Catholic Church was the only church to maintain its autonomy from the Leninist regimes in Eastern Europe. Out of the underground war networks, the Church rebuilt itself into what Osa calls an "activist church," emphasizing its flexible episcopal strategy and loosely coupled formal and informal structures that allowed it to adapt to the adversity of state socialism and to broaden its social bases of support (1989: 296). The activist model of the Church led to a two-tiered organization: the cautious episcopate or national hierarchy on one tier, and an activist base of local clergy on the other. The role of the lower clergy can be seen in the way that Zbigniew Bujak became involved in the opposition. He explained:

> [T]here was the question of how to connect with these people who work in the opposition, who edit underground newspapers. I started to think, are there people that I could contact. And I remembered listening to the sermons of a priest, Kantorski, in the town that I lived in. I thought these are not usual sermons. These are sermons which

are based on the underground press and when I met him, I asked him, if he would give me some of those papers. I said it was because I can hear in your sermons that you use that press. He looked at me very long and he knew my family. He knew that my father was a member of the AK [the Home Army, part of the underground resistance during World War II]. Then after thinking a little about it, he gave me the papers. He also made contact with the people at the press for me. (Hedberg, 1992: 96)

This enabled the Church to play its unique role as mediator between the regime and society. Cardinal Wyszyński could "bargain and compromise strategically with the state, and . . . assert his control over the activist base of lower clergy only when politically necessary" (Osa, 1989: 298). In the years leading up to 1966 (the millennium anniversary of the founding of the Polish nation and its conversion to Christianity), the Church undertook a series of national mobilizations under the name of the "Great Novena," which, although not explicitly political, demonstrated its ability to mobilize the public outside of the political sphere (Osa, 1996). After martial law, church services continued to serve as meeting places. One member of the democratic opposition commented at that time that "in hundreds of churches there are what [amount] to constant demonstrations [on] behalf of Solidarity."[26]

Although I highlight the congruency between the civil society master frame and the Church, the rapprochement between the Church and the democratic opposition did not represent unconditional support for the opposition or a merging of the aims of both groups. This was always an alliance, and often a delicate one. In the 1970s, a rapprochement took place between intellectuals and the Church, as both sought to provide assistance to striking workers. Adam Michnik's book *The Church and the Left* reflects his conscious efforts to redefine the image of the Church from that of a conservative institution to that of a protector of human rights in the history of Poland. In so doing, he sought to redefine the relevant political identities within Poland. He argued that "the central con-

[26] Borusewicz, quoted in Lopinski et al., 1990: 135.

flict in Poland is the conflict between the totalitarian authorities and a society systematically deprived of its rights" (1993: 182). He described the Church as both a "security umbrella" that helped curtail the repression and a "model of civil disobedience" (ibid.: 236). Ash observes that "the Poles have a remarkable ability to hear what they want to hear from their Church leaders, and disregard the rest. Thus young Poles love and venerate the Pope, but lustfully ignore his teachings on sexual morality. The workers respect the Primate, but cheerfully ignore his warnings against the strike" (1983: 58). Michnik himself argued that the result of such a rapprochement "would not be a political alliance but a community in humanist values, whose consistent advocate would be a Church loyal to the spirit of the Gospels" (1993: 203). Regarding the dissidents, Ash suggests:

> The *rapprochement* with the Church from the Left took place at several levels. For Leszek Kolakowski it was a stage in a profound philosophical quest. . . . For the young historian Adam Michnik it followed rather from the historical discovery that the Church had been the single most important defender of human and civil rights against totalitarian encroachments in Poland. . . . For KOR's most dynamic political activist, Jacek Kuroń, it was probably more a calculation of political tactics. (1983: 20–21)

Similarly, a leader of a Solidarity chapter in southern Poland commented, "I know that in order to avoid subordination to Communists, cooperation with the Church was necessary." He explained: "[T]he authority of the Church was not powerful enough. What was needed was a push from both sides. Only the alliance of the authentic social movement with the Church's ethical authority could bring about this much desired change."[27]

Nor was the Church of one voice about this rapprochement. Father Josef Tischner, an influential theologian from Cracow, argued against Michnik's portrait of the evolution of the Catholic Church in Poland (Michnik, 1993; Michnik and Tischner, 1995). He argued that Michnik's distinction between a good church that emphasizes human rights and a bad church that represents chauvinism

[27] Quoted in Kubik, 1994: 226.

misrepresented the Church's values, which are not limited to human rights but extend to the establishment of a Christian moral order. He accused Michnik of focusing only on the Church's activities that were compatible with Michnik's liberal conception of the political sphere. For Tischner, the dissident intellectuals were out of touch with "the nation, the so-called 'ordinary people,' [who] fill the churches and pilgrimage sites."[28] Further, Cardinal Glemp, the successor to Cardinal Wyszyński, was not the unequivocal supporter of the opposition for which his predecessor had been so loved. He acted under what he described as the three guiding principles of the Polish Catholic Church: that the Church is not of this world, although it is in this world; that it depends more on listening to God than to people; and render that unto the emperor which is the emperor's and that unto God which is God's (Raina, 1985b: 89). When asked what "tactics" the Church had employed in late 1982, Glemp retorted, "Where did you get this phrase, from what radio station? . . . To speak clearly, the Church must rather be itself. The Church can not bring in a political partnership" (ibid.: 293). In a 1984 interview in Sao Paolo, Brazil, he said that Wałęsa had lost control of Solidarity because the union "was a sack into which everything had been thrown, all the opposition Marxists, Trotskyites, and then all the careerists and Party members."[29]

Charter 77 and "Living in Truth"

Unlike Solidarity in Poland, the civil society master frame in Czechoslovakia remained within the sphere of a small group of dissidents who focused on signing petitions rather than organizing protest. The emergence of a master frame concerned with human rights can be traced to the publication of a document entitled "Charter 77" on January 1, 1977, that petitioned the Czechoslovak government to honor its signing of the Helsinki Accords in 1975, committing it to protect human rights. The original document had

[28] Quoted in Michnik, 1993: 13.
[29] Quoted in Stokes, 1993: 113.

239 signatures and identified its three spokespersons as the former minister of foreign affairs in 1968, Jiří Hájek, the playwright Václav Havel, and the philosopher Jan Patočka. Charter 77 declared that it was not an organized movement with a registered membership or organizational body, but rather a broad association of people joined only by the individual act of signing the charter. It described itself as "a free, informal, open community of people of different convictions, different faiths, different professions united by the will to strive, individually and collectively, for the respect of civic and human rights in our own country and throughout the world."[30]

The emergence of Charter 77 illustrates how political actors seek to exploit changes in international alliances by framing their claims in particular ways. The original proclamation proclaimed that Charter 77 emerged in direct response to the signing of the Helsinki Accords. Within Czechoslovakia, the impulse came in 1976 from the government's arrest of the members of a rock band, the Plastic People of the Universe, and the sentencing of four members for eight to eighteen months in prison for "disrespect of society" and for being "filthy" and "obscene." Havel later stated: "Jiří Němec and I both felt that something had happened here, something that should not be allowed simply to evaporate and disappear but which ought to be transformed into some kind of action that would have a more permanent impact, one that would bring this something out of the air onto solid ground" (1990a: 132).

Consistent with the agency claim of the civil society master frame, the signatories of Charter 77 insisted that they did not seek to convince others to participate in political activity. Its philosophical leader, Jan Patočka (1981), argued that Charter 77 was apolitical because its signatories were joined not by political beliefs but by the moral conviction that human society could not function satisfactorily in the absence of an ethical foundation under the Leninist regime. This was a matter of inner decision among those who took part, something prepolitical. That is, although it may have formed

---

[30] Quoted in Skilling, 1981: 211.

the basis for political behavior, it was not in itself political. For Havel, Charter 77 was not an act of "political manipulation: canvassing people, persuading them and making promises. All he had ever done was to tackle his own personal problem. He did not offer 'life in truth' as a political commodity. Having no desire to be manipulated himself, he had no intention of manipulating the consciousness of others" (Šimečka, 1991: 79). Charter 77 insisted that it was "not an organization. It has no rules, permanent bodies, or formal membership. It embraces everyone who agrees with its ideas, participates in its work, and supports it. It does not form the basis for any opposition political activity."[31]

The rejection of political aims may have been an attempt to avoid repression from the authorities, but this provides only a partial insight into its intentions. It clearly failed to prevent repression, nor did Charter 77 change its framing strategy following repression. The antipolitical claim reflects a deeper understanding of its intended audience, which lived under the policies of "normalization" pursued in Czechoslovakia after 1968. In the absence of fiscal crisis and continued repressive policies, Charter 77 had fewer than two thousand signatories by 1989. Not only was it virtually impossible for Charter 77 to mobilize the broader population to revolt, it could hardly reach agreement among its members. One charter member observed that a planned document about the communist takeover in 1948 "proved too hot to reach a consensus. Obviously, a 40 year-old Catholic who has never been a member of the Communist Party can never agree on this subject with a 65 year-old ex-Communist" (Urban, 1988: 32).

The civil society master frame of Charter 77 was not accepted by all members of the democratic opposition. Milan Kundera, the novelist, derided Havel's stance as unrealistic and foolish in the face of overwhelming odds. Frustration at the lack of response from the general population led Václav Benda to argue in 1978 that the individual "liberation" that came from signing the charter (emphasized by Havel as the key to change) "gradually gave way to disillusion-

---

[31] Quoted in Skilling, 1981: 212.

ment and deep skepticism" (1991: 36). In response, he declared that the opposition in socialist Czechoslovakia should commit itself to "join forces in creating, slowly but surely, parallel structures that are capable, to a limited degree at least, of supplementing the generally beneficial and necessary functions that are missing in the existing structures, and where possible, to use those existing structures, to humanize them." Ten years later, Benda conceded the limits of what Charter 77 could accomplish in Czechoslovakia even given changes in the international sphere: "[T]he destruction of totalitarianism cannot be brought about merely on the basis of a program, since the powers-that-be—even in their most difficult periods—are so strong that they are capable of defeating all attempts at resistance at an early stage" (1988: 13). He concluded, "[U]nder no circumstances should the charter become a political movement, i.e. an opposition with a clearly defined political program. This would lead to the loss of its identity—and if internal strife did not eventually lead to its demise, it would doubtlessly be coerced and effectively suppressed by the authorities" (ibid.: 13).

Two new movements emerged probing the limits of the civil society master frame in the late 1980s but were greeted by repression and failed to attract any significant attention: the Democratic Initiative and Movement for Civic Freedom. In October 1987 the Democratic Initiative (*Demokratická Initiativa*) emerged as part of an attempt to unify the democratic opposition with a letter to members of the Czechoslovak federal parliament calling for the democratization of public and political life. Drawing upon the repertoire of petition actions in Czechoslovakia, its first letter identified itself only as the "initiative of fifty signatories," including several prominent members of Charter 77.[32] The letter was broadcast on Radio Free Europe, but this and subsequent letters received no apparent response from the authorities. In a letter to General Secretary Jakeš in January 1988, the authors of the letter announced that they were sending their "proposals and suggestions with the name democratic

---

[32] Quoted in Hlusičková and Otáhal, 1993: 24.

initiative."[33] On October 28, 1988—the seventieth anniversary of the founding of Czechoslovakia—the Democratic Initiative called for participation in its only public demonstration in Wenceslaus Square, which led to immediate police attention and persecution of its signatories. As a result, its spokesperson canceled all activity and prepared a publication in November 1988 that explained why Democratic Initiative was stopping its activity (Mandler in Otáhal and Sladek, 1990: 613). By late 1989, Democratic Initiative existed only in name and in the person of its spokespersons, who continued to publish proclamations and letters. Some members of Charter 77, such as Havel, were no longer associated with it (in part due to a history of personal antagonism between Havel and Mandler that dated to both men's participation in the literary journal *Tvář* in the 1960s).[34]

In 1988, several Charter 77 signatories sought once again to unify the opposition and create an explicitly political movement inspired by but independent from Charter 77, the Movement for Civic Freedom (*Hnutí za Obćanská Svoboda*, hereafter referred to by its Czech acronym, HOS). Many of the original signatories, including Havel, had also been involved in the original efforts of Democratic Initiative. In contrast to Charter 77's deliberately antipolitical nature, HOS's manifesto began: "[T]he time has now come to start working in earnest in the political sphere" and contained ten points about changes in Czechoslovakia.[35] The movement sought to draw upon the interwar tradition of democracy led by president Tomáš Masaryk and called for the abolition of Article 4 of the Czechoslovak Constitution, which guaranteed the leading role of the Communist Party. Without the accompanying change in the political opportunity structure, however, HOS gained little public support, gathering only 949 signatures (Hlusičková and Cisarovská, 1994: 15). *Rude Pravo* denounced the manifesto as a "counterrevolutionary pamphlet." Its signatories were also subject

[33] Quoted in ibid.: 30.
[34] Havel, 1990: 86–87.
[35] *East European Reporter* 3, no. 4 (spring/summer 1989).

to persecution by the secret police, who arrested one hundred of them within two weeks of the manifesto's publication in October 1988. Havel commented in December 1988: "Only time will tell what contribution HOS might make in this country. . . . Maybe like Charter 77 it will soon become an integral part of Czechoslovak public life, in spite of the displeasure of the powers that be. Maybe it will remain only the seed of something that will not bear fruit until much later. Maybe the whole initiative will be harshly suppressed. . . . Be that as it may . . . the exclamation that the King is naked will reverberate in the ears of those who see that he is indeed naked" (1989: 54).

The Czechoslovak regime became increasingly isolated over 1989 as neighboring Leninist regimes weakened and fell in Poland, Hungary, and East Germany. Although the policy of repression continued until the student demonstration on November 17 that led to the general strike, several petitions attracted support that laid the groundwork for later activity. In the summer of 1989, in response to Havel's imprisonment, a new petition entitled "Several Sentences" emerged that became the first openly political petition to attract support from outside of the dissident circles—namely from the cultural community, which would prove critical to the successful mobilization by Civic Forum in November. It was released by the theater community on June 29, 1989, and was deliberately named to recall an earlier statement entitled "Two Thousand Words," which had served as one of the pretexts for the intervention by the Warsaw Pact armies in 1968.[36] "Several Sentences" began by proclaiming "there is a danger of an open crisis. None of us wants such a crisis."[37] In the tradition of its antecedent, Charter 77, and its successor, Civic Forum, it proclaimed that "anyone who is in agreement with us is welcome to express . . . support by adding his or her signature" and called upon the leadership to enter "genuine dialogue." By summer 1989 "Several Sentences" had collected forty thousand signatures, far superseding Charter 77, but without any

[36] Havel, 1991: 379.
[37] Quoted in *Uncaptive Minds* (Aug.–Sept.–Oct. 1989): 35.

accompanying political mobilization or activity that could organize the signatories. In comparison to the hundreds of thousands demonstrating in East Germany by the summer and fall of 1988, such activity seemed almost insignificant.

Setting the Stage

The announcement of the Sinatra doctrine and the fall of the Berlin Wall in East Germany in November 1989 ended all illusions that the East European Leninist regimes could count on Soviet support. This created incentives for insurgency and pressure for change, but variation in Poland and Czechoslovakia has illustrated that changes in international alliances did not determine what followed, nor did it alter the regime's ability to repress challengers. If the regimes had simply been weak, we would expect any challenge to have led to their overthrow. The breakup of the April 1988 strikes in Poland illustrate that the regime, however, pressured by economic crisis, had not lost the capacity to repress protest. Similarly, the repression of the Palach Week demonstrations in January and of protests on the national anniversaries in August and October of 1989 in Czechoslovakia illustrate that this was not true. Even after the announcement of the Sinatra doctrine, members of the democratic opposition meeting in November 1989 estimated that it would take two years for fundamental change to occur in Czechoslovakia.[38]

In this chapter, I have analyzed the three features of political opportunities as complementary, demonstrating that the Leninist regimes did not lose the capacity to repress challengers but became vulnerable in light of changes in international alliances and economic crisis. Attention to patterns of insurgency demonstrates the mutual influence of political opportunities and movements: while changes in political opportunities create incentives for insurgency, movements can influence the definition of existing opportunities through framing strategies. The arguments in this chapter highlight

[38] Quoted in Otáhal and Sladek, 1990: 580.

the absence of prior unconditional support or organizational readiness of the opposition. If the general population had been so discontented with the system, one might expect them to express their discontent at any chance that did not entail high risk. This claim is flawed because it rests upon a simplistic presumption of antistate sentiment resembling Cold War anticommunism. Further, it is not supported by voting behavior in Poland in the 1987 economic referendum. As noted earlier, voters had two ways they could express dissent: by voting against the government's program or by abstaining from participation altogether (as Solidarity urged them to do). Voting in this case was relatively low risk, but Polish voters did not choose to express their dissatisfaction as this claim would predict. According to official estimates, 68 percent of the electorate voted (an estimated higher percentage than in the 1989 partially free elections), and two-thirds of those voters voted in support of the government's program, even if that did not result in the necessary level of approval by a total majority of voters.

Thus in the late 1980s, neither Solidarity nor Charter 77 was an organized political faction awaiting an opportunity to seize power. As I have argued, one must ask how Solidarity and Civic Forum were able to organize supporters so rapidly, lacking the institutional resources of the regimes they were facing, and how the terms of negotiations were set and structured potential outcomes. As the case studies in the next four chapters will show, the legacy of opposition in general and the civil society master frame in particular influenced the choices considered by the movements once the regime had weakened. The civic movements did not call for violent revolution as in Hungary in 1956, for reform from above as in Czechoslovakia in 1968, nor for redressing corruption as in China in 1989. Although this new master frame provided a common symbolic language in the late 1980s, the framing strategies of the civic movements in each country varied in light of perceived political opportunities and the events that precipitated insurgency. With the arguments of this chapter in mind, I turn to the case studies and contrast the pattern of the "democratization from above" in Poland with the "democratization from below" in Czechoslovakia. I begin each case study with an analysis of the potentials for insurgency created by changes in political opportunities and contrast the mobilization and bargaining processes by which this potential was transformed in differing forms of reconstruction of the state.

CHAPTER THREE

Framing the Roundtable in Poland

We utter grand words, but what Poland needs are bold decisions and wise and energetic actions.
—Lech Wałęsa, opening the Polish roundtable, February 8, 1989[1]

DESPITE THE LONG history of political struggle in Poland
after World War II, the negotiated agreement for partially free
elections in early 1989 has been widely perceived in the scholarly
literature as an instance of a pacted transition whereby elite negotiations led to an agreement in which the old regime retained significant positions of power.[2] With the failed regime-sponsored referendum in 1987 and failed Solidarity strikes in April 1988, a political
impasse had been reached in the late 1980s whereby neither the regime nor Solidarity could mobilize sufficient popular support to resolve Poland's increasing economic problems. In the public statements of both sides, the notion of an "anticrisis pact" emerged, in
which the impasse would be resolved by a limited opening: the Solidarity trade union would be legalized in exchange for support for
the government's proposed economic reforms and limited participation in parliament. By ending unplanned strikes in the name of an
honorable compromise in August 1988, Solidarity leaders set limits
to the political agenda for an agreement with the regime; further, by
excluding from the roundtable negotiations the possibility that the

[1] *Uncensored Poland News Bulletin*, no. 25/89 (July 2, 1989): appendix, p. 9.
[2] Bunce, 1999; Linz and Stepan, 1996; Staniszkis, 1991. For a contrary
view that emphasizes public protest, see Ekiert, 1997.

Leninist regime could lose elections, Solidarity transformed the negotiations from an attempt at co-optation into an opportunity for political competition.

The uncertainty of the moment for both sides can be neither overestimated nor forgotten, as there was no blueprint for what was to follow. Indeed, in late 1988 few believed that these negotiations would lead to competitive elections or seriously challenge the regime's authority. Analysis of the roundtable indicates that the pathbreaking agreement for partially free elections was not determined by the weakening of the Leninist regime or changes in the international sphere but was the result of bargaining among political actors seeking to mobilize public support on behalf of their aims. In the process of bargaining, the principal political actors were themselves transformed. Wałęsa's repeated slogan in the 1980s, "There is no freedom without solidarity," may have been effective, but it begged the question: who was "Solidarity" at the end of the 1980s? Polish national discourse has tended to emphasize the continuity of Polish resistance to communism, culminating with the re-emergence of Solidarity after the rise of Mikhail Gorbachev in the Soviet Union (Bernhard, 1993; Ekiert, 1996; Karpiński, 1982; Kubik, 1994; Ost, 1990; Staniszkis, 1991). By contrast, this chapter suggests that the Solidarity that participated in the roundtable negotiations in 1989 was vastly different from the Solidarity that organized strikes in 1980–81.

Below, I focus on three areas: (1) the anticrisis pact and August 1988 strikes; (2) competing attempts to frame the roundtable, in which I contrast the "honorable compromise" framing strategy of Solidarity leaders with the competing framing strategies of Polish patriotism by the Leninist regime and Polish independence by nationalist groups; and (3) setting the agenda for participation in partially free elections. In conclusion, I consider alternative explanations and counterfactual evidence for the outcome of the roundtable.

The Anticrisis Pact and August 1988 Strikes

As discussed in Chapter 2, the failed 1987 economic referendum and April 1988 strikes had demonstrated that neither the Leninist regime nor Solidarity could unilaterally mobilize sufficient political support to resolve the problems facing Poland. In the late 1980s, the notion of an "anticrisis pact" emerged in the public statements by the state and Solidarity, in which Solidarity would agree to partici- pate as a limited voice in the government in exchange for the legali- zation of the trade union. On December 13, 1987, the historian Jerzy Holzer published an open letter to Wałęsa and Jaruzelski in *Tygodnik Powszechny* and *Polityka* in which he called for "a final attempt to enable representatives of those in power and of those who, for some millions of people, symbolize the solicitude for the working people's interests to meet without preliminary conditions, but with good will."[3] This idea was furthered in February 1988 in the journal *Konfrontacje* when Bronisław Geremek stated that an anticrisis pact was possible by which Solidarity would "accept a program for social, economic, and political reforms and, in doing so, . . . recognize the government."[4] In this scheme, the party would retain control over foreign policy, national defense, and internal se- curity; the opposition would gain influence over questions of social policy, and Solidarity would be conditionally relegalized.

The regime's vision of an anticrisis pact was announced by the call for the creation of a "proreform coalition" in the May 5 edition of the party newspaper, *Trybuna Ludu*. At the same moment as the regime repressed strikes in Gdańsk, this call sought to redefine Geremek's proposed pact into the co-optation of the opposition in the government. As an internal document produced by the Ideologi- cal Committee of the Communist Party observed, this difference was not merely semantic but a deliberate attempt to exclude the part of the opposition (such as the Confederation for an Independ- ent Poland and Fighting Solidarity) that rejected any cooperation

[3] *Uncensored Poland News Bulletin*, no. 3/88 (Feb. 4, 1988): 14.
[4] *Uncaptive Minds* (June–July–August 1988): 7–8.

with the regime.[5] A June 14, 1988, Politburo report from the Seventh Plenum announced the possibility of holding roundtable negotiations: "On the question of political pluralism in Poland manifesting itself in the existence of most diverse associations, which is an important issue for different communities and groups, we wish to declare our openness for businesslike discussion on concrete future policies in this respect. It could be useful to call a round-table meeting of representatives of a broad spectrum of existing and proposed associations."[6] The importance of Gorbachev's policies as a statement of approval for these developments was explicit: "We ascribe particular importance to the changes introduced by the CPSU [Communist Party of the Soviet Union]. The philosophies of Polish renewal and Soviet perestroika are ideologically homogeneous and aimed in the same direction."[7]

These ideas were limited to discussion in the mass media until August 15, when miners in Jastrzebie went on strike and were joined three days later by an inter-factory strike committee in Szczeciń. On August 22, the workers at the Gdańsk Shipyard once again went on strike. Like the earlier failed strikes in April, these were neither organized nor led by the leading Solidarity figures, but by contrast, the first postulates of many August strike committees across Poland called for the "legalization" or "reactivation" of Solidarity or the "introduction of trade union pluralism."[8] Although it cordoned off the shipyard and declared the strikes illegal, the Leninist regime feared that it could not resolve these strikes without the assistance of Solidarity leaders. Discussion began between the regime and Wałęsa through the mediation of the president of the Warsaw Club of Catholic Intelligentsia, Andrzej Stelmachowski.[9] On August 25,

[5] In Perzkowski, 1994: 9.
[6] *Uncensored Poland News Bulletin*, no. 110/88 (June 14, 1988): 14.
[7] Ibid.: 20.
[8] See the list of cities and enterprises whose first demand was the legalization of Solidarity in the Political-Organizational Committee of the Communist Party's report in Perzkowski, 1994: 27–30.
[9] My account draws upon an interview with Andrzej Stelmachowski, July 10, 1995.

Stelmachowski traveled to Gdańsk under the authority of the Church and was permitted to enter the striking shipyard. He read a statement in which the regime proposed to discuss trade union pluralism, including the legalization of Solidarity, social-political pluralism for clubs and associations, and an "anticrisis pact," meaning elections to the lower house of parliament, or *Sejm,* on a common platform of "reform" (Tabako, 1992: 242). Declaring the situation to be "abundantly dangerous," Wałęsa suggested that a roundtable could be the first step in resolving the crisis; such negotiations would concern three areas: (1) the "fulfillment of the demands of workers and citizens in the area of trade union pluralism"; (2) the "fundamental broadening of social-political pluralism"; and (3) a "common statement on the way out of the current crisis as well as on economic reform" (ibid.: 248–49). This last area would include steps to build social trust as well as a common declaration on democracy and strengthening the role of the *Sejm.* Negotiations "would therefore be a means of realizing civic principles of shared responsibility for the development of the country." The Catholic Church, "whose authority and role in the public life of Poland [are] universally recognized," would serve as an observer and guarantee the good conduct of both parties. With this, on August 31, on the eighth anniversary of the signing of the Gdańsk Accords, Wałęsa announced that the strikes would end. He announced a meeting with General Kiszczak and Polish bishop Dąbrowski about the formation of a roundtable concerning "cooperation for economic, social, and political reform for the good of the country."[10]

Consistent with the anticrisis pact, the regime and opposition entered into a bargaining process concerning elections through which the opposition would participate in the government and thereby offer legitimation for the government's policies, and Solidarity would be relegalized. Central to this process was competition over the political agenda, especially the interpretation of the aim of

[10] "Oswiadczenie Lecha Wałęsy," Aug. 31, 1988. Photocopy, Citizens' Committee Archives, Polish Senate.

the negotiations and a redefinition of identity and of the political resources each participant could bring to bear at the table. At its most
basic level, it necessitated a change in the identity of the "other"
from an untrustworthy enemy to a political partner. This meant
agreeing upon a common language. As one Solidarity leader observed: "Now both sides have started using the same language, and
finally some of them mean the same things. Until very recently, the
word 'democracy' meant its absence, 'fraternal assistance' meant
armed intervention, and 'security' meant danger."[11]

Competing Attempts to Frame the Roundtable

By comparing (what I refer to as) the honorable compromise
framing strategy with which Solidarity sought to mobilize support
with attempts by the regime and nationalist groups, I explain the
agreement for partially free elections as an outcome of bargaining in
light of perceived support from collective actors. Because such support was conditional, framing strategies constrained the choices
that challengers were willing to consider and accept. Notably, each
of the three competing groups sought to construct an image of the
Polish "nation" that they claimed to represent. Further, in situations where the regime initiates negotiations from above, it com-
petes to influence the outcome of state reconstruction by defining
who will be permitted to participate in the political sphere and on
what terms, as well as by mobilizing its own supporters.

Although in retrospect it may seem to have been inevitable, in
the fall of 1988 the nature and extent of public support for Solidarity was unclear. Increasing public unrest did not necessarily trans-
late into support for the proposed anticrisis pact or roundtable negotiations, in light of Solidarity's inability to mobilize the country
for earlier strikes (especially when Solidarity had not even organized the strikes that led to the roundtable). A portrait of an uncertain public divided around the best path for the future is supported

[11] Jacek Kuroń in Wałęsa, 1992: 178.

by state public opinion polls, which, as noted in Chapter 1, can be taken as only general portraits of trends rather than precise indications of individual attitudes. For example, when asked in July 1987 if the activities of Lech Wałęsa and those around him were in the interests of society, only 5.8 percent of respondents said decidedly yes, while 22 percent said decidedly not. The largest percentage, 35.8 percent, reported that it was difficult to say. These percentages remained fairly constant through August 1988, when 7.4 percent responded that Wałęsa's activities were in the interests of society, 26.1 percent responded decidedly not, and 29.1 percent felt it was difficult to say (CBOS, 1994: 366). State public opinion polls in September 1988 suggest that a majority of the public viewed the August 1988 strikes as manifestations of economic rather than political protest: nearly half of all respondents in Poland (48.2 percent) felt that the political demands of the August strikes were "not justified," while only 29.2 percent felt the demands were "justified" (ibid.: 362). By convincing the younger workers to end their strike in August, Wałęsa demonstrated his authority to speak for Solidarity and strengthened his bargaining position with the regime. This authority, however, was far from unconditional or secure. The gulf between the leaders of Solidarity from 1980–81 and the younger leaders of the April and August strikes was not easily bridged. Wałęsa was jeered as a "traitor" by some shipyard workers when he called for the end of strikes in August 1988 (Tabako, 1992: 345). He reported with surprise that he thought he had proved himself to be a trustworthy leader, but "the young people at the shipyard now do not think much of experienced people, and they simply ignore previous merits. All they want are palpable effects. . . . They have their own visions, their own objectives, and they are determined to fight for them."[12] His decision to enter into negotiations with the regime was hotly debated among the opposition. Wałęsa , in turn, declared, "I would negotiate with the devil himself if it would help Poland."[13]

[12] In *Uncensored Poland News Bulletin*, no. 20/88 (Oct. 31, 1988): 7.
[13] Quoted in Stokes, 1993: 124.

TABLE 2

Competing Framing Strategies and Networks, Poland, 1989

Challenger	Injustice	Identity	Agency	Networks
Leninist regime "Polish patriotism"	External crisis	Polish nation united in the face of danger	Co-optation	Party structures and media
Solidarity "Honorable compromise"	Crisis due to party, martial law	"Society" as citizens	Compromise, legal means of change	National Executive Commission, publishing ties
Nationalist state groups "Polish Independence"	Foreign domination	Poles as ethnic identity	War against the state	Small groups

In Table 2, I compare these framing strategies along the dimensions of injustice, identity, and agency, as well as pre-existing networks of members that they could mobilize in their support.

Below, I argue that the success of the honorable compromise framing strategy was the result not simply of its superior resonance but also of its ability to link its claims to a network of public support.

THE LENINIST REGIME'S FRAME OF POLISH PATRIOTISM

In contrast to the typical image of a monolithic party regime, analysis of bargaining necessitates a conception of the regime as an actor composed of diverse constituencies whose support is necessary for it to undertake certain actions. The chair of a politburo committee concerned with political strategy in 1989 identified at least three constituencies within the regime with whom he consulted—the decision-makers in the politburo, the military, and the regional party secretaries—each of which had different perceptions of the situation.[14] Similarly, another regime negotiator argued that it

---

[14] Interview with Janusz Reykowski, Oct. 10, 1994.

was a mistake to see the government coalition "as a monolith entering the negotiations with a thought out and fully prepared plan of action. Whereas in reality there was no such plan. A leading centre also did not exist. There were at least two, if not more, 'staffs' and a general lack of co-ordination between them. The exchange of information between the particular groups, sub-groups or negotiating groups was practically non-existent" (Gebethner, 1992: 56). The regime itself formally included not only the Polish United Workers Party (PZPR) but also two satellite parties (the United Peasant Party and the Democratic Party) and several small allied Catholic organizations (such as PAX). The official trade union (OPZZ), while insisting on its independence at the negotiations, can also be considered a regime constituency.

Earlier, I defined framing strategies as claims concerning injustice, identity, and agency. The regime's framing strategy attempted to redefine the political and economic situation in Poland as an external threat to the Polish nation so disastrous that everyone had either to pull together or to go down together. As one member of the government coalition side of the roundtable argued, the regime entered negotiations convinced that the worsening economic situation created "the necessity to achieve some agreement which would prevent mass protest with consequences which might lead to a national tragedy" (ibid.: 52). This idea of a national crisis represented an attempt to reframe the notion of injustice from the illegal opposition to that of an external disaster. The ambiguity surrounding responsibility for this crisis "obscured the real relationship of the party leadership to the economic, political, and social conditions of the 1980s" (Holc, 1992: 129).

Similarly, by identifying itself as the "government coalition," the regime sought to obscure its identity as the Communist Party whose leading role was guaranteed by the Constitution. In this way, the identities of both participants would be redefined: the communist regime would not meet with an illegal opposition to contest the political boundaries of the state, but rather, in the language of Polish patriotism, "Poles would meet with Poles." As the regime declared in the final accords:

> Aware of differences, occasionally conflicts . . . but also respecting each other's identities, participants in the debates tried to find the most efficient ways of putting the Polish state in order. In keeping in the spirit of 1980, they began a dialogue about what unites Poles— their sense of responsibility for Poland's future, for the Polish economy and Polish culture, for the Polish people and the Polish state, for all Poles and their family.[15]

The effort to link nationalism and socialism had a long history whereby the regime sought to portray the Polish People's Republic as "the only rightful heir to all progressive (that is, socialist or Communist) traditions ever developed by the Polish nation" (Kubik, 1994: 64; see also Szporluk, 1988). This entailed a construction of the Polish nation as ethnically and religiously homogenous (described by Kubik as the Piast tradition), rather than the Polish-Lithuanian Commonwealth (or the Jagiellonian tradition) that characterized Poland from approximately 1400 to 1945. Simultaneously, the regime also sought to frame the identity of its opponent as the "constructive" opposition. Thus, in his announcement of the roundtable, General Kiszczak declared, "I do not lay down any preliminary conditions either as to the subject of the conversations or as to the composition of the participants. . . . I exclude, however, the possibility of participation by individuals rejecting the legal and constitutional order of the Polish People's Republic."[16] In light of years of seeking to discredit the opposition as anarchists intent on destroying the country, this attempt was largely unconvincing and "regarded as a symptomatic example of manipulation" (Janowski, 1992: 164).

Finally, for the party this was not a path to revolution but an attempt to create a "Polish humane and democratic model of socialism."[17] This approach was based on the assumption that the party

[15] *Uncensored Poland News Bulletin*, no. 65/89 (April 7, 1989): 4.

[16] Quoted in Janowski, 1992: 163.

[17] Czyrek in *Uncensored Poland News Bulletin*, no. 15/88 (Aug. 18, 1988): 18.

was strong enough to maintain control over limited democratization. The party proposed that the opposition would participate in "competitive" but "nonconfrontational" elections. This was to be a controlled opening by which the regime would maintain the authority to implement reforms and rule in exchange for granting a minority voice to the opposition. As an internal document produced by the secretariat of the Central Committee explained, there would be multiple candidates for available seats, but participants in the elections would abstain from the following: any kind of attack on the basic political institutions (including the leading role of the Communist Party and unity with the USSR) or on the origins of the People's Republic of Poland; discussion concerning responsibility for mistakes of the past, responsibility for the 1981 conflict and martial law; or calling for a negation of the previous forty years. By contrast, there was to be a declaration of the "understanding of Poles acting in their higher interests and in the aims of the entire nation."[18]

With this framing strategy, the regime sought to mobilize its supporters and thereby strengthen its hand at the roundtable. It continued to control the institutions of public policy and military control. Jaruzelski told East German leader Erich Hoenecker as late as May 27, 1989, that the "situation in the army, in defense, is good. Even the opposition knows it."[19] Yet the Leninist regime faced constraints of its own. Despite Gorbachev's declared support for reform, the regime feared economic and political ostracism in Eastern Europe, given the lack of enthusiasm for reform among its trading partners in the Warsaw Pact, such as East Germany and Czechoslovakia. Further, the regime feared a negative reaction from within itself that in the worst case could lead to civil war. Although Generals Jaruzelski and Kiszczak had reluctantly concluded that negotiations were necessary, the broader party membership and regional secretaries were divided. For example, a poll carried out in early 1988 indicated that the legalization of the opposition was

[18] In Perzkowski, 1994: 289.
[19] In ibid.: 366.

supported by 38 percent of the PZPR and 41.6 percent of OPZZ members (Rychard, 1992: 141); at the same time, however, one politburo member estimated that a majority of the regional secretaries opposed liberalization.[20] As a government negotiator warned Solidarity:

> You often say that you have your social basis that you have to be accountable to. . . . But we also have our basis, and it is not only the Party. I do not need to remind you about the things that are happening now. But you need to take into consideration our position. We have to concede, for otherwise there will be no agreement.[21]

Finally and most basically, the regime feared chaos. In the words of the regime's representative at the table on political reforms, "I thought that democracy can not be described and reduced to some simple event such as free elections."[22] To satisfy its supporters in the nomenklatura, the government intended to create guarantees that nothing would happen too quickly.

The regime's concessions to the nomenklatura in the fall of 1988 seemed to be designed to throw roadblocks in the path of negotiations. On September 27, 1988, Mieczysław Rakowski was named prime minister, a controversial choice at such a moment given his history of bitter, anti-Solidarity comments as the editor of a party weekly. At the same time, Rakowski was aware of the need for reform and had previously warned the regime in an internal memorandum that if socialism did not revitalize itself, "it will see upheavals and revolutionary outbursts initiated by an increasingly better educated populace."[23] In a move seemingly intended to alienate the democratic opposition, Rakowski declared that the government would not negotiate with several key Solidarity leaders (such as Michnik and Kuroń) and that he could solve the economic problems without roundtable negotiations. He proceeded with audacity to

---

[20] Ciosek in *Tajne Dokumenty Państwo-Kościół 1980–1989*, 1993: 558.
[21] Cypryniak in Osiatyński, 1996: 50.
[22] Interview with Janusz Reykowski, October 10, 1994.
[23] Quoted in *Uncensored Poland News Bulletin*, no. 10/88 (May 27, 1988): 17.

announce the decision to liquidate the Lenin Shipyard in Gdańsk (the birthplace of Solidarity in 1980) as unprofitable, provoking Solidarity leader Bujak to declare that "the very idea of coming to an agreement . . . is politically and socially finished."[24]

In the context of the apparent inability of both sides to agree upon the terms for negotiations, the regime permitted Wałęsa to participate in a televised debate with the chair of the government trade union (who boasted that he would make "marmalade" of the Solidarity leader). In Wałęsa's words, it was clear that the government "was counting on 'Mr. Wałęsa's weaker intellectual capacity'" to humiliate him publicly and diminish his stature prior to the roundtable (1992: 167–68). Coached by media advisors such as film director Andrzej Wajda, however, Wałęsa sought to present himself as trustworthy, while his quick and lively responses to his duller opponent highlighted the difference between Solidarity and the regime. Public attention to the debate on November 30, 1988, was enormous. State polls afterward showed that 78 percent of all Polish adults watched this debate, and, according to a government survey, 68.8 percent of Warsaw households felt that Wałęsa represented himself better, compared with 5.8 percent for the head of the government trade union (CBOS, 1994: 384). The regime's attempt to downplay Wałęsa's authority failed dramatically and, if anything, offered Solidarity its first opportunity to demonstrate itself as a political actor on the national stage, bolstering the perception that the opposition might succeed in the negotiations.

The regime sought to mobilize its own members in support of the roundtable at the Tenth Plenum of the Communist Party, held in two parts, in December 1988 and January 1989. At these meetings Jaruzelski sought to gain the full support of the party by eliminating divisions within the party elite. At the first part, he removed the so-called hard-liners from the Central Committee, and in the second part he recruited new members, some of whom would represent the party on key issues at the roundtable (such as Janusz Reykowski, the government coalition's representative at the table on political

[24] Quoted in Stokes, 1993: 123.

reforms). When faced with resistance, Jaruzelski, Kiszczak, and others in the top leadership threatened to resign if the party did not accept the legalization of Solidarity. With that threat, they exited the room, leaving the Central Committee to debate among itself what to do. At this key moment, the remaining hard-liners in the Central Committee lost an opportunity to influence the path of events by voting 142 to 32, with 14 abstentions, to lift, "in conditions of national agreement, restrictions on creating new trade unions."[25] Restrictions upon negotiation included that Solidarity had to define itself as part of socialism, break relations with extremist groups, and forgo foreign financial aid; in turn, Wałęsa accepted the restrictions not as conditions but rather as the regime's statement of its negotiating position.

THE HONORABLE COMPROMISE FRAME
OF SOLIDARITY

With what I will refer to as the "honorable compromise" framing strategy, Solidarity sought to mobilize public support for its decision to end strikes and enter into negotiations, despite years of rejecting participation in official political structures. To do so it had to insist on clear symbolic boundaries concerning the source of the problems facing the country, its identity as the representative of Solidarity, and the limited nature of the agreement. This did not mean that the opposition accepted the regime's claims that a national crisis united them. Geremek, among others, argued, "The situation in which people find themselves is deteriorating: the material situation, the ecological situation and everything else—and it is deteriorating ever more swiftly. There is no hope, no prospects."[26] Even so, the opposition focused responsibility for the crisis firmly on the policies of the regime.

The central issue for the opposition concerned their identity as representatives of Solidarity at the roundtable. How could they

[25] Quoted in ibid.: 124.
[26] Quoted in *Uncensored Poland News Bulletin*, no. 16 & 17/88 (Sept. 10, 1988): 23.

claim to officially represent a trade union that remained illegal? Rejecting the framing by the regime that Poles would meet with Poles, opposition negotiators insisted on their identity distinct from and outside of the regime, that they would not join the government but would participate in it only as outsiders. Geremek argued that the term "pact" "contains no notion of coming to an agreement. No—this is a pact of two sides of divergent interests."[27] Given the presence at the roundtable of the government trade union, Solidarity leaders did not define themselves as a trade union to avoid debate over which union had greater support. To this end, the official name of the Solidarity delegation to the roundtable was "the Solidarity and opposition side." During negotiations, Solidarity leaders often argued that any agreement must be acceptable to "society" or it would be worthless for both sides. As one Solidarity leader argued across the roundtable, "If we agree to such a compromise, it will be useless for you . . . for if society does not accept the deal, you would sign a contract with a partner that has ceased to exist."[28] Drawing upon the civil society master frame, Solidarity negotiators emphasized the unity of "society" or the nation against a foreign state. It drew upon the romantic tradition in Polish history, which emphasizes "that society possesses a natural organic unity; that loyalty to the nation is more precious than life itself; that Poland has a special, divinely ordained destiny; that patriotic and religious commitment are closely akin" (Król, 1994: 88).

This broad mandate from society blurred the distinction between trade union members of Solidarity and their intellectual advisors, in contrast to the negotiations between Solidarity and the regime in 1980–81 (where the identities of union members and intellectual advisors was always sharp). The creation of a clear opposition identity against the regime has been called the "squaring [of] the roundtable": unlike the regime's vision of a roundtable around which many groups (including the communist trade union, wom-

---

[27] Quoted in *Uncensored Poland News Bulletin*, no. 16 & 17/88 (Sept. 10, 1988): 24.
[28] Bujak in Osiatyński, 1996: 49.

en's groups, and Catholic groups) would have an equal seat, the opposition sought to redefine a negotiating table at which only two sides would face each other, the regime and the opposition. At the final negotiation on January 27, 1989, before the convening of the roundtable meetings, a compromise was reached at which the Solidarity trade union would not be relegalized prior to the roundtable; its relegalization would be an outcome of the negotiations leading to elections.

The agency component of the framing strategy necessitated a decisive shift from the civil society master frame by accepting participation in politics, but it emphasized that this was a one-time, limited compromise based on respect for legal means of change. The emphasis on nonviolence and legal change drew on the civil society master frame. As Adam Michnik observed, "Taught by history, we suspect that by using force to storm the existing Bastilles we shall unwittingly build new ones" (1985: 86). Others have suggested that martial law had taught Solidarity leaders that "symbolic and emotional support cannot prevail over pure might. . . . [This experience] helped some of the leaders of the opposition put aside their 'all or nothing' approach" (Osiatyński, 1996: 24). For some critics of Solidarity the notion of "compromise" was viewed with mistrust, as a sign of weakness. Michnik insisted:

> My vision of compromise certainly adopts realism as the starting point. The geo-political reality is that we are not strong enough to drive the Red Army out of Poland. But my vision of compromise has another starting point. It is based on my conviction that pluralist democracy necessitates compromises in the face of complex realities. (1988: 27)

In contrast to the more abstract pronouncements of Solidarity's intellectual leaders, Wałęsa declared that it "must be a constructive kind of a compromise, provided it is not a cheap deception trick but covers all aspects of real life and puts everything in good balance."[29] This would remain a delicate balance throughout the roundtable,

[29] Quoted in *Uncensored Poland News Bulletin*, no. 20/88 (Oct. 31, 1988): 8.

leading to several extremely subtle distinctions that the opposition sought to maintain. At a meeting the week before the roundtable, future prime minister Mazowiecki insisted to his negotiators that "the entry of the opposition into parliament does not mean the entry into the government."[30]

With the honorable compromise framing strategy, Solidarity sought to mobilize support and gain access to institutional resources it lacked. Its principal constraint was at the same time its main resource: the authority of its name to represent the legitimate voice of society against the regime. Geremek described this as its "moral capital," which was controlled by the leaders of Solidarity in 1980–81, but which might also be squandered if its identity as the opposition became blurred through the impression that it was becoming part of the establishment (1990: 34). Thus Solidarity leaders placed enormous weight on the open nature of the talks by which it would maintain and increase its public support as a legitimate political force. This emphasis on openness drew upon the civil society master frame and shaped the behavior of all participants. Indeed, on a typical day of negotiations there might be as many as six roundtable press conferences, including the government coalition, the opposition, the two satellite parties, the official trade union, and perhaps one of the small regime-allied Catholic organizations.

Although Solidarity had always been a broad movement whose supporters understood it differently, the honorable compromise framing strategy continued the transformation of Solidarity from a trade union, protecting workers' rights, to a political movement, challenging the Leninist regime. This shift began under martial law, which some have argued "caused underground activists to believe that the goal of their struggle was the destruction of communism, not the defense of the workers' interests" (Modzelewski, 1994: 69). Thus, rather than mobilizing strike committees in workplaces, Solidarity activists created a new organization for the purpose of par-

[30] See Czyrek's report of the meeting at the secretariat of the Communist Party, January 23, 1989, in Perzkowski, 1994: 234.

ticipating in the roundtable: the "Citizens' Committee under Lech Wałęsa, NSZZ Solidarity." In contrast to 1980, when "intellectuals" acted as advisors for the striking workers, these intellectuals were now the principal negotiators with the regime for elections in which they would compete, not the workers. An earlier incarnation of this group in 1987 had led to the "Appeal of the 60" in which members of Solidarity and opposition intellectuals declared that "restructuring of our social life and of the economy should be based on social agreements between the authorities and genuine representatives of social milieux."[31] In December 1988 this group convened in a meeting that one of the participants referred to as the formation of a "shadow cabinet."[32] Fifteen "commissions" were appointed and called upon "to prepare roundtable talks," headed by individuals who would later represent the opposition at the corresponding roundtable groups.[33] With only ten workers, the list of proposed candidates for the elections prepared by the Citizens' Committee further illustrated the shift away from Solidarity's trade union identity. It is notable, however, that some of the same players were active as both members of the Solidarity National Coordinating Commission and the Citizens' Committees. Their arguments during negotiations that they could not make decisions without consulting one side or another conjures up the image of them switching hats as they move from meeting to meeting, perhaps with Wałęsa as the man wearing all the hats at the same time.

THE FAILED FRAME OF POLISH INDEPENDENCE

The honorable compromise framing strategy was not shared by all members of the opposition. A range of smaller groups, such as

[31] "The Appeal of the 60," in *Uncensored Poland News Bulletin*, no. 23/87 (Nov. 30, 1987): 15.

[32] Marcin Król, in *Uncensored Poland News Bulletin*, no. 2/89 (Jan. 31, 1989): 10.

[33] "The Resolution on the Formation of the Citizens' Committee," in *Uncensored Poland News Bulletin*, no. 24/88 (Dec. 31, 1988): 9.

the Confederation for an Independent Poland (*Konfederacja Polski Niepodległej*, hereafter referred to by its Polish acronym, KPN), the Young Poland movement, and "Fighting Solidarity," rejected the notion of compromise as the recognition of a fundamentally illegitimate state, calling for independence for Poland. Although these groups emerged from diverse histories and ideologies, the broad similarities in their rejection of compromise in the name of an independent Poland joined them and occasionally led to explicit cooperation among them. Founded as a political party dedicated to "the war for the recovery of independence" in 1979, KPN had an extensive hierarchy of associations and affiliated groups, as well as its own publishing house for books and newspapers.[34] Similarly the Young Poland movement was formed in 1979 to undertake a "war for the moral face of the nation, defense of the identity of national culture, the dissemination of access to knowledge and information as well as the elaboration of national thought and political program[s]" (Cecuda, 1989: 97). Founded as a regional splinter from the Solidarity trade union in 1982, Fighting Solidarity also declared its aim to wage a "war for the recovery of independence," and it had an active publishing house and radio, with its own youth movement (ibid.: 108).

The call for Polish independence linked itself to the interwar tradition of General Piłsudski in Poland, which emphasized Polish independence against foreign dominance. In the same journal in which Solidarity advisor Geremek announced its willingness to participate in an anticrisis pact, the leader of the Young Poland movement rejected the civil society master frame, arguing:

> [The opposition] cannot limit itself to the organization of external pressure on the structure of the state and toward efforts . . . to form a spiritual sovereignty aside from and in spite of the state. . . . The currently existing state is a real, although very imperfect form of the Polish state. The opposition . . . should undertake the battle for the

[34] See Cecuda, 1989: 46–50. Notably, KPN survived as a political force into the postcommunist period and continued to win seats in parliamentary elections in Poland as late as 1995.

state to become a genuinely effective tool for the realization of the national interest of Poles.[35]

Rather than compromise, he argued for the "recovery" of the state by society, identifying the goal of the opposition as being "a civil state, in which power grows from a wide social base."[36] For example, at a meeting with the striking workers in the Gdańsk Shipyard in August 1988, a KPN representative declared that the demands for independent trade unions and political pluralism should be linked to a third—that of an independent fatherland.[37] The leaders of "Fighting Solidarity" called for a boycott of the negotiations and elections, proclaiming that negotiations with the Communist Party were "tantamount to reconciliation with captivity."[38] This, they argued, necessitated continued organization along the lines of the underground army during World War II. In 1988, its members had been arrested on charges that they were responsible for explosions outside the Communist Party building in Gdynia. Together with other right-wing groups, KPN and Fighting Solidarity published a competing call for the opposition to unite within the framework of the so-called Independent Opposition and Parties Alliance (Siedlecki, 1989).

Although the call for independence draws upon traditions in Polish history and can therefore be said to have a potential measure of resonance, these groups failed, first, because their ambiguous stance toward violent tactics prevented them from gathering broad public support while the regime targeted them for repression; and, second, because their rejection of negotiations clashed with the sense of economic crisis vividly illustrated by the failed 1987 referendum and the April 1988 strikes. As noted earlier, the regime sought to influence the opposition by repressing those groups that it felt threatened social order through potentially violent tactics. Kennedy notes how harshly the regime treated the radicals of Fighting

[35] Aleksander Hall in Holc, 1992: 137.
[36] Quoted in ibid.: 138.
[37] Wagner in Tabako, 1992: 233.
[38] Quoted in Stokes, 1993: 126.

Solidarity and KPN, while it "lambasted the youth-based, independent peace movement WiP [Freedom and Peace] as traitorous to Polish society" (1992: 57). Their sometimes ambiguous stance toward violence also prevented these groups from forming alliances with the Catholic Church, whose institutional network would prove essential to the Citizens' Committees in the June elections. Evidence for the Church's rejection of these groups can be seen in records of negotiations with the regime, where the Catholic Church responded to the news of the arrests of the leaders of "Fighting Solidarity" by declaring, "God protect us from terrorism in Poland," and re-emphasizing Solidarity's rejection of violence (Raina, 1995: 219). Finally, although these groups failed to mobilize public support on behalf of "independence," their vocal presence nonetheless influenced the choices made by both the Leninist regime and the democratic opposition by strengthening their commitment to negotiation. Because these groups had institutional resources sufficient to maintain organized adherents, publish proclamations, organize demonstrations, and even run candidates in the June elections, they served as a reminder of the threat of chaos should negotiations fail to produce an agreement.

Setting the Agenda for Partially Free Elections

As Jon Elster observes, "[T]he Polish round table talks did not have a very ambitious aim at the outset."[39] At the beginning of the negotiations, it appeared that the table on trade union pluralism would be the place of Solidarity's greatest victory, achieving relegalization. Analysis of the outcome, however, demonstrates that it was the table on political reforms that transformed an attempt at co-optation into an opportunity for electoral competition. At the opening of the roundtable, the regime proposed that elections would be conducted as previous elections had been: voters would receive a single list of candidates to accept or reject, only this time there would be Solidarity candidates on the list. Solidarity candi-

[39] Elster, 1996: 11.

dates would be included in the regime's list of candidates as 35 percent of the seats in a single house of parliament, and parliamentary seats would be allocated on the basis of a plan specified beforehand. At the close, the terms were competitive: Solidarity candidates would compete on their own lists against regime candidates for 35 percent of the seats in a lower house of parliament, as well as for 100 percent of the seats in a new upper house. In turn, the opposition agreed to the creation of a presidency whose six-year term would outlast the four-year term of the new parliament.

The outcome was premised upon the exclusion from the agenda of the possibility that the regime could lose the elections. With the advantage of hindsight, it is worth observing that there were no provisions in the election laws for dividing the seats in the lower house of parliament among the coalition partners (who would later defect and join Solidarity to form a government), nor for the replacement of defeated candidates on the National List (several of the most notable of whom failed to gather the majority needed). No provisions were made for the replacement of the nomenklatura in key positions in government. The absence of such provisions suggests clearly that neither side anticipated either the results or the need to take precautions against a defeat of the government coalition. The Senate election ordinance consisted of ninety-eight senators, two from each of the forty-nine voting districts, to be chosen in the same manner as the seats in the *Sejm* open for competition. This clearly gave disproportional advantage to the rural areas, where the party foresaw stronger support.

The commitment to bargaining fundamentally altered the impact of the political resources that each side could bring to bear upon the outcome. The regime's control of the military, its national party structure, and the mass media would be less important than the ability to present arguments on behalf of particular plans of action in light of public support. As Castle observes, the regime "had committed itself to an arena in which its resources had only limited utility. The opposition, on the other hand, had entered an arena in which its weaknesses became strengths" (1995: 98). Attention to

bargaining demonstrates how the conditional nature of public support constrained the choices the negotiators perceived they could
accept, although arguments by negotiators based on the constraints
of supporters must be evaluated in light of the likelihood that they
could lead to actual rejection of the negotiations (and were not
merely a tactical move). Osiatyński argues that, because of the mutual interest in compromise by both sides at the roundtable, threats
of withdrawal from the talks based on the constraints of their con-
stituents were rarely used, but that "Solidarity felt that its threats
and arguments were more credible for its adversaries than vice
versa" (1996: 51).

Below, I analyze the three features to the political agreement of
the Roundtable Accords: the competitive election of candidates, the
creation of a presidency, and the re-establishment of a Senate in the
parliament. No single source contains a comprehensive documentation of the Polish roundtable, with its plenary sessions and three
subtables that met over two months. In my analysis, I rely upon
notes from the private meetings between regime and Solidarity negotiators (Dubiński, 1990), internal documents from both sides
(Perzkowski, 1994, and documents from the Solidarity Citizens'
Committee archives), interviews and statements by participants, as
well as media and secondary sources (Castle, 1995; Elster, 1996;
Osiatyński, 1996; Stokes, 1993).[40]

1. Competitive elections of candidates: The decisive feature of
the Roundtable Accords was the agreement that the parliamentary
seats allotted to Solidarity would be filled through competitive elections, rather than assigned by the regime according to prior agreement. Negotiations involved thirty-six participants, which met nine
times over a period of two months. The proposal by the government-coalition side at the first meeting of the table on political reforms on February 10 was that the negotiated elections were to be
conducted like the previous elections: voters would receive a single

[40] Marjorie Castle's unpublished dissertation (1995) presents perhaps the
most detailed and thorough analysis of the roundtable negotiations, to which I
am indebted.

list of candidates to accept or reject, only this time there would be Solidarity candidates included on the list. Parliamentary seats were to be allocated on the basis of a plan specified beforehand. The opposition was to be entitled to 35 percent of the seats in the *Sejm*, and the party, as specified at the last pre-roundtable Magdalenka meeting, would retain a 53 percent majority of parliament, relying upon its coalition partners for a governing majority. This step was based upon the assumption that these satellite parties would remain loyal, disciplined coalition partners, an assumption the opposition appeared to share, showing no interest in how the seats for the coalition would be divided up.

For the opposition, however, participation in the elections and acceptance of its limited role in the state was a price to be paid for the legalization of Solidarity, not a benefit. They saw no chance for systemic change in such a role, rather only the legitimation of the leaders of the Leninist regime who were guaranteed a majority in the new parliament. The strategy that emerged was that they would accept participation in the elections on the principle that they would run only for seats in which there would be free competition. This was entirely consistent with their mandate not to appear to become part of the establishment or risk the moral capital that was their only resource. As one Solidarity negotiator declared across the negotiating table, "Keep your controlling mandate and give the rest not to us, but to society."[41]

Furthermore, the election agreement had to be explicitly stated to be a one-time deal, and there should be a commitment that the next elections would be fully democratic. The actual division of the seats must be made publicly and openly. In Geremek's words: "[O]therwise we would have had to pretend that we suddenly fell in love with the Communist Party and of our own sincere will wanted to give it sixty-five percent of the seats in the Sejm" (1990: 120–22). There would be no common platform nor single ticket of candidates. As Michnik said, "I can't imagine any of my colleagues from Solidarity who would agree to let his name be placed on the list.

[41] Lech Kaczynski in Dubiński, 1990: 54.

And I wouldn't even feel that I should try to convince them into it."[42] Finally, Solidarity absolutely had to be legalized before the election campaign.

The party appeared to understand and agree with the opposition's need to prevent the impression that it was becoming part of the establishment. In an earlier meeting of the Joint Council of the government and Episcopate on January 23, 1989, the Polish archbishop referred to talks in which the regime indicated it understood that an independent church was better than a subordinate one because it could do more for the common good. He continued, "[If] they [the opposition] have greater autonomy, they would also be more real." Asked if he understood, the regime's representative replied, "Absolutely."[43] The creation of a *Sejm* in which the opposition appeared to have no independence would merely support the opposition's claim that the regime was not worthy of social support. On the other hand, it did not want to create a *Sejm* in which opposition deputies were democratically elected while party deputies were not. To this end, it proposed at the second meeting of the table, on February 18, that there be competition even for the seats guaranteed to the regime, so that multiple candidates could run for each seat, provided that each was a party member. This appeared to be an opportunity for the party to demonstrate its conviction to transform itself into a genuine political party. It appeared to be a "safe experiment in democracy, a way to bring in new blood and promote the smartest and most energetic party activists, those capable of appealing to the electorate, all this without the risk of competing with the opposition" (Castle, 1995: 114). The only exception was the National List, which guaranteed seats for the party leadership and made up no more than 10 percent of the seats. Still, agreement to making the division of parliamentary seats dragged on into March, until both sides agreed at the March 20 meeting to make it public and official. The one-time nature of the election was written into the legislation as the "ordinance to the Tenth *Sejm*," and the final

---

[42] Quoted in Castle, 1995: 117.
[43] Ciosek in *Tajne Dokumenty Państwo-Kościół 1980–1989*, 1993: 561.

agreement of the table on political reforms stated that the "signatories to the agreement are going to do their best to make sure that the composition of the next *Sejm* is determined by voters only."[44] The government-coalition side even agreed to the use of political symbols on the election ballot that would distinguish the candidates. The opposition won access to the mass media and agreement for the creation of a newspaper for the election campaign.

2. The creation of a presidency: The impasse created by the regime's proposal for a presidency with broad powers illustrates the contestation over the extent of the "honorable compromise" that Solidarity could accept and the guarantees that the regime demanded to reassure its nomenklatura base. As part of the guarantee of its position after the elections, the government-coalition side presented at the February 18 meeting a proposal for the re-establishment of the office of the president, which had been abolished in 1952. This meant that the existing head of state, the chair of the Council of State, would be replaced by a position with more authority in matters of the military, internal security, and foreign affairs. It was to serve as the guarantor of constitutional order and, in that way, was essential to reassure conservative elements within the regime who feared that the elections might set off social instability. For the party, in the words of Janusz Reykowski, its chair of the table on political reforms, "the next step toward democracy [must] not be a step toward destabilization."[45] The eventual proposal was for a president with a six-year term, which would ensure his continuity past the first new parliament, which would be elected for four-year terms. Initially this new office was seen as far too high a price to pay for participation in the elections, and the opposition rejected the proposal at the same meeting it was proposed, declining even to set up a working group to consider the question. Geremek threatened to withdraw Solidarity's support for earlier agreements about the seats in parliament:

---

[44] *Uncensored Poland News Bulletin,* no. 65/89 (July 4, 1989): 6.
[45] Quoted in Wałęsa, 1992: 178.

If we cannot reach an agreement and you are unable to make concessions, then we will probably have to return to another way of thinking about political reforms. . . . We may need to begin the reform of the state with a contract about the distribution of the seats in the *Sejm*, and to leave the other two elements, i.e., the presidency and the Senate, for constitutional changes that are to be introduced in 1991.[46]

Geremek's threat and the postponement of debate by the leader of the regime team of negotiators illustrate the limits to the agreement Solidarity perceived it could accept in exchange for re-legalization of the union.

3. The Senate: Faced with the impasse over the presidency, Wałęsa and Kiszczak (who had until this point remained outside the negotiations) met again at Magdalenka on March 2 to discuss a resolution to the problem. At this meeting, Kiszczak proposed the re-establishment of the Senate, which would be appointed by the president and would serve consultative functions, a proposal rejected by Geremek as a third price for the re-legalization of Solidarity. According to the published notes by the secretary of the regime, after eight hours of discussion, the meeting appeared to be at an impasse until suddenly one of the regime negotiators asked what the opposition would say if the second chamber were chosen by free elections.[47] Wałęsa and Geremek both quickly said that this might make an acceptable political package. The creation of the freely elected Senate was later called by Wałęsa "our greatest success."[48] An interview by Castle with Kwaśniewski suggests that the proposal for a freely elected Senate was his idea alone, but that "the warm reception of this suggestion by the otherwise unyielding opposition made it imperative that the regime give serious consideration to making this the basis for a new proposal" (1995: 128).

The final package designated a president with strong executive powers, clearly designed for General Jaruzelski to reassure the interests of the nomenklatura. It would be elected by an absolute

[46] Quoted in Osiatyński, 1996: 50.
[47] Aleksander Kwaśniewski in Dubiński, 1990: 76–77.
[48] Quoted in Stokes, 1993: 125.

combined majority of the *Sejm* and Senate (based on the 65 percent of the seats guaranteed to the government coalition in the *Sejm*). The president would be chairman of the Committee on National Defense and commander-in-chief of the military. The president could veto legislation produced by either house, although this veto could be overruled by a two-thirds majority in the *Sejm*. Further, the president was empowered to dissolve parliament if it were unable to form a government within a three-month period, unable to pass a budget, or encroached upon presidential authority. Finally, the president could declare a state of emergency for up to three months, although that could be extended only with approval from the *Sejm* and the Senate. On the other hand, the newly re-established Senate was given the mandate to "control the activities of the state" (Osiatyński, 1996: 57). It could introduce legislation and would have veto power over the *Sejm*, although, like the presidential veto, it could be overruled by a two-thirds majority of the *Sejm*.

The key to the acceptance of this package by Jaruzelski was his calculation of the balance of resources that each side would bring to the election campaign. The party maintained control over the media and its national network of local party structures. The nature of the roundtable agreement suggests that the party genuinely believed that it would be rewarded by being re-elected in return for its efforts at liberalization. The Senate election ordinance consisted of ninety-eight senators, two from each of the forty-nine voting districts to be chosen in the same manner as the seats in the *Sejm* open for competition. As noted, this was intended to give disproportional advantage to the rural areas where the party foresaw stronger support. Wałęsa himself was to declare that Solidarity was capable of winning Senate seats in only eighteen of the forty-nine voting districts (Koseła, 1990: 126).

Conclusion

The agreement for partially free elections at the roundtable was premised on expectations concerning likely political scenarios, namely that the Leninist regime would continue to control the political sphere in Poland in the near future. Their self-limiting nature may seem naïve in retrospect, given the rapid fall of neighboring Leninist regimes in which the new democrats had greater space for constructing new political institutions. Thus, I have sought to reconstruct the perceptions of what was possible in Poland at the time in light of a stalemate whereby neither side could resolve the situation alone and an international context in which the Warsaw Pact remained intact. I have argued that collective actors influenced the path of democratization in Poland by altering the range of outcomes considered by elites needing to maintain the support of the groups they represented. In the late 1980s, Solidarity did not seek to disrupt the political order through strikes but rather to demonstrate its trustworthiness in negotiations concerning democratization in Poland. As Ost observed:

> Solidarity ceased to exist as a trade union when martial law was imposed. By the mid-1980s no one could point to a viable Solidarity, not even those most committed to finding one. In 1987 the underground press was marked by one persistent theme: Solidarity was dead. . . . Paradoxically, however, it was this very weakness that became Solidarity's new strength. (1989: 84)

Notably, the two sides were unable to agree upon the direction for economic reform, even as economic crisis had driven both sides to the negotiating table. Thus, while the agreement at the table on political reforms radically altered subsequent political competition and the relegalization of Solidarity took place in a relatively straightforward manner, the table on economic reforms was unable to produce an accord. At this table, the official trade union (OPZZ) asserted its autonomy, calling at times for greater benefits for workers than the Solidarity side. Although its dissent on the question of indexation delayed the signing of the final agreement, this ultimately did not threaten the legitimacy of the agreement, nor significantly influence the path of change.

Solidarity leaders insisted upon an agenda that would not compromise its conditional support or its "moral capital" but would lead to an "honorable compromise." The commitment to bargaining in light of conditional support made certain outcomes more likely (such as the agreement that all seats for which Solidarity could run would be contested competitively) while excluding others (such as the initial proposal of a strong presidency and Senate to be filled by the old regime). Analysis of the table on political reforms demonstrates how collective actors enabled and constrained the alternatives considered, producing an electoral agreement in which Solidarity could demonstrate public support rather than the effort at co-optation intended by the Leninist state. I have argued that the misperception of the strength of the position of the government was critical to the agreement at the roundtable.

The nature of the election package agreed upon by both sides suggests that neither side predicted Solidarity's sweep of the election. As noted, there were no provisions for the possibility that the Leninist regime might lose the elections, suggesting clearly that neither side anticipated the results or the need to take precautions against a defeat of the government coalition. The failure of nationalist groups advocating Polish independence suggests that a more radical framing of events would not have received the support of the public or might have provoked a backlash against reform by hardliners within the government. At key turning points in the process leading up to and during negotiations, the consistency of the framing strategies of the participants influenced their respective support for events. If in August 1988 the younger striking workers had failed to support Wałęsa's call for negotiations, the Solidarity leaders might not have been able to demonstrate their ability to speak for society and quiet economic upheaval. If the conservatives in the politburo had accepted Jaruzelski's resignation at the second part of the Tenth Plenum, even the limited opening for the opposition might have been rejected and the regime further isolated. Finally, if the offer for free elections to the Senate had not been made and accepted by the government, Solidarity negotiators had indicated their willingness to withdraw their support for the compromise elections.

By analyzing how bargaining can lead to unexpected outcomes, this book rejects alternative explanations of the roundtable negotiations as an agreement by which the state elite agreed to relinquish power in exchange for political leniency or economic advantages. For example, Zubek declares that the Polish state had sought to exploit the weakness of the Polish opposition in the late 1980s by negotiating a pact whereby state elite would be guaranteed the ability to take over formerly state-owned properties as privately owned companies (1994: 813). He emphasizes:

> [In] the summer and early autumn of 1988, the communist leadership undertook a massive campaign of semi-official overtures and preliminary negotiations with some of these former leaders [of Solidarity], forming a resurgent leadership milieu. . . . After the fundamentals of the agreement had been established . . . the agreements were concluded amidst the pomp and circumstance of the "round-table" negotiations in the spring of 1989. (1996: 277–78)

Similarly Jadwiga Staniszkis uses the phrase "political capitalism" to describe the process by which the former nomenklatura was made owners of previously state-owned property (1992). Although this explanation may have appeal in light of the apparent ability of certain elites of the old regime to capitalize upon new economic opportunities, it lacks theoretical justification as well as historical corroboration. The supposed threat of force and organizational superiority of the regime cannot explain why events did not turn out the way the regime intended: while the Polish leaders of the Leninist regimes offered the democratic opposition a limited voice in parliament, the successful election campaign and defection of the satellite parties resulted in a new Solidarity-led government. Zubek's explanation falters when he must explain what he refers to as the "devastating defeat" of the Communist Party in the June elections. The opposition's weakness, which had previously enabled the state to impose an agreement, suddenly became a powerhouse, a "steamroller . . . [that] managed to easily sweep most districts" (1996: 280). Finally, despite incentives to reveal such an agreement in the post-communist period that could discredit the participants, no evidence for such an agreement has come to light.

Instead, the eight weeks of negotiations "produced significant changes in the capabilities and interrelationships of the actors" (Castle, 1995: 145). Some 58.7 percent of respondents in a national survey felt that Solidarity, rather than the regime, had gained greater social support as a result of the talks (CBOS, 1994: 408). Solidarity had used the public nature of the roundtable to establish itself as a serious negotiating partner with the regime, worthy of the trust of the country. Ultimately, the agreement provided it with a key opportunity, which I turn to in the next chapter: an opportunity to use the election campaign to mobilize society, or, in Wałęsa's words, "to wake society up" (1992: 185).

CHAPTER FOUR

The Pacted Resolution in Poland

The legalization of Solidarity is only the first relatively easy period of the war of the opposition against the government. The
next period will be harder for us.
                              —General Kiszczak in September, 1988[1]

IN THIS CHAPTER, I explain unexpectedly successful mobilization of voters in the partially free elections in June 1989 and
the pacted resolution of the challenge based on the Roundtable Accords. To the surprise of observers and participants alike, Solidarity
candidates won ninety-nine out of one hundred seats in the Senate
and all of the seats for which they competed in the *Sejm*. The main
puzzle is how Solidarity was able to exploit a limited opportunity to
mobilize the public to vote for its candidates: whereas it lacked the
material and organizational resources emphasized by social movement research, its far-better-financed adversary (the Leninist regime) controlled a national network of party and mass media structures. By examining the diffusion of the movement, I analyze how
Solidarity leaders mobilized support throughout the country on the
basis of a unified electoral strategy that transformed the network of
Catholic Church parishes into local Citizens' Committees. I examine how the constraints of the honorable compromise framing strategy and uncertainty surrounding the international response to the
election results led to the resolution whereby General Jaruzelski was
elected president with the assistance of Solidarity deputies, and a

[1] Quoted in Perzkowski, 1994: 63.

grand coalition government headed by Solidarity prime minister Mazowiecki was formed with the unforeseen defection of the former satellite parties.

In this chapter I examine four areas: (1) the honorable compromise framing strategy and mobilization in the election campaign; (2) transformation of local parishes and diffusion of the movement; (3) the regime's electoral campaign; and (4) the unexpected outcome and formation of the Mazowiecki government in August 1989.

The "Honorable Compromise" Framing Strategy in the Election Campaign

The roundtable agreements transformed the political landscape in Poland, making the ability to secure votes in elections the aim of mobilization, rather than striking in factories or protesting on the street. Analysis of the election campaign leading to the pacted reconstruction of the state thus necessitates bridging the literatures on contentious politics and voting. Although voting is typically less risky than protesting, voting cannot be explained solely on the basis of aggregate individual predispositions, since voters must actually go to the polls for these predispositions to have political consequences, especially in novel, uncertain, and urgent circumstances. Solidarity perceived itself to be at a disadvantage given the constraints of the roundtable agreement for nonconfrontational elections, the international political opportunity structure (since the neighboring Leninist regimes remained intact), and the absence of pre-existing organizational structures. As one analyst observed, "Solidarity . . . cannot count on mass enthusiasm to make up for its organizational disadvantages."[2]

Having previously urged the population to boycott elections, Solidarity would now have to urge the population to vote, and to vote for the package agreed upon at the roundtable. It had to explain to voters the nature of this agreement and convince them that

---

[2] Quoted in Stokes, 1993: 126.

they should participate in what were admittedly only partially free elections. At the same time, the opposition sought to avoid appearing to antagonize the state, so that the relegalization of the Solidarity trade union on April 17 took place quietly, without the celebration one might have imagined. The fulfillment of the long-standing slogan "There is no freedom without solidarity" had few immediate consequences upon the political environment, which was focused on the elections. Wałęsa commented later upon the Poles' love of dramatic victory, observing that the actual relegalization of Solidarity appeared to be only an "administrative" victory that could not generate much enthusiasm (1992: 186).

In this and the next section of this chapter, I examine the process by which Solidarity sought to transform its "moral capital" into votes. I argue that the claims of the honorable compromise framing strategy (discussed in Chapter 3) influenced the selection and presentation of candidates to voters, as well as the decision by many of Solidarity's prominent leaders not to run in the elections. The election campaign had two phases: the nomination of candidates on the basis of collecting voter signatures, until May 10, 1989, and the twenty-five-day campaign, ending June 4.

With the announcement of the Roundtable Accords, debate emerged within the opposition that revealed competing strategies for the election campaign. At a debate on April 8, three scenarios were proposed: first, elections could be held under the banner of Solidarity. This was rejected as failing to represent the changes that had taken place in Poland since 1981 regarding pluralism of opposition opinion. Second, the Citizens' Committee could head the elections only formally, while all candidates would be chosen by national and regional committees set up by Solidarity. Thirdly (a model advocated by Aleksander Hall), the Citizens' Committees would appeal for a democratic coalition of various oppositional groups that would propose candidates.[3] After debate, the second model was agreed on by vote: candidates would be selected by regional committees created by Solidarity and the Coordinating

[3] *Uncensored Poland News Bulletin*, no. 8/89, 16 May 1989: 13.

Commission of the Citizens' Committee "Solidarity." The decision was consistent with the honorable compromise framing strategy emphasizing Solidarity's identity as "society" against the state (rather than its being a trade union), but firmly anchored in the legacy of the symbols and personalities of Solidarity. The agreement upon the selection of candidates exposed divisions within Solidarity. Three members of the original Citizens' Committee—Mazowiecki, Hall, and Marcin Król—resigned in protest against the undemocratic means by which candidates would be chosen. At this meeting it was already clear that the opposition perceived these elections as a compromise and did not expect to be forming a government after the elections. Thus Wałęsa declared that he would not run for any seat, in case they failed: "Someone must be in reserve to save you and the country," he explained.[4] Similarly, although perhaps for different reasons, many of the prominent leaders of the Solidarity trade union—such as Bujak and Frasyniuk—declined to run in the elections. Bujak argued that his proper place was "in the Union," from which he could defend what everyone expected would be the minority in parliament.[5]

Drawing upon the roundtable negotiations, Solidarity relied upon the honorable compromise framing strategy as a simple and clear way of identifying and distinguishing its candidates as the embodiment of the moral capital of Solidarity representing a united society. During the short election campaign, the only thing that could unite and mobilize people in such a short time, argued opposition activists, was the names of "Solidarity" and of Lech Wałęsa. In the words of the secretary of the Citizens' Committee, Henryk Wujec:

> They had structure and organization. They had money, of course. We hadn't, and we were afraid. . . . Our arm, our force was the name Solidarity and the name Lech Wałęsa. We said, it's not important, my name is Kowalski, Wujec, Rokita. What's important is that I am the candidate of Solidarity. . . . You should vote only for Solidarity.

[4] *Uncensored Poland News Bulletin*, no. 8/89 (May 16, 1989): 14.
[5] Quoted in *Karty '89* [Ballot '89], the election newspaper in Cracow of the Committee of MKO "Solidarity," Issue 1 (April 25, 1989): 1.

> Maybe my partner from the Communist Party is more famous, but he is not from Solidarity.[6]

Thus, rather than focusing on personalities (with the exception of Wałęsa), Solidarity's election campaign maintained its collective identity, which distinguished the bearers of Solidarity's moral capital from their competitors. This connection was made visible to voters by the creation of campaign posters for every Solidarity candidate with Lech Wałęsa, with his signature on the bottom and a statement of support such as "Jan Jozef Lipski: That's my candidate, Lech Wałęsa ."[7] Solidarity sought to identify itself (as all participants in the election did) as the representative of the national legacy, invoking the historical association of society and the nation against the state in posters such as those that declared, "Vote for your Poland, Solidarity" or "Let Poland be Poland, Solidarity."[8] As I will argue in the next section of this chapter, the symbolic link between society and the nation against the state was completed by the historical association with the Catholic Church, which would provide many local Citizens' Committees with the institutional resources needed for the election campaign.

Public statements to voters stressed the identity of the opposition outside of the state and the nature of the compromise the elections represented, creating a delicate balance of participation in the state without accepting responsibility for its policies. Candidates stressed the one-time nature of these elections and the four-year term after which completely free elections would be held, arguing that this was an unprecedented (if limited) opportunity to vote for actual representation in parliament that would create an evolutionary path to structural change. The Citizens' Committee election platform, straightforwardly entitled "Why we vote," declared its intention that the "independent minority in parliament will not form the government and will not appoint the president in accordance with our wishes, but it will lawfully and loudly express the will of

---

[6] Interview by author with Henryk Wujec, October 28, 1994.
[7] Photocopy from Citizens' Committee Archives, Polish Senate.
[8] Quoted in Boni, 1990: 13, 24.

the Polish people and mobilize the public."[9] Across the country Wałęsa proclaimed, "[We] are the opposition outside the system, not parliamentarians."[10] Similarly, the opposition declared on television, "[We] are irrevocably outside of the system which came from the East."[11]

Consistent with the honorable compromise framing strategy's stress on legal means of political change, the second issue of the newspaper created for the election, *Gazeta Wyborcza* (literally *Election Newspaper*), declared in a paraphrase of Karl Marx: "A spectre is haunting Europe and other continents . . . a spectre of the end of a military form of communism." It continued, "[We] want to replace [the totalitarian system] with parliamentary democracy. However we reject revolution and violence, since we are aware that it is easy to replace one dictatorship with another."[12] Thus, disruptive protest would not be part of Solidarity's tactics (indeed, it often sought to prevent such disruptions by striking workers or other groups). Rather it emphasized orderly meetings to present its candidates and inform potential voters about the election.

The first task of the Citizens' Committees was to nominate local candidates of Solidarity for parliament, and then to collect the three thousand signatures necessary for the candidates to be placed on the official voting list. A handout by the Group for the Promotion of the Election of the Citizens' Committee identified activities that "every one of us" must do, including wearing Solidarity pins, speaking with people, spreading information about the election, organizing pre-election meetings, bringing information to Citizens' Committees, and organizing the sale of Solidarity election shares to help pay for the campaign.[13] Young people, drawing from the student

[9] *Uncensored Poland News Bulletin*, no. 79/89 (May 27, 1989): 1.

[10] Quoted by Kiszczak at a meeting of the secretariat of the Central Committee on May 2, 1989, in Perzkowski, 1994: 335.

[11] Quoted by Baka at a working meeting of the secretariat of the Central Committee on May 10, 1989, in Perzkowski, 1994: 342.

[12] "The election campaign," *East European Reporter* 3, no. 4 (spring–summer 1989): 35–36.

[13] Photocopy from Citizens' Committee Archives, Polish Senate.

movements and others such as Freedom and Peace, provided an energetic network of activists across the country. On April 23 an election program was proposed and a list of candidates—one for each
of the 161 seats in the *Sejm* and 100 seats in the Senate that Solidarity candidates contested—agreed upon. Seventeen days later, on
May 10, all of the necessary signatures were submitted, and the
election campaign focused on staging election rallies and public
meetings. Given the newness of having the opposition on the ballot,
the Citizens' Committees distributed flyers instructing voters on
how to vote for Solidarity candidates. The ballots contained the
names of all candidates and, in the tradition of voting under the
communist regime, voters were to cross out all candidates whom
they did not support. In the past voters might have simply placed
their ballots in the voting box without crossing off any names (since
all were party candidates), but these elections offered a situation in
which the voters could express their support through what Timothy
Garton Ash called "the glorious work of deletion" (1990b: 27).
One flyer from the region around Łódź displayed sketches of the
ballots for the *Sejm* and Senate with the names of all but Solidarity
candidates crossed out. It announced, "[B]eware! On the list of
senators you will find not crossed out only these two names. You do
the crossing out."[14]

The Transformation of Local Parishes and
Diffusion of the Movement

According to Geremek, Solidarity faced enormous obstacles:
"We can exploit this piece of freedom, but we have only a sketchy
organizational structure and extremely limited access to the media."[15] The adoption of a centralized electoral strategy posed significant challenges for Solidarity in the absence of a pre-existing national structure. The Citizens' Committees were not based in facto-

[14] Photocopy from Citizens' Committee Archives, Polish Senate.
[15] Quoted in Wałęsa, 1992: 183.

ries or enterprises that had formed the network of Solidarity strike committees in 1980–81, nor in underground units of martial law. Instead, they had to create a new network of Citizens' Committees to provide support for Solidarity candidates and mobilize voters across the country. In these circumstances, the key to their success was the transformation of the national network of local parishes and Clubs of Catholic Intelligentsia into local Citizens' Committees on the basis of the congruency between the claims of the honorable compromise framing strategy and the identity of the Polish Catholic Church as the bearer of national tradition. As argued earlier, the use of the claims of the honorable compromise framing strategy by Solidarity candidates increased the likelihood of the "attribution of similarity" between the leaders of the movement at the roundtable and local voters. Having discussed the history of the relationship between Solidarity and the Catholic Church in detail in Chapter 2, I focus here on the support by the hierarchy for participation in the elections (and sometimes explicitly for Solidarity candidates) and the organization of local Citizens' Committees. To support my argument, I analyze the election campaign in two cities that represent different traditions in Polish history, social and economic structure, and legacy of opposition activity: Cracow and Wrocław. Rather than a unidirectional process of diffusion outward from Warsaw, the diffusion of Solidarity's electoral strategy might be better seen as nodal, or composed of a center with several key points where regional cities also provided assistance to nearby localities. My account relies upon primary documents gathered in the archive of the Citizens' Committee at the Polish Senate, including questionnaires sent from local offices from each of the forty-nine voting districts to the central committee in Warsaw, election flyers and posters, and local newspapers.

SUPPORT BY THE HIERARCHY

Having served as a mediator between the state and Solidarity during the roundtable negotiations, the behavior of the Church hierarchy in the election campaign was an essential part of the calculation of both the state and the opposition. The state strategy of co-opting the opposition rested upon the assumption that the Church would maintain its role as mediator, urging caution and a long-term perspective on Polish interests. General Jaruzelski assured Czecho-slovak Communist Party leaders during his visit to Prague on February 1, 1989, that the Church was interested in maintaining peace in Poland, that it had moderated the opposition and would not "encourage an antistate mood" (in Perzkowski, 1994: 260). This proved to be a mistake, since during the campaign, candidates for the Citizens' Committees benefited from many public displays of the Church hierarchy's support.

Thus, on April 18, after the official re-legalization of Solidarity, Wałęsa and the opposition leaders of the three main tables of the roundtable flew to Rome where they were publicly received by the Pope, who encouraged their efforts. The Polish hierarchy itself announced its support for the elections. In Bulletin 234 of the Episcopal Conference of May 2, 1989, the Episcopate expressed its view that "by ending the monopolization of power, elections represented an important step on the road to self-government."[16] Consistent with the honorable compromise framing strategy, the bulletin called for the *podmiotowość* of the nation and society, a term David Ost defines as "subjectivity" and elaborates as "the creative, active process whereby people become the 'subjects' of history rather than its passive 'objects.'"[17] On the eve of the election, Primate Glemp publicly received Jacek Kuroń and Adam Michnik, two of Solidarity's prominent non-Catholic leaders.

Solidarity flyers were full of images and words of the Church to emphasize its support. One such Solidarity poster shows the Pope apparently whispering in Lech Wałęsa's ear, with the equation underneath: "Solidarity = trust."[18] Another quoted the Primate's Social Council (whose chair also served as one of the chairs of the

[16] Quoted in ibid.: 201.
[17] Photocopy from Citizens' Committee Archives, Polish Senate; and Ost, 1990: 4.
[18] In Boni, 1990: 7.

roundtable plenary sessions) declaring that "it is necessary for Catholic society to fulfill the voluntary election by voting."[19] By linking support for Solidarity with the Church, voting became part of the duty of all Catholics in Poland.

Organizing Local Committees

The creation of a national network of Citizens' Committees "Solidarity" relied heavily upon the Church for institutional support, especially in the countryside and smaller towns where it was weakest. Parishes not only permitted gatherings in a relatively free space but also held regular services accessible to all Poles with a symbolic religious language in which support for Solidarity could be expressed. This drew upon the legacy of martial law in the 1980s, when local parishes continued to serve as a haven for activity that was forbidden outside their walls, including discussion groups, theater performances, and art exhibits. For example, the Church had held so-called Weeks of Catholic Culture in which political discussions took place and in which the honorable compromise framing strategy emerged. Organized by the Catholic Ministry for Creative Artists, intellectuals associated with Solidarity met on October 9, 1986, in the Church of Our Lady in Warsaw, as part of a cycle entitled "The Difficult Art of Compromise."[20] The meeting attracted two thousand people. At this meeting, Bronisław Geremek expressed the views of many concerning Solidarity in the 1980s: "One cannot speak of an opposition in Poland in the sense that there exists a force waiting to take power. More accurately, it is a certain state of alertness in society, an all-embracing state of communion. . . . What remains is the realism of understanding both the geopolitical situation and the aspiration of society." Wojciech Lamentowicz, formerly a lecturer at the Central Committee's School of Social Sciences, noted the impasse in Poland: "The ruling team undoubtedly

[19] Photocopy from Citizens' Committee Archives, Polish Senate.
[20] Quoted in *Uncensored Poland News Bulletin,* no. 21/86 (November 16, 1986): 31, 32.

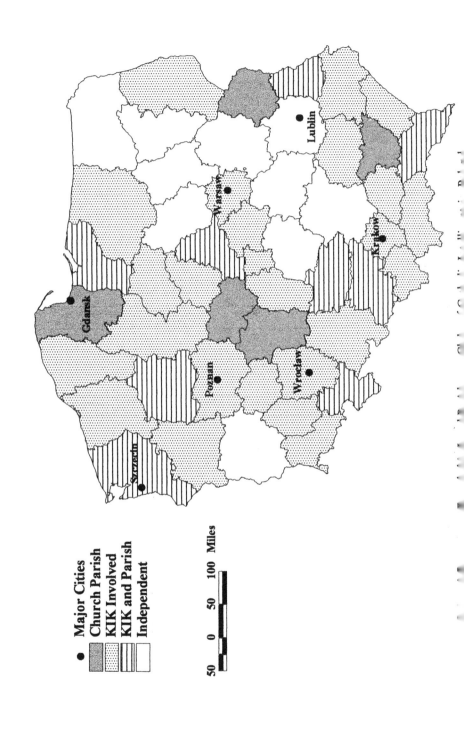

Major Cities
Church Parish
KIK Involved
KIK and Parish
Independent

50   0   50   100   Miles

has the power to block attempts at criticism and association, but at the same time they do not even have the power to carry out their own programmes." He suggested, "[S]ome space should be reconstructed, in which a dialogue could be held where the two sides could at least listen to each other."

The transformation of the church-based network in the election campaign was one of Solidarity's first goals. Indeed, the Warsaw headquarters began organizing the election campaign by preparing a map of Poland that showed all the voting districts and dioceses of the Catholic Church. Kosela argues, "[M]ost of the [citizens'] committees began their activities in church halls . . . [and] at least half of all committees were . . . using church premises from the beginning of the campaign" (1990: 128). The claim that local parishes formed branches of the movement is corroborated by records of a survey sent to the Warsaw headquarters by each of the Citizens' Committees in the forty-nine voting districts of Poland, in which twenty-three out of forty-nine explicitly identified their location in local parishes or Clubs of Catholic Intelligentsia, whose assistance was identified by thirty-five out of forty-nine voting districts.[21] The voting districts in which branches of the Citizens' Committees were established in local parishes or branches of Clubs of Catholic Intelligentsia are highlighted in Map 1.

A Group for Aid to the Regions was established at the Warsaw headquarters of the Citizens' Committees that oversaw the activity of local branches. This enabled them to take the first steps in the creation of local Citizens' Committees in every voting district, based on the provision of the roundtable agreement that required local authorities to provide them with furnished offices and communications equipment such as telephones and telexes. Kosela details eighteen "organizational solutions" by the Church during the pre-election campaign, including the schooling of many of the election activists (since the vast majority of those composing the civil com-

---

[21] Citizens' Committee Surveys, in Citizens' Committee Archives, Polish Senate.

mittees were also members of the Catholic Intelligentsia Clubs or people involved in industrial or peasant missions), priests helping to initiate and to organize the activity of some of the local civil committees, use of church halls for meetings, use of pulpits to inform local people about the establishment of Solidarity's civil committees, the nomination of local candidates, and gathering of signatures to place such candidates on the official voting list (ibid.: 128–30).

The activity by the Church in support of Solidarity candidates was noted with concern by the state, since the neutral position of the Church was "essential" to the state's election campaign.[22] At a May 2, 1989, meeting, General Kiszczak warned that the Church was offering support for the registration of candidates, although Jaruzelski dismissed the report, claiming it had only "moderate effects" and calling for more talks with the Church.[23] By May 24, however, the Office of Denominations outlined in a letter to Jaruzelski the steps it had undertaken to neutralize the activity of the Church, including written protests and information sent to the primate, the establishment of talks between the provincial party leaders and bishops calling for the separation of "moral principles in public life" from "party-oriented political options in the election," and meetings between politburo members and Bishop Dąbrowski.[24] On May 31, 1989, the government explained to the Joint Commission on the Government and the Episcopate that it was "counting on the Church to be a neutral, corrective moral force" and requesting that there be no political agitation in parishes on election day, only to be told by Bishop Dąbrowski that this was outside the domain of the Church, since no one is allowed to agitate on that day according to the election law.[25]

[22] Notes from a CBOS election report to the Central Committee, in Perzkowski, 1994: 356.

[23] Quoted in ibid.: 335.

[24] Quoted in ibid.: 373.

[25] Ibid.: 376–77.

DIFFUSION OF THE MOVEMENT:
CRACOW AND WROCŁAW

By examining the election campaign in Cracow and Wrocław, I analyze the diffusion of the centralized Solidarity election strategy and the successful mobilization of voters beyond the central headquarters in Warsaw. Analysis of these two cities cannot represent the entire country, especially one with as large a rural population as Poland. Yet because the two cities reflect meaningfully different traditions in Polish history, they illustrate the similarities that come from the centrally organized election campaign as well as the differences deriving from their geographical and historical uniqueness. Cracow, the regional capital of Małopolska in the southern part of Poland, was part of the former Austrian partition in the eighteenth century and had a long tradition of Solidarity activism in the working-class suburb of Nowa Huta, as well as dense church and university networks. By contrast, Wrocław, in the so-called Western Territories, became part of Poland after 1945 as part of Poland's changing borders after World War II. While Solidarity had been strong in Wrocław in 1980–81, it was led not by Wałęsa but by its own charismatic leader, Władysław Frasyniuk, and did not participate in the strikes of 1988.

Cracow: The Małopolski regional Citizens' Committee "Solidarity" was founded on April 10, 1989, in Cracow by the representatives of independent groups invited by the spokesperson for the regional Solidarity organization, Stefan Jurczak. My account draws upon analysis of the election newspaper *Karty '89* [*Ballot '89*] in April–May 1989. The transformation of local parishes is evident in the first issue, which identifies three Information Centers for "Solidarity": the Regional Organizational Center was at the Club for Catholic Intelligentsia in the city center, and the district centers in Nowa Huta and Krowodrza Podgórze were both in local parishes. The symbolic linking of the Solidarity candidates and the Church can be seen in the headline story in the second issue, which reprinted a telegram sent by Solidarity candidate Mieczyslaw Gil to the Pope with best wishes. In that issue, an article entitled "Excitement" describes the public processions taking place at churches: "After masses celebrated in the churches, we leave in streams of rain in a many-thousand mass of people frequenting all places of worship in which we used to be when the ZOMO [the riot police] commonly broke up all progress, like the church in Kalinowy, as in Arka and Szklane Domy."[26] The spokesperson for the Citizens' Committee in the nearby district of Nowy Sącz declared that the collection of signatures for candidates in the first part of the election campaign was taking place "mostly in churches."[27] Later articles describe the churches as virtual campaign centers for Solidarity, covered with Solidarity posters with slogans like "Vote Only for Solidarity" and "Cross Out All But Solidarity."[28] The public support of the hierarchy was also demonstrated when on May 12, the cardinal of Cracow received the Solidarity candidates, expressing confidence in the Episcopate's statement and stressing that "the Church sees in the coming elections a chance to lead the Fatherland to the path of proper development."[29] When asked in a newspaper interview what he expected from the elections, Father Jozef Tischner of Cracow displayed the modesty of the honorable compromise framing strategy: "I do not have big expectations. I do not think that economic miracles will take place or Finlandization, but it seems to me that thanks to new people in the *Sejm* and Senate there will be a little more truth in our country."[30]

In their pre-election meetings the candidates stressed the honorable compromise framing strategy as they explained the elections and sought to garner support. At one meeting, on May 1, 1989, for Solidarity candidate Jan Maria Rokita at the Lokomotywownia Prokocim, Rokita declared:

> The elections are not fully democratic. Even if we win, we will not have a majority in the *Sejm*, only 35 percent. We just however accept the risk, even a risk of losing. The signed accords give us a new possi-

[26] *Karty '89* [Ballot '89], Issue 2: 1.

[27] Ibid., Issue 4: 3.

[28] Ibid.: 3.

[29] Bulletin from press office MKO "Solidarity" in Cracow, May 12, 1989. Photocopy, Citizens' Committee Archive, Polish Senate.

[30] *Karty '89* [Ballot '89], Issue 4: 1,3.

bility to solve the conflicts with the government on a parliamentary route—a possibility we have never had before. We must no longer strike over everything.[31]

In a newspaper interview, Krzysztof Kozlowski responded to the question of whether he felt the communists would freely give up the government: "[Of] course not. The communists have never given up a government freely." But he argued that it was possible and worthwhile to create a situation in which they would be faced with the presence of the opposition in parliament.[32] Solidarity candidate Jerzy Zdrada linked voting for Solidarity to the nation, declaring at a pre-election meeting that the election was not a question of cosmetic changes but "of building a sovereign Fatherland."[33] Activity that did not use the honorable compromise framing strategy was met with repression, most notably in the breakup by the militia of a demonstration outside the Soviet Embassy on May 17 organized under the slogan "Soviets Go Home." The response by the Citizens' Committee deplored the use of force and stressed that Solidarity had always been a speaker for "social peace," calling on all forces in Poland for "similar responsibility."[34]

The difficult balance between the declared openness of the Citizens' Committees to independent candidates and the unity of the Solidarity list is especially evident in Cracow, where the leader and founder of KPN, Leszek Moczulski, competed for a seat in the *Sejm* against Solidarity candidate Jan Maria Rokita. A report for the Málopolski Citizens' Committee on a pre-election meeting of the two candidates on May 29, 1989, reveals the competing framing strategies.[35] In contrast to Rokita's introduction of himself as the candidate of the Citizens' Committees, Moczulski sought to challenge the Solidarity strategy by simultaneously blurring the distinction between the

[31] Ibid., Issue 2: 4.
[32] Ibid., Issue 6: 2.
[33] Ibid., Issue 6: 4.
[34] Ibid., Issue 7: 1.
[35] Memorandum, Małopolski Citizen's Committee "Solidarity," "Pre-election encounter of Jan Rokita and Leszek Moczulski," May 29, 1989. Photocopy, Citizens' Committee Archive, Polish Senate.

two groups and stressing the positive differences of KPN. Referring to Polish history, he argued that there were two political orientations in interwar Poland: independence, represented by Piłsudski, and compromise. "We see that both paths were needed," he argued, attempting to make an analogy in the emphasis on independence by his party, KPN, and the compromise line of the Citizens' Committees. Although the group in the Citizens' Committees may have gained advantageous results for Poland, he continued, "it can lead to the impression that after forty-five years Poles are accepting the system. The position of KPN in the elections contests this manipulation." Moczulski concluded by declaring that in all of Poland people should choose to vote for Solidarity, but "in the seventeen regions in which KPN is running they will have to achieve something higher." In response, Rokita rejected Moczulski's frame as relying upon the language of the state: "I do not understand the distinctions made by the Polish communists: constructive-confrontational. This distinction means nothing in the Polish reality. . . . The term independent opposition also means nothing." He sought to reinforce the distinction between himself as the Solidarity candidate for whom people should vote and Moczulski's candidacy for KPN: "Please do not say that the programs of Solidarity and KPN are not rivals but complementary. . . . [F]or mandate number 200 there is only one representative seat, and we cannot sit in it at the same time. . . . [L]adies and gentlemen . . . it is a choice between two people, Rokita and Moczulski. It is a choice between two political profiles for parliament."

Wrocław: The Citizens' Committee in Wrocław was founded on April 26, 1989, and led by Solidarity activist Władysław Frasyniuk, who, like Wałęsa, had declined to run for elected office. My account draws upon *Gazeta Wyborcza*, the election newspaper of the Citizens' Committee in Wrocław (with the same name as the national newspaper). The transformation of the pre-existing church network in Wrocław, as in Cracow, is evident in a newspaper article identifying "Information Points of the Citizens' Committee 'S' in Wrocław."[36] The headquarters of the Citizen's Committee was identified

[36] *Gazeta Wyborcza Wrocław*, Issue 5: 2.

as the Club of Catholic Intelligentsia, with three Information Points for the voting districts (with their hours of operation) at the parishes of St. Clement Dworzak, St. Augustine, and Sts. Jacob and Christopher. In each issue, pre-election meetings with the candidates were announced, with meetings nearly every day held in parishes, as well as Houses of Culture, schools, hospitals, and community centers. As in Cracow, the Cardinal of Wrocław received the Solidarity candidates on May 18 and was even more explicit in his support for Solidarity, assuring them that "'Solidarity' can always count on the active support of the Church."[37] At this meeting, Solidarity candidate Duda drew on the tradition of Polish romanticism, defining the period as the end of an epoch in which Poland was ruled by foreign powers; the Church, he asserted, "has always been accepted in the role of the interrex," the temporary political authority in the transition period between Polish kings.

The honorable compromise framing strategy is evident from the first issue of the election newspaper, in which Frasyniuk declared:

> The elections will not be completely democratic. . . . We declare that this does not lead us to resignation from this possibility. These should be the last elections in which some kind of contract. . . . We want the next to be free. . . . The condition is that we take advantage of the possibility, the support of our candidates for 35 percent of the seats of representatives and to gain a majority in the Senate. . . . We must very quickly, beginning from the not great technical and organizational basis, which we succeeded in rescuing from martial law and later built underground, create our own possibility, which the government has had and dispersed since the 1940s.[38]

In a series of "Talks with the Candidates" published in the election newspaper, Karol Modzelewski, candidate for senator, declared: "The Roundtable Accords are perhaps the only chance to avoid the very tragic event in the life of the nation. It is a way out to the path of hope, to hold back economic collapse. It is also hope for evolutionary change of the structures of the state."[39]

[37] Ibid., Issue 10: 1.
[38] Ibid., Issue 1: 1.
[39] Ibid., Issue 9: 1.

The activity of competing groups such as Fighting Solidarity and the Polish Socialist Party can also be found in Wrocław. While the first issue of the election newspaper observed that all opposition political groups have the right to put forth candidates for the elections, the May 10 issue described a meeting in which a Citizens' Committee candidate accused a Solidarity member who was running independently for office that he was "disorienting people . . . leading to the division of votes for the opposition."[40] At a meeting on May 10, representatives of smaller opposition groups accused the Citizens' Committee of being "undemocratic," leading to calls for a boycott of the election.[41] Solidarity candidate Modzelewski responded that the compromise gained at the roundtable had opponents in the state as well as the opposition, with both sides declaring the compromise to be a betrayal: "The call for a boycott threatens this chance. The 'roundtable' accords give the opposition . . . the veto of the Senate," he declared, adding that he finds it difficult to believe that Fighting Solidarity and the Polish Socialist Party do not understand the arithmetic of the proportion necessary for the veto.[42] As in Cracow, independent activity outside of the honorable compromise framing strategy was met with repression. On May 1, a demonstration organized by Fighting Solidarity and the Polish Socialist Party was broken up by the militia police, leading to protest actions against the intervention.

The Regime's Electoral Campaign

As Heyns and Bialecki observe, "[In] theory, the government should have been far better prepared to wage a political campaign than were the ad hoc civic committees set up by Solidarność, even with the organizational assistance provided by local parishes" (1991: 354). Although the regime had never had to organize an election campaign against an opponent before, it had a network of

[40] Ibid., Issue 6: 2.
[41] Ibid., Issue 7: 1.
[42] Ibid., Issue 8: 1.

party structures and control over the national media at its disposal. Yet by all accounts its campaign was curiously lackluster by contrast to the flurry of energy and symbolic action of its opponent (Castle, 1995). Analysis of the state's election strategy creates a somewhat surprising contrast. Whereas Solidarity chose its candidates by internal nomination and ran a centralized campaign stressing unity, the government coalition chose to have its candidates nominated at the voting district level and ran a decentralized campaign highlighting the diversity of beliefs of its candidates. Its declared aim was to revitalize the party as a democratic force for reform through competition for the strongest candidates. At the party congress in May, Jaruzelski declared that the "pulse of the party is starting to beat more strongly, to put forth a new strategic initiative for the leading of the process of reform."[43] Yet the regime's failure to defeat Solidarity for any of the contested seats suggests that it failed to perceive the possibility that it *could* lose, expecting that it would be rewarded for its decision to convene the roundtable. Ultimately, it failed to realize that resources and strategies that had been more or less successful under conditions of political monopoly would not create the same advantages under conditions of competition. Below, I examine the framing strategy of Polish patriotism with which the state sought to garner public support and its impact upon the decisions for selecting candidates.

The plan for the election campaign prepared on February 15, 1989, by the Political-Organizational Committee of the Communist Party declared that all activities of the party had to serve the following aims: showing that the changes in Poland were the consequence of the party reform program prepared at the Ninth and Tenth Party congresses, the deepening of the process of national understanding into a broad foundation, especially the linking of the constructive opposition in a pro-reform coalition, and the gaining of approval by the party and society for the rest of the roundtable.[44] In its electoral program, prepared just before the election on May

---

[43] Quoted in Kaluza, 1989: 31.
[44] In Perzkowski, 1994: 293.

30, the state identified itself as "a coalition of three parties and three associations of lay Catholics and Christians with our own identity and sovereignty." It declared that the party would be the guarantor of stability during democratization and defined its "number one task" as "improving the living standards for Polish families."[45] State election flyers characterized the PZPR as the "initiator" of the roundtable, as wanting radical changes in the economy, changes in the means of behavior of the government, and fair living conditions for the entire society.[46] It sought to use the language of patriotism, insisting that "we are linked by Poland, for the good of Poland, its development and its secure and successful development."[47]

Many of the claims made by the state during the election campaign raise questions of resonance—that is, whether they corresponded to the beliefs and experiences of those it sought to mobilize. For example, by means of its framing strategy of Polish patriotism, the state sought to portray itself as diverse, drawing upon the national traditions of Poland. This was a claim difficult to support, given the postwar history of one-party rule in Poland. As Koseła notes, non-Solidarity candidates sought to use the symbols and images of the Church, using photographs taken with the Pope (1990: 130). Again, this would be hard to square with the history of persecuting the Church as the legitimate spokesperson for the nation. How would a party that had maintained an official policy of atheism be able to claim the support of the Pope, while local parishes were serving as local branches of the Citizens' Committees? The state even sought to use the language and strategy of the Citizens' Committees to its own ends. It responded to Solidarity flyers on voting with its own, explaining "[h]ow to vote, who[m] to support." One flyer (printed by the ambiguously named Citizens' Committee of Candidates) announced, as did the Solidarity flyers,

[45] Quoted in *Uncensored Poland News Bulletin*, no. 10 & 11/89 (June 15, 1989): 7.

[46] Photocopy from Citizens' Committee Archives, Polish Senate.

[47] Quoted in *Uncensored Poland News Bulletin*, no. 10 & 11/89 (June 15, 1989): 8.

that voters should cross out all names but those of its candidates, and that it was "better not to cross out anyone" on the National List.[48] Ultimately, it was simply confusing to voters to find a flurry of symbols and messages for the candidates of the "government coalition" in the face of the clear, united Solidarity slate. Jaruzelski himself acknowledged inside the party that the opposition would find themselves in a more advantageous position when presenting their case to the public:

> [We], not wanting to lead to the breakdown of the roundtable at the start, use certain kinds of generalizations. They are euphemisms. . . . But people won't read them, for people it is black and white. One says, there will be Solidarity, and another says that there will be some sort of talks and there will be a "roundtable" and that there will be some model of cooperation.[49]

Yet resonance alone cannot explain the failure of the regime (since the state proved capable of mobilizing nearly two-thirds of the electorate to vote in the 1987 economic referendum despite Solidarity's call for a boycott). These symbolic claims must be linked to the tasks of the nomination and presentation of candidates.

The state's electoral strategy relegated the task of mobilization to the electoral districts, creating unforeseen opportunities for divisions within the government coalition that would become problematic after the election. Even when it was clear that the opposition would run a united campaign, the regime failed to use its Twelfth Plenum in April 1989 to mobilize the party for the campaign. Instead it declared the need to prepare for another meeting the next month. Misunderstanding the threat of competitive elections, the regime permitted more than one candidate to run for some seats, suggesting that it failed to see that multiple candidates might confuse voters and splinter the support for their candidates. Not only were there multiple candidates from the PZPR, but also from its satellite partner parties and from associated organizations, including the official trade union and other social and religious groups af-

---

[48] Photocopy from Citizens' Committee Archives, Polish Senate.

[49] Quoted in Perzkowski, 1994: 107.

filiated with the regime. The final numbers are staggering. On the final ballot, there were 681 PZPR candidates for the party's 156 *Sejm* seats, an average of 4.4 per seat; there were 284 Polish Peasant Party candidates, an average of 4.2 per seat; and 84 Democratic Party candidates, an average of 3.5 per seat. Among the 558 candidates for the Senate seats, there were 186 PZPR members, 90 Peasant Party, and 69 Democratic Party members (Castle, 1995: 170).

Thus, one could actually conclude that the regime's multiplicity of candidates were more democratic than Solidarity's, insofar as the regime sought to permit the representation of diverse voices at the regional and local level. Yet this would fail to understand the specific requirements and demands of an electoral campaign—namely to present candidates clearly and mobilize voters' support on their behalf. Expecting a nonconfrontational campaign on the basis of far greater material resources, the regime did not recognize that it might not be rewarded for its democratic gestures but instead that it could fail to present a clear case for support under conditions of (even limited) competition against a united Solidarity.

The Unexpected Outcome and Formation of the Mazowiecki Government

The result of the June elections was that Solidarity won all but one of the seats it contested, giving it 99 out of 100 seats in the Senate and all 161 of the competitive seats in the lower chamber, the *Sejm*. Not only was this outcome unexpected by both sides, but only two candidates on the National List chosen by the regime received a sufficient majority to enter parliament (an outcome not foreseen nor provided for in the roundtable agreement). In light of its overwhelming electoral success, Solidarity's adherence to the roundtable agreement and assistance in fulfilling guarantees for the Leninist regime is striking; the self-limiting character of the democratic opposition would subsequently be challenged as moving too slowly and too leniently upon the regime. Returning to bargaining, I analyze the uncertainty of international constraints and the influence of the honorable compromise framing strategy upon negotiations whereby, rather than the proposed minority voice co-opted into parliament, Solidarity formed a new government.

After the election results were announced, Lech Wałęsa observed, "I face the disaster of having a good crop. . . . Too much grain has ripened for me, and I can't store it all in my granary."[50] Although unprecedented, the results did not initially seem to threaten the regime, which had been guaranteed its 65 percent majority in the *Sejm*. Despite signs from the USSR that the Soviet Union would respect the Polish election results, neighboring Leninist regimes announced that they would not follow the Polish path. Jaruzelski declared that the results of the election should not interfere with "the bold historical experiment which we have begun"; "the presence of Gorbachev makes our situation easier, because it underlines the correctness of our path of reform."[51] In his June 6, 1989, editorial in *Gazeta Wyborcza*, Michnik highlighted constraints upon the choices facing the opposition:

> Poland's geopolitical situation remains, after all, unchanged; the repressive apparatus remains in the hands of the same people as before. We are entering a time of hope, but also a time of danger. The fatal shots recently fired in Tblisi and Beijing show the dangers that we need to avoid. Solidarity will adhere to the roundtable agreements, and we expect the authorities to do the same. (1998: 126)

After a June 6 meeting with Solidarity leaders, General Kiszczak held a meeting of the Military Council of National Defense in which he communicated to the Council that "the opposition does not intend to take over the government, does not intend to form its own government, and is willing to respect the contract agreed upon at the roundtable regarding the proportion of seats in parliament" (Raina, 1995: 450). At a public session of the Commission for Understanding that same day, General Kiszczak soberly confirmed the decision by the party to abide by the election results. He also ob-

---

[50] Quoted in Stokes, 1993: 127.

[51] "After the elections," *Uncensored Poland News Bulletin*, no. 10 & 11/89 (June 15, 1989): 20, 21.

served that all involved should be warned by the "Beijing solution," in which demonstrations in China were ended by military intervention, especially students in Cracow who had taken inspiration from the Chinese students (ibid.: 452).

In this light, Solidarity insisted on procedural, legal means of fulfilling the roundtable agreement. It permitted the regime to fill empty seats from the National List and to alter the electoral rules to fill the allocated regime seats in the second round of voting. Initially any signs that Solidarity would assume positions of authority in a new government were greeted critically within the democratic opposition. The expectation that Solidarity would be a vocal opposition in the government, not form the government, caused some to react negatively to Adam Michnik's proposal in *Gazeta Wyborcza* that a new government be formed with "your president, our premier." As late as July 25, Wałęsa declared that the "force which enjoyed the support of the majority of society" was not prepared to form a government: "We will remain the opposition."[52] Further, the fulfillment of the Roundtable Accords initially appeared in jeopardy when Jaruzelski declared that he was no longer willing to accept the presidency in light of the declared reluctance to support him by the two satellite parties, who were newly aware of their independence after the electoral campaign. Although he changed his mind after declarations of support from George Bush, the Warsaw Pact leaders, and even Wałęsa, Solidarity representatives, and senators found themselves in the awkward situation whereby their votes were needed to elect the president. In the end, nineteen Peasant Party members (out of seventy-six) voted against him or abstained, and three were absent; seven Democratic Party members (out of twenty-seven) voted against him or abstained; one Solidarity representative voted for him and eighteen invalidated their ballots for the presidency, resulting in Jaruzelski's election. The crumbling of the regime coalition (unforeseen in the roundtable agreement) meant that General Kiszczak was unable to form a government with the sup-

[52] Quoted in Pernal and Skorzyński, 1990: 127.

port of the satellite parties in July, raising the question of how a new government would take shape.

On August 7, Wałęsa surprised many by announcing that Solidarity would be ready to form a "broad coalition" with the former satellite parties that would produce a parliamentary majority for an opposition-led coalition government. The lingering influence of the Soviet Union can be seen when, on August 22, at Prime Minister Rakowski's request, Gorbachev telephoned. According to Rakowski, Gorbachev indicated his continued support for Jaruzelski, saying that only if Solidarity specifically turned against the Soviet Union would its policy toward Poland change. The autonomy of the new Solidarity-led parliament was immediately clear in their repudiation on August 17 of the Warsaw Pact invasion of Czechoslovakia in 1968. On August 24, Tadeusz Mazowiecki was named prime minister and inaugurated the coalition government with the declaration that "we will enjoy our newly regained freedoms for only a short time if we do not surmount the economic crisis" (1989: 10).

Conclusion

In this chapter, I have argued that the transformation of local parishes into Citizens' Committees by Solidarity was the key to its electoral success, given the conditional nature of public support and the uncertainty surrounding the outcome. I emphasized the congruency between the honorable compromise framing strategy of the Solidarity candidates and the Church's perceptions of the need for procedural, democratic political change, as well as the claim to represent "society" against an illegitimate state. Admittedly, Solidarity's success at the polls must be qualified by a voter turnout of only 62 percent (less than the regime reported participating in the 1987 economic referendum whose boycott Solidarity had urged). As Heyns and Bialecki comment, "It is difficult to know, considering the dearth of comparable elections, whether one should be surprised that a vigorous social movement could not pull more votes, or impressed by the electoral support a nascent political organization received in the teeth of state power" (1991: 357). The outcome of state reconstruction with the formation of the Mazowiecki government was not determined by voting alone but through further negotiations in the summer of 1989. Given its overwhelming support in the election, Solidarity could well have claimed the right to reject the guarantees for the government in the roundtable agreement. I have argued that, rather than power-seeking behavior, the perceived constraints of the international arena and the honorable compromise framing strategy explain why Solidarity did not demand renegotiations of the Roundtable Accords on the basis of its electoral success.

An alternative explanation for the results of the June 4 elections might rest solely on broad antistate sentiments among the population that were given safe expression through voting. Although support for Solidarity is difficult to separate from antistate sentiment (ibid., 1991), individual sentiments are insufficient to explain voting patterns and must be supplemented with attention to mobilization. My claim that Solidarity's success in transforming the networks of the Catholic Church into local Citizens' Committees explains the successful mobilization of voters is supported empirically by Koseła, who analyzed the percentage of votes for Solidarity, a measure of social integration, and the number of clergy in each district. He concluded that the covariance of the number of clergy and the proportion of votes won by a Solidarity candidate was sufficiently strong to support a relationship (1990: 135). He cautioned that the success of Solidarity was equally a failure by the Leninist regime to mobilize its supporters, but he argues that the clergy's support for Solidarity candidates was most visible in the rural counties in eastern and central Poland where "the network of social organisations was smashed in the 1940s and 1950s" (ibid.: 132). In a postelection evaluation of the election for the Central Committee, politburo member Reykowski also concluded that the activity of parishes "did not only create an organizational infrastructure for the opposition but it was also a tremendous influence upon the opinions and position of voters."[53]

---

[53] In Perzkowski, 1994: 449; see also Reykowski, 1993.

This claim is supported further by analysis of relative support for Solidarity and the government across voting districts in Poland. Jasiewicz and Zukowski (1992) argue that Solidarity candidates in the Senate elections received the strongest support in those regions of Poland where church attendance was highest and a strong mass peasant opposition tendency existed from 1944 to 1947. Thus Solidarity had higher support in southeastern Poland: Galicia and the inhabitants of Podlasia, Warsaw, Upper Silesia, and the Lublin Lands, as well as in the better socially integrated and less collectivized parts of the Western Territories. Heyns and Bialecki agree that in the countryside in this area "it is difficult to exaggerate the importance of the local parish for communication and mobilization" (1991: 364). In contrast, the authorities had greater support in Greater Poland, Pomerania, Żielona Góra, Warmia-Mazuria, and the Zagłębie Basin. The highest abstention rate was achieved in central Poland: in Mazowsze, leaving out the major cities—Warsaw, Kujawy, and Łódź. The influence of the link between the Church and Polish national tradition is further supported by the relatively high abstention rate in areas of mixed ethnic composition, where support for Solidarity was lower than in neighboring areas (including Chełm and parts of the Opole regions, Upper Silesia, and the Polish-Byelorussian territories of Białystok).

The perception of Solidarity's success, for all its political imagination, would however quickly be overtaken by international developments. With the dramatic capitulations of the neighboring regimes in the fall of 1989, Poland suddenly slipped from being the front-runner in democratic change to lagging behind, with a parliament in which the president was a communist, the Communist Party still held a plurality of seats in parliament, and the opposition ruled in coalition with the former satellite parties (Gross, 1992). This created immediate tensions between the roundtable agreements and subsequent calls for "acceleration" in reform, to which I will turn in the concluding chapter.

CHAPTER FIVE

Rapid Mobilization in Czechoslovakia

"I don't understand. We had reports that everyone was terrified."
—One Czechoslovak Communist Party member to another while
walking toward an empty horizon in a 1989 cartoon by Jirásek[1]

C ZECHOSLOVAKIA WAS one of the most repressive states in Eastern Europe before 1989, with a weak and fragmented democratic opposition; yet, strikingly, the reconstruction of the state took place faster there than in other Eastern European countries and arguably led to more radical changes. This chapter analyzes the insurgency of Civic Forum and Public Against Violence, sparked by the repression of a student demonstration on November 17, 1989, and culminating in the peaceful general strike ten days later. By comparing competing attempts to mobilize public support in a dynamic political environment, I demonstrate that the general strike was not the only possible outcome from changes in the international arena or the breakdown of the Leninist state; rather it was the result of successful mobilization by the civic movements that linked their demands for gradual, legal change on behalf of the nation with striking theater networks that served as the organizational basis for a general strike.

I focus on four areas: (1) international isolation and the repression of the student demonstration; (2) competing attempts to frame the opening; (3) the transformation of theater networks and diffusion of the movement; and (4) mobilization in the squares and the general strike.

[1] Reprinted in Whipple, 1991: 218.

International Isolation and the Repression of the Student Demonstration

While the fall of neighboring Leninist regimes in Eastern Europe in late 1989 isolated Czechoslovakia and created pressure for change, these events did not determine what followed. As discussed in detail in Chapter 2, after the Warsaw Pact invasion in 1968 Czechoslovakia imposed a policy known as "normalization," which entailed an attempt to repress public dissent and buy off the population with material goods without modifying the party's monopoly over power. Although there were changes in the leadership of the state and party in response to the calls for perestroika in the Soviet Union in the 1980s, the new leaders were as conservative as their predecessors. The Czechoslovak prime minister, who would soon be sitting across the negotiating table from Václav Havel, referred to him in the Austrian press as late as October 22, 1989, as an "absolute zero" (Draper, 1993a: 16). The announcement of the Solidarity-led government on August 20, 1989, did not deter the Czechoslovak state from repressing a demonstration in Prague on August 21, the twenty-first anniversary of the Warsaw Pact invasion. Similarly, even with East Germans occupying the West German embassy in Prague in late October, a demonstration held on the anniversary of the founding of the Czechoslovak state on October 28, 1989, was met with force. This highlights the need to distinguish between the domestic political opportunity structure (which did not show any signs of weakness, as the state never lost control over its military and administrative apparatus) and international polity (since the state became vulnerable in the context of the rapid and unexpected fall of neighboring Leninist regimes).

Unlike in Poland, where the leaders of the Solidarity movement were a visible potential partner for the state to negotiate with, no organized political alternative to the Leninist regime waited in the wings for an opportunity. Charter 77 resolutely refused to support organized political action, while new political initiatives in the late 1980s (such as the Movement for Civic Freedoms or Democratic

Initiative) were repressed swiftly. As Václav Havel observed in 1988, "When the friends from Polish Solidarity, whom we meet occasionally at the Czech-Polish border, ask how many people Charter 77 has behind it, I feel like answering that if there are millions of people behind Solidarity, only millions of ears stand behind Charter 77" (1988b: 12).

THE "MASSACRE" OF THE STUDENT DEMONSTRATION

The policy of repression continued until November 17, 1989, when the military police intervened against a student demonstration commemorating the fiftieth anniversary of the killing of a student by the Nazi government. The students had received official permission from the Socialist Union of Youth for a demonstration that grew to approximately fifty thousand people and, after leaving its original location and marching toward the city center, was forcefully dispersed by the riot police at 8:40 P.M.[2] By the time Civic Forum had announced itself, two days later, there had been two noteworthy developments. First, on November 18, Radio Free Europe reported that one student demonstrator had been killed by the police, a report that later turned out to be false but that heightened the feeling of crisis. Second, that same day, much of the Czech theater community gathered at the Realistic Theater in Prague, where one of the demonstrators from the theater academy read the students' proclamation calling for a general strike on November 27. The same afternoon, the coordinating committee of Prague students was formed, composed of two representatives of each faculty. It prepared the first program of the students, entitled the Proclamation of the University Students to the Workers and Peasants of Czechoslovakia (Wheaton and Kavan, 1992: 198–99). That evening, members of the theater community at the Realistic Theater prepared a

[2] For a minute-by-minute account of the student demonstration on November 17, see Otáhal and Sladek, 1990: 16–19.

proclamation declaring themselves to be on strike and in support of the student demands, including the general strike.

Initially the state continued to defend itself by defining who would be permitted to participate in political change and on what terms. The Czech prime minister appeared on television on November 19 and sought to discredit the dissidents, who, he proclaimed, had:

> misused the action of November 17. [Everyone] must be shocked by the disinformation that one student died in the intervention. . . . It shows who is who, who is after power and why, who misused the students, artists and young people. I declare that nothing in these reports is true. No armed units took part in the police action. The spread of mendacious and untruthful rumors of dead and injured has impressed many and influenced their attitudes. (Wheaton and Kavan, 1992: 58)

On Tuesday, November 21, the Czechoslovak prime minister met with spokespersons for the student, artistic, and civic circles of the Prague public. He refused to meet with Havel and announced that, although force would not be used to disperse demonstrators as it had been in the past, "we will protect socialism, about which no discussion is possible" (Otáhal and Sladek, 1990: 137). He later stated that he alone had made the decision not to use force, having been convinced by the repressions of the demonstrations in January and throughout 1989 that a peaceful solution was needed (ibid.: 558). At no point did the state lose control of the police or military. The available evidence suggests that they remained active in the early days of the revolution, halting a student demonstration from continuing toward Prague Castle on November 20 and infiltrating the striking theaters. According to a subsequent investigation into the activities of the Czechoslovak People's Army, tanks and soldiers were deployed to Prague and a security measure entitled Intervention was prepared by the minister of national defense; the Ministry, however, awaited orders from the Central Committee, which opted for a "political" rather than a military solution to the problem (Začek, 1994: 9). By controlling the mass media and distribution of newspapers in the days immediately after November 17, the party sought to prevent Civic Forum from spreading to the rest of the country.

Transcripts from the Central Committee meetings held on November 24 and 26 reveal the inability of party members to agree upon a solution or to establish ties with other groups (such as the Obroda group of former communists expelled from the party after 1968). General Secretary Jakeš opened the extraordinary session by announcing bravely that the party had underestimated the activity of its enemies, but that he was "convinced that it is . . . solvable, but under the conditions that the party go on the offensive, show its capability to gain serious and careful access to the majority of workers, especially the young" (Krtilová 1992: 6). Even after Jakeš's replacement as general secretary, however, the party appeared unable to make a decision, leading one member to exclaim despairingly, "[T]his is already a discussion club, it's not a responsible organ for resolving the situation in the state" (ibid.: 178). The extent of the party's inability to perceive the threat was visible in the new general secretary's conclusion that they should resolve the problem at a special meeting of the Communist Party to be held on January 26, 1990. By that point, Civic Forum and Public Against Violence would be seated in the cabinet posts of their former adversaries.

Thus, in contrast to explanations that emphasize the role of declining state repression in creating opportunities for mobilization, it was the *continued* state repression that provoked the emergence of Civic Forum and Public Against Violence. An opportunity was created first, by the repression of the student demonstration in a dramatically changed international context, and second, by the subsequent failure of the state to use its repressive capacity, which was perceived by the new movements as a sign of state breakdown.

Framing the Opening: Failed Attempts and the "Civil Society" Framing Strategy

With the successful general strike on November 27, Civic Forum demonstrated its capacity to disrupt the political order and thereby established itself as the legitimate spokesperson for the "nation" in negotiations with the state. To avoid explaining the democratic outcome exclusively in terms of state breakdown, I must reconstruct the uncertainty of November 1989 and introduce the failed attempts by smaller, lesser-known groups to influence the outcome. Because none of the challengers existed with public support before the repression of the student demonstration, they had to locate or create the resources needed to mobilize support. One member of Civic Forum commented, "I thought that to call a general strike on Sunday night for the next Monday, meaning in eight days, was nonsense, that it was suicide, that nothing will happen. We will call a strike and it won't happen and we will lose. They will say, so you see, a few fanatics!" (Otáhal and Sladek, 1990: 588). Mobilization was neither inevitable nor effortlessly achieved, but rather the result of competition among challengers seeking to influence the outcome. I contrast the successful challenge by Civic Forum with the failed attempts of two competing challengers—socialism with a human face by reform communists and rapid democracy by the Democratic Initiative—and a counterfactual challenger that failed to emerge—Slovak nationalism. In Table 3, I compare these challengers along the three dimensions of framing—injustice, identity, and agency—as well as in terms of pre-existing networks of members they could mobilize in their support.

This table suggests that, while the injustice claim is largely similar among the challengers (with the exception of the counterfactual Slovak nationalist movement), identity and, most importantly, agency differ. Attention to pre-existing networks makes possible comparison of potential organizational advantages. It suggests that, prior to the repression of the student demonstration, no group had overwhelming resources, although reform communists might have mobilized those purged after 1968. Attention to framing and networks suggests that the failure of the competing groups was not simply the result of the superior resonance of the civil society framing strategy, but of their inability to link their claims to the dynamic political environment after November 17 and, critically, to the

TABLE 3

Competing Framing Strategies and Networks, Czechoslovakia, 1989

Challenger	Injustice	Identity	Agency	Networks
Reform communist "Socialism with a human face"	Stalinism, 1968	Ex-party, working class	Reform, social democracy	Obroda, ties to current party
Democratic Initiative "Rapid democracy"	Massacre, 1968	Members of new political parties	Immediate elections in early 1990	Small, national network
Slovak nationalist (counter-factual)	Czech centralism	Slovak ethnicity	Constitutional change	Non-existent
Civic Forum/ Public Against "Civil society"	Massacre, 1968	Citizens with human rights	Strike, pressure the state to make changes	Isolated dissidents

striking network of theaters that could provide the organizational resources to mobilize the population for the strike. Once the theater strike had begun, the group able to link its claims to this network would have a formidable advantage that would prove impossible to challenge.

COMPETING CHALLENGERS

First, given the prestige associated with Alexander Dubček, why was he unable to mobilize support for an opportunity to implement socialism with a human face (consistent with Gorbachev's policies)? This framing strategy identified the source of injustice in the Stalinist deformations of socialism and called for a renewal of socialism upon the principles of the Western European socialist parties. It called for greater discussion and openness in political life, which would include associations outside the party but within the general framework of the existing political system. A natural network of former communists purged after 1968 had begun to organize in early 1989, forming the Obroda movement for Socialist Renewal. Obroda had even previously met in 1989 with members of the

Communist Party to discuss the development of reconstruction and perestroika in Czechoslovakia. Dubček had begun to appear in public for the first time since the early 1970s, granting an interview to the Hungarian press and even being notified on November 17 that he would receive the Sacharov Prize, granted by the European Parliament to leaders in the efforts by nations for democracy, progress, and freedom. In November 1989 a new group, which referred to itself as the Democratic Forum of Communists, emerged with a program that rejected the leading role of the party and sought to build new political structures out of the basic organizations of the Communist Party.

The socialism with a human face alternative failed, I argue, for two reasons. Although this group had potential organizational advantages, its claims for a revitalization of socialism had limited appeal after twenty-one years of "normalization" and prevented it from establishing ties with the Communist Party, which had replaced it in 1968. Dubček's appearances in Wenceslaus Square were received enthusiastically by the crowds, but the announcement of the resignation of the Central Committee of the Communist Party on November 24 demonstrated the weakness of the party and an opportunity for Civic Forum to press for changes beyond socialism with a human face. At that day's press conference of Civic Forum, Dubček's first press conference in twenty years, he was the focus of attention and asked whether he would become general secretary of the party or president. He told journalists, "I have always stood for and continue to stand for a reform, renewal of socialism." Before any further questions could be asked, however, there was an interruption by a Czech journalist who announced the resignation of the Central Committee, and the room erupted with euphoria and champagne. When calm returned, however, all of the journalists' questions were now directed to Havel, who declared forcefully, "[In] the Czechoslovak language context [the term socialism] has lost all meaning."[3] Similarly, a former leader of the Prague Spring in 1968 appeared on Czechoslovak television on December 7 calling

---

[3] Unpublished transcripts of Civic Forum press conference, November 24, 1989, as translated at that time for the Western press by Rita Klimová.

for tolerance and more time for Prime Minister Adamec to form a new government. In response, a headline article in the Civic Forum Information Service criticized this as a "basic misunderstanding of the situation in which we live" and called for continued pressure on the government it identified as "totalitarian."[4] Secondly, the bitter history of party purges after 1968 made it difficult for cooperation to be established between those reform communists purged after 1968 and the current party responsible for the purges. Transcripts from the Central Committee meeting held on November 26 reveal the antagonism between these groups. One Central Committee member announced that he met with members of the Obroda club in an attempt to "lead a dialogue with those who are for socialism." The difficulty of establishing any such dialogue surfaced when the members of Obroda raised the issue of how the events of 1968 would be interpreted. The Central Committee member retorted acidly: "To this, I, comrades, stated the viewpoint that it certainly is possible to discuss this question of 1968 . . . but above all about its end and who is to blame that '68 happened as it did" (Krtilová, 1992: 168). Even when faced with a revolution, the reform communists of 1968 in the Obroda club and those communists in power in 1989 were unable to go beyond assigning blame for earlier events and establish what could have been a powerful counterforce to Civic Forum and Public Against Violence.

Second, given the widespread support for greater democracy, why did the call for immediate elections among political parties fail? In contrast to Civic Forum's rejection of party politics, a group called Democratic Initiative argued that there was no need for intermediate steps to democracy, such as "forum" organizations or negotiations with the communists. Political pluralism could be achieved directly by forming political parties that would compete in immediate elections along the model of Western democracies. The leaders of Democratic Initiative presented three demands on November 19: the resignation of the government effective November 25; the formation of a temporary government composed of non-

---

[4] Informační Servis no. 23, December 8, 1989.

compromised members of the current government, leaders of the Prague Spring such as Alexander Dubček and leaders of the opposition such as Václav Havel; and free elections for the Federal Parliament to be held on February 1, 1990 (Hlusičková and Otáhal, 1993: 205–6). Democratic Initiative had been created in 1987 and had a national, if small, network of supporters. It identified itself as "an independent political party with a concrete program for peaceful transition to democracy which would result in free elections and the creation of a pluralist society" (ibid.: 206). It announced its support for the demands of Civic Forum and the students but rejected as insufficient Civic Forum's call for negotiations with the old government about its reconstruction. Instead, it insisted that the communists should simply resign. In response to the argument that free elections would not be possible in such a short time, one of its leaders responded, Why not? It was possible in Poland and East Germany; "why wouldn't it work here when so many hands were willing to help?" (Otáhal and Sladek, 1990: 618).

The radical democrats failed because, although the call for immediate elections had appeal, its claim to represent political parties relied upon traditional conceptions of political competition at a time when the experience of communism led Czechs and Slovaks to view parties as symbols of the politics of the past. Further, Democratic Initiative was unable to establish ties with the striking theaters, nor mobilize its fragmentary networks as a viable alternative. First, the appeal to mobilize as political parties was weak because Czechs and Slovaks had lived in a one-party state for forty years. Czech Prime Minister Petr Pithart argued in 1990:

> [T]he dominant feature of public political opinion is distrust and even unwillingness to participate in political parties. This is true even among people who are politically active. This is the reflection of an instinctive distaste for political parties in general, and for everything that is associated with party apparatuses, discipline, leaders' privileges, perks and so on. These are vague, over-generalized dislikes, and spring from the experience of Communist rule.[5]

[5] Quoted in Whipple, 1991: 173.

Even so, Democratic Initiative requested in December 1989, in a letter to the new government, that it be registered as an independent party.

Second, Democratic Initiative was unable to establish cooperation with other groups. Civic Forum argued publicly against the call for immediate elections, declaring that the "entire effort of the opposition is directed toward *free* elections" (emphasis added) but that *immediate* elections would be premature and "would lead to a divisive battle."[6] In an interview, the leader of Democratic Initiative observed that the question at that time was securing political allies, and that "Havel made a coalition with cultural figures."[7] While theaters could serve as "forums" throughout the country, it is difficult to imagine that the rapid democracy framing strategy could transform striking theaters into local branches of political parties. Thus, although Democratic Initiative could have offered what might be seen as a more radically democratic form of reconstruction of the Leninist regime, it was unable to exert any influence, being forbidden from speaking on the balcony of Wenceslaus Square by Civic Forum members who refused to permit any indication of "politics" among the groups. One member of Civic Forum later explained that Democratic Initiative had "broadcast that their only existing party was poorly represented" and that "others tried to rid [its leader] of his party-fixation and reasoned from the standpoint of Civic Forum as the goal" (ibid.: 633).

Third, why was the appeal to ethnic nationalism notably absent from the framing efforts of Public Against Violence in Slovakia (which remained closely tied to Civic Forum)? In many cases, political crises have offered minority, ethnic groups opportunities to mobilize and make claims, as the ethnic republics did in the dissolution of the former Soviet Union (Beissinger, 1996). In 1989, Czechoslovakia was composed of two republics representing ethnic groups with distinct languages, histories, and traditions. Differences in the economic and political experiences of socialism in each republic

[6] *Informační Servis* no. 14, Dec. 2, 1989.
[7] Quoted in Otáhal and Sladek, 1990: 616.

could have created opportunities for Slovaks (whose population was roughly one-third of the total population) to argue that the injustice for Slovaks was linked to their experience under the federal state, and that Slovaks should mobilize to form an independent state in which their interests would be met. The potential resonance of Slovak nationalism can be seen in the demonstration four months later, in March 1990, demanding the hyphenation of the proper name of the country, Czecho-Slovakia, which drew tens of thousands of Slovaks back into the streets.

I argue that ethnic nationalism was absent in the framing strategy of Public Against Violence because the injustice claim, although potentially resonant, clashed with the close cooperation between Czech and Slovak leaders of the civic movements that enabled them to mobilize the entire country. One of the founders of Public Against Violence later commented, "[W]ithout . . . the massive demonstrations in Prague's Wenceslaus Square, Slovakia would hardly have been able to start a fundamental transformation" (Butora and Butorová, 1993: 76). Indeed, in Bratislava on November 16 a student demonstration had also been held in memory of the death of the student killed by the Nazi government in 1939. Unlike the events in Prague, the demonstration in Bratislava took place without major incident (Gál, 1991: 14). The day after the repression of the student demonstration in Prague, news of the police repression and apparent student death spread to Slovakia through students and the theater community, including the return from Prague by a Slovak actor to Bratislava with news of Civic Forum's founding. Several small groups met separately to discuss the events in Prague, including environmentalists, artists, representatives of the underground Catholic church, and social scientists (each of whom would become part of Public Against Violence), but without any coordination until a meeting was held on November 19 at the Umelecká Beseda (Artists' House) (Antalová, 1998). The media broadcast of demonstrations in Prague further served to orient public attention, even in Slovakia, to the national capital. Interestingly, while Public Against Violence was founded in Bratislava, a branch of Civic Forum was initially founded by local activists in the Eastern Slovak capital of Kosice that had better contacts with their counterparts in Prague than in Bratislava. Thus, rather than ethnic nationalism, Public Against Violence's founding proclamation was consistent with the civil society framing strategy (which I will elaborate in the next section) and had close ties to the striking theaters. It announced:

> Provoked by the violent intervention against the recent peaceful student demonstration in Prague, representatives of the cultural and scientific public have met and decided to create the association PUBLIC AGAINST VIOLENCE. Our aim is to contribute to the ending of the violence and turning away from social change. We are deeply uneasy about the state of Czechoslovak society. (Feldek, 1990: 11)

Rather than the experience of Slovaks under the federal state, the injustice claim of Public Against Violence focused on the student demonstration in Prague. Similarly, the identity claim was not ethnic Slovaks, but the "public," composed of citizens, concluding: "As citizens, we are taking matters into our own hands!" (Antalová, 1998: 306). The agency claim directed efforts toward peaceful dialogue to resolve the situation facing both Czechs and Slovaks. As one of the leaders of Public Against Violence announced on November 24 in Bratislava, "Our revolution is not a revolution of violence, it is a revolution of understanding, reconciliation, love, and trust" (Feldek, 1990: 31). Many of the demands in the program of Public Against Violence, prepared in cooperation with the Coordinating Committee of Slovak Universities on November 25, 1989, were aimed at changes on the federal level, such as the cancellation of the constitutional clause guaranteeing the leading role of the Communist Party in political life (ibid.: 35).

To sum up in theoretical terms, among the competing challengers, those with the greatest potential for success were those that distanced themselves from traditional conceptions of politics and that aligned their claims with the already striking theaters and students. The socialism with a human face alternative, despite its potentially formidable networks, can be seen (in Diani's terms) as a "realignment" framing strategy, while the Democratic Initiative presented a "revitalization" frame inconsistent with the identity and demands of the largest potential network, the striking theaters (Diani, 1996). Only the counterfactual Slovak nationalist frame could have offered an "antisystem" alternative, but it had no prior history of organization, nor did it emerge to compete with the close ties across republics of the civic movements.

THE CIVIC MOVEMENTS AND THE SUCCESSFUL GENERAL STRIKE

By contrast, the civic movements succeeded in mobilizing support for the general strike because their "antipolitical" claims offered a clear alternative to the political experiences of Czechs and Slovaks under communist rule, while their claim to represent "citizens" against an illegitimate state could incorporate competing challengers (such as the reform communists and Democratic Initiative). Critically, the symbolic link between "citizens" and the nation was congruent with the identity and demands of the striking theater network, and the transformation of the theaters into local branches of the movement enabled them to overcome their organizational deficiencies in the mobilization for the general strike. Because the link between the civic movements and the striking theaters calls for elaboration, I will consider it separately below.

Earlier I proposed that framing strategies are characterized by claims about injustice, identity, and agency. Rather than generalized grievances against the system, the element of injustice is sharply focused on what the founding proclamation of Civic Forum describes as "the brutal massacre of a peaceful student demonstration."[8] Whether or not the repression was objectively as brutal as earlier repressions in Prague (such as in January 1989) or in other settings (such as Tiananmen Square in China), Civic Forum sought to heighten the sense of moral outrage by emphasizing the non-

[8] The complete text, with the divergent translation of "Občanské Forum" as "Citizens" rather than "Civic" Forum, is in Wheaton and Kavan, 1992: 202–3.

violence of the demonstrating students (in contrast to an unruly demonstration by professional agitators). In a small theater in Prague, Civic Forum announced itself as the "spokesman" on behalf of the part of the Czechoslovak public that was "increasingly critical" of the regime and "shaken" by the repression of the student demonstration. In the atmosphere of Prague after November 17, with the rumor circulating that one student had been killed, there were few people who would claim not to be critical or shaken.

Central to the civil society framing strategy is the identity of its adherents as a united citizenry endowed with human rights whose will the movements claimed to represent against the state. This identity claim drew upon the historical dichotomy in Eastern Europe of an oppressive state against "society," which represents the nation. It challenged the vision of socialism as the fulfillment of national history and the ability of the state to represent the aspirations of the working class, recalling earlier democratic periods (such as the interwar Czechoslovak republic led by President Masaryk). Consistent with this, membership in Civic Forum was "open to all sections and forces in Czechoslovak society on which our country depends, to initiate the process of finding ways by peaceful methods to a democratic social order and with it, prosperity." In contrast to party politics, membership was not obligatory, nor controlled by a central organization, but simply a matter of personal decision or declaration in support of the stated aims of the founding proclamation. This framing drew upon Charter 77's identity as a wide range of individuals loosely united around a broad definition of the defense of human rights rather than a partisan movement (Skilling, 1981). Civic Forum's founding proclamation sought to demonstrate its ability to represent society by identifying its participants as eleven independent organizations, members of two satellite parties, the church, artistic and other associations, some former and present members of the Communist Party, and "other democratically inclined citizens."

The agency component of the civil society framing strategy was defined as peaceful participation in the general strike and negotiations with the state, at which Civic Forum would pressure the state to make the necessary changes. Havel insisted at a press conference on November 23, 1989, that "Civic Forum . . . is only a foundation whose sole purpose is to unite people, to create . . . an atmosphere of effective pressure upon the existing government so that the government [will] create sufficient space for a pluralistic society."[9] In this way, Civic Forum sought to thwart the state's definition of all opposition as enemies or hooligans without regard for law and order. The emphasis on nonviolence and peaceful methods filled the public statements of Civic Forum, which announced in its daily news service, "[L]et us refuse any form of terror and violence. Our weapons are love and nonviolence."[10] A common poster at the time showed Havel smiling, below which it was written, "[T]ruth and love shall triumph over lies and hatred." This claim was antipolitical not in the sense that it was directed against the state but in that it claimed not to seek political power for itself. As one member of Charter 77 said in 1988: "I do not believe it is the opposition's job to solve the state's problems. It is our job to make problems for the state. Of course, we can point out existing problems, we can discuss the methods by which to solve the problems—but it is the government which must solve them" (Urban, 1988: 32). In its founding proclamation, Civic Forum declared itself "competent to negotiate immediately with the state leadership concerning the critical situation in our country, to express the present demands of the public, and to seek ways to their solution." In so doing, it initially presented four demands:

1. resignation of members of the Communist Party involved in "normalization" after 1968;
2. resignation of those responsible for the repression of demonstrations;
3. establishment of a commission to look into these events, on which Civic Forum must be represented; and
4. release of all prisoners of conscience.

[9] Unpublished transcript of Civic Forum press conference, November 23, 1989, as translated at that time for the Western press by Rita Klimová.

[10] Informační Servis no. 14, Dec. 2, 1989: 1.

These demands are notable for their modesty. Despite the fall of the Leninist regimes in neighboring countries, the founding proclamation did not call for fundamental changes in the system, but almost a reformist spirit calling for the redress of human rights abuses.

The Transformation of Theaters and Diffusion of the Movement

The framing of the repression of the student demonstration by the civic movements, however powerful in symbolic terms, would have been insufficient in itself to garner support for the general strike. Mobilization would not have succeeded without sufficient institutional resources that shaped the ability of the civic movements both to deploy framing strategies and to form strategic alliances among social groups. Civic Forum could not simply frame events as dissidents had in the past. As one of the dissidents observed, he and others had prepared "the usual protest" to read to the students and actors after the police repression, but the strike changed everything: "It was something unheard of until that time. To read the Charter document no longer made sense. After two hours, it was completely outdated."[11]

In the previous section, I argued that the alignment of its claims with the demands of the striking theaters would prove crucial to the success of the general strike. I should emphasize that Civic Forum and Public Against Violence emerged *after* the theater strike had begun. Whereas a structural approach to emergence would emphasize pre-existing ties between members and recruits, I examine the process by which such ties are established through framing strategies that create a common perception of the situation, an activist identity of participants, and shared aims. By framing their identity as "citizens" without political aims, however, the civic movements aligned their claims with the demands of the striking theaters historically associated with the birth of the nation. This enabled them

[11] Quoted in Otáhal and Sladek, 1990: 661.

to overcome their organizational deficiencies and gain access to local activists, meeting places, and communication resources with which they could spread their message and mobilize others outside of Prague. Further, while both students and theaters were essential to the early period of mobilization of the public, the students maintained their own independent identity and goals apart from Civic Forum, while striking theaters were transformed into smaller, local branches of Civic Forum itself. Branches of Civic Forum in theaters were also distinguished from those founded in factories, research institutes, or schools, because they did not represent one group of society but rather, like their parent body, a forum in which members of all groups of society met regularly.

WHY THEATERS?

Attention to the role of theaters links them by analogy to the discussion in Chapter 2 of the Catholic Church in Poland as "free spaces" or "havens for opposition" that provide the networks on which social movements often draw in the early stages of emergence. To explain why theaters (and not other networks, such as the Church or factories or universities) formed the local networks for Civic Forum, I examine the link between the theater and the birth of the nation historically, as well as nascent network ties between the dissident and cultural communities in more recent history.

In the nineteenth century, when the area that would become Czechoslovakia remained under the control of the Austro-Hungarian Empire, theater was widely understood as a tool for awakening national consciousness, since Czech could be spoken in the theaters while German was the official public language. A network of state theaters was established in nearly every small town, leading one Civic Forum activist to comment, "Czechoslovakia has the densest theater network in Europe" (Oslzlý, 1990: 104–5). The building of the National Theater in Prague was a symbolic event in which representatives from every region of the Czech lands arrived in Prague with local contributions (Agnew, 1993: 147–48). It was widely portrayed in Czech history as a visible manifestation of the creation of the nation, bearing the maxim "A nation in itself." In this sense, Holý argues that the symbolic link between Civic Forum and theaters drew upon the resonance of the Czech concept of the nation regarding the state, as well as the self-image of the Czechs as "a highly cultured and well-educated nation" (1993: 208).

After the Warsaw Pact invasion in 1968, theaters acted as public spaces for political expression because they had a degree of institutional autonomy lacking in factories and churches and a theatrical language that enabled them to express opinions in a manner difficult for the state to control. As a whole, the theater community in Czechoslovakia was not very different from the rest of society; as playwright Pavel Kohout has commented: "Opportunists immediately sold themselves to their new masters, the frightened majority offered their sacrifices to the emperor and, secretly, to God, and the tiny minority decided to live in truth with all the risks this implied" (1990: 7). This created a division between the official theaters, known as "stone theaters," and alternative theaters, known as "small theaters," for the small spaces in which they frequently performed (Chtiguel, 1990: 89). These small theaters have been characterized by:

> their flexibility; they have no fixed program, no professional necessity to tie themselves to a specific plan. If, for some reason usually unknown to them, they fall under official displeasure, they can disband and regroup under another name when their case has been forgotten. They are capable of adapting to performance in a variety of different venues. (Day, 1985: 36)

These theaters had to develop a means of expression that would survive political scrutiny: "a theatrical language . . . that would be very clear to sympathetic spectators but unintelligible to the totalitarian watchdogs of culture" (Oslzlý, 1990: 99). Subtle subtext through tone of voice, gesture, and symbolism were the tools of this theater, which has been described as "true paradise for a semiotician, but a nightmare for a literary censor" (Deak, 1990: 43). The resulting style relied not on traditional texts and scripts or psychological portrayal of reality, which would be easy targets for censorship, but on visual and metaphoric imagery, and the nonverbal art forms of dance and music, which depended on interpretation by the audience to be understood. Jeremy Adler describes the Ypsilon Theater in Prague's performance when Brezhnev died:

> *Macbeth* was duly done, with inordinate pauses at the relevant points, and a full minute of silence after "Yet who would have thought the old man to have had so much blood in him?" [He adds, it] was a black mass. A tacit conspiracy developed between actors and their public, and particular theaters earned the national credibility on which they capitalized in recent events. (1989: 1413)

In the face of repression, the avoidance of political themes can be seen as an obvious survival mechanism, although Havel describes their inspiration as one of affinity:

> The humor was described as pure, as an example of l'art pour l'art, as dadaistic, as being an end in itself, but, oddly enough, this humor, which apparently had no connections with "burning events" of the time, as the phrase is conventionally understood, gave expression, strangely and indirectly, to the most urgent matter of what man really is. And without necessarily being intellectuals, perceptive members of the audience felt that even the most grotesque escapade by Vyskočil touched something essential in them. (1990: 52)

Havel himself added that these theaters relied upon "an increasingly sophisticated set of ciphers, suggestions, indirect references, and vague parallels," declaring, "sometimes they are so refined and convoluted that even someone as open to everything as I am can scarcely understand them" (1990a: 55).

In the late 1980s theaters were politicized through their increasing contact with dissident networks. Links were established between the official and unofficial cultures through the creation of a journal, *About Theater*, dedicated to Havel (who served as its chief editor) on his fiftieth birthday. Subsequent issues contained articles by representatives of both unofficial and official cultures, encouraged by Havel's efforts. His official biographer emphasizes:

> Václav knew how to attract people and blend them together, young and old, dissidents and *strukturaks*, reform Communists and the un-

> derground; and this was of paramount importance. He crossed the
> border between the forbidden on the one hand, and the permitted or
> tolerated on the other. He widened and diluted the borders of the
> ghetto. (Kriseová, 1993: 222)

As a result of these ties, the cultural community was prominent in
the signing of the petition to free Havel from prison in early 1989.
This politicization made them more receptive than other parts of
society, and the theaters began to test the limits of state control by
preparing productions of Havel's plays. According to the dramaturg of Theater on a String, his theater arranged in the late 1980s to
perform a production entitled "Rozrazil" (which contained a section written by Havel) in Prague on the prominent anniversaries in
Czechoslovak history, including November 17. This may explain
the immediacy with which theaters went on strike in support of the
students, even before Civic Forum had been created.[12]

Below, I analyze three aspects of the mobilization process in
November 1989: the trips by actors and students to factories and
the countryside, the theater strike in the form of public discussions
in place of performances, and diffusion of the movement from
Prague to the countryside. I demonstrate the regional diffusion of
Civic Forum with reference to developments in Plzeň, the capital
of Western Bohemia; Brno, the capital of Southern Moravia; and
České Budějovice, the capital of Southern Bohemia.

SPREADING THROUGHOUT THE COUNTRY:
THE "ACTION ELEPHANT"

To succeed in mobilizing the country to participate in a general
strike, Civic Forum had to rely upon the activities of the actors and
students who made these trips to those outside of Prague. The civil
society framing strategy is evident in the available record of these
trips, whose purpose was to mobilize the public against the old regime, especially the so-called working class whom the Communist

---

[12] Interview with Petr Oslzlý, November 24, 1993.

Party claimed to represent. On Monday, November 20, the first trips were organized from Prague in which a small group (composed at first of an actor and a student who had participated in the November 17 demonstration, and later also a lawyer or an expert from another field) traveled to factories outside of the cities to spread information about the events to the working class.

Initially many of the actors were not welcomed at some of the factories where they traveled. One member of the strike committee reported that the gates at the Tatra factory in Prague were closed to the actors, and the workers called out to them, "[D]on't poison us here!"[13] He describes the actors as "agitators" and reports gradual success at gaining access, with the help of members of the Socialist Union of Youth who worked at the factories. Gradually this changed as more information about what happened on November 17 became available. A letter from the strike committee of the Municipal Prague Theaters to the CKD Dukla plant in Prague on November 20 argues that the "intelligentsia" must not be divided from the "workers" as they have been in past months (Otáhal and Sladek, 1990: 96–97). It announces public evenings to be held in their theaters and invites the employees to participate. A newspaper article on November 21 reports the visit by two members of the Realistic Theater and three architecture students to the CKD-Diesel Engine plant in Prague, where the group "tried to explain that it is not good to divide people into intelligentsia, students, and working class; on the contrary we would like to be united" (ibid.: 183–84).

The Theater Institute in Prague served as the information and documentation center of the Czech theater community for these trips, and their archive contains the most systematic information about them. Although it is impossible to know precisely how many trips were taken, a memorandum written on November 26, 1989, details the systematic role of the Prague actors in providing assistance to the regional theaters. The memorandum (Theater Institute archive, Prague, Document #134) reports:

[13] Karel Steigerwald, in Hviždala, 1990: 42.

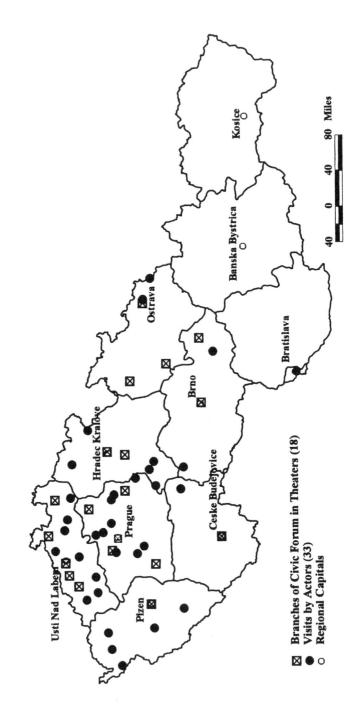

MAP 2. Civic Forum and Public Against Violence Branches Founded in Theaters, Czechoslovakia

The Realistic theater sent its actors to assist:	Gottwaldov and Příbrami
The National Theater – " –	Ostrava, Hradec Králove, Pardubice
Theater na Vinohradech	Liberec, Cheb, Karlový Vary
Theater E. F. Burian	Uherské Hradiště, Jihlava
Municipal Prague Theater	Šumperk, Český Těšín, and Opava
Theater S. K. Neumann	Oloumoc, Kolín
Theater of J. Wolkr	Most
Theater on the Balustrade	Ustní nad Labem
Semafor	Kladno, Teplice
Drama Club	Plzeň, České Budějovice

The above memorandum contains the capitals of each of the six regions of the Czech Republic and smaller cities within them. In addition to the above list, the Rokoko and ABC theaters in Prague also report trips to forty-five cities, twenty-three universities and high schools, and seven enterprises in Prague.[14] The network of local branches of Civic Forum founded in theaters and trips by actors to the countryside is illustrated in Map 2.

THE THEATER STRIKE: PUBLIC DISCUSSIONS IN PLACE OF PERFORMANCES

After the declaration of the strike at the Realistic Theater in Prague on November 18, other theaters followed quickly. One member of the strike committee of Czech theaters explained that it was agreed that closing the theaters would play into the hands of the regime; rather, the theaters would open their stages to public discussions.[15] Many Prague theaters went on strike immediately. Members of the Theater on a String and HaTheater from Brno formed strike committees in their city. In the smaller city of Kladno, the director

[14] "Diskusní večery na scenách Rokoka a ABC [Discussion evenings on the stages of Rokoko and ABC]," Theater Institute archive, unnumbered document.

[15] Karel Steigerwald, in Hviždala, 1990: 40. See also Adler, 1989; Chtiguel, 1990; and Oslzlý, 1990.

Hana Burešová canceled her premiere for the strike. By the morning of November 26 the Theater Institute in Prague recorded branches of Civic Forum in fourteen theaters in Prague and in eighteen cities outside of Prague, including the capitals of the six regions of the Czech Republic.[16] Slovak theaters, with which the Czech theater community had excellent contacts, followed quickly.[17] This provided an important network of communication throughout the country, located in places that would be familiar to all citizens (who might not, for example, know where the university or a particular factory room would be) and would be heated (which was important, since it was, after all, November). In the packed theaters at night, people from all parts of society came to listen or to present information about the situation and to discuss the course of events.

At these discussions, the actors were able to speak about the rapidly changing events to large groups of people in ways that many dissident intellectuals simply lacked the skills to do. As one Slovak actor and Public Against Violence spokesperson observed, discussions in the theaters did not merely repeat public slogans but "helped larger groups of people create a somehow united, common opinion" about what should be done (Kňažko, quoted in Antalová, 1998: 26). These evenings played an important role in setting the tone for the revolutionary events, which came to be known for their "merry-ness." The most detailed account of these evenings is in the book published by the Semafor theater in Prague (which fittingly dubbed itself "Civic Semaforum"), containing the programs and discussions in the theater during the strike, from November 18 to December 10, 1989 (Novotný, Černý, Kopačková, and Pražak, 1990). This account makes clear that the theaters did not cause or direct the events but rather played an important role in spreading information, at a time when the mass media were controlled by the Communist Party, and mobilizing people to participate in the demonstrations. In fact, it was through the efforts of the members of the

----

[16] Theater Institute Archive, photocopied document no. 124.
[17] Interview with Martin Porubjak, dramaturg, December 14, 1993; see also Antalová, 1998.

Semafor theater that the first strike declarations by students and theaters reached Slovakia. On November 18, they telephoned Studio S, a theater in Bratislava, and read both proclamations (Novotný et al., 1990: 28).

Each evening at Semafor began with the broadcast of the television news, analyzed and supplemented by uncensored information about current events. Afterward, prominent members would read the proclamations of the students and theater communities and later of Civic Forum. The evenings continued with the presentation of, or telephone calls to, guests, including students who had participated in the November 17 demonstration, legal experts, economic experts from the Forecasting Institute, and cultural figures. Members of the audience were invited to speak about their personal experiences or ask questions, which were moderated by the actors on stage. Many of these evenings had a curious quality to them, a cross between a political rally, a therapy session, and a cabaret.

After the television networks had agreed to broadcast information about the political situation, one such evening at Semafor was televised nationally, enabling an entire nation of television viewers to observe these public discussions. The cabaret-like quality can be seen when on November 26, 1989, after a long discussion about the economic situation, Jiří Datel Novotný proposed that they sing a song. Another of the leading actors agreed, but added, "We are doing this only to lighten the mood here. . . . Don't take it as an artistic appearance but as an injection in order to continue on" (ibid.: 134). The next day students from the faculty of journalism appeared to announce the creation of the so-called Committee for a Merrier Strike, which satirized the seriousness of political discourse and slogans, proclaiming that "we are deeply dissatisfied with the decision of several members of the Communist Party to resign. We need decent conditions for their work! We come from the reality that the most suitable conditions would be created by oppression and a government of misunderstanding" (ibid.: 165). Even in the negotiations and internal discussions of Civic Forum, the sense of humor that characterized the theaters is visible. Timothy Garton Ash describes

a brief entre-act that occurred at the height of the Civic Forum negotiations at the Magic Lantern theater:

> [B]efore anyone can discuss this, a group of students come on stage,
> dressed comically as young pioneers: white blouses, red bows, the
> girls' hair in pigtails. It is the students' Committee for a More Joyful
> Strike. We have come, they say, to cheer you up—and to make sure
> that you don't turn into another politburo. Then they hand out little
> circular mirrors to each member of the plenum. (1990a: 112)

In their welcome to the final evening at Semafor after the announcement of the Government of National Understanding, Novotný announced their call for a "merry discussion."

DIFFUSION FROM THE CENTER TO THE COUNTRYSIDE: PLZEŇ, BRNO, ČESKÉ BUDĚJOVICE

Although developments in Prague were key to Civic Forum's
success, trips by actors and students and similar evenings in theaters
outside of the capital played a crucial role in mobilizing the regions
and smaller towns. Public opinion surveys taken by the Institute for
Public Opinion prior to November 1989 show the radicalizing effect of these experiences upon residents of Prague.[18] Yet, if the
movement were not to remain isolated and vulnerable, it had to
spread from Prague to the rest of the country whose residents had
little experience or information about the events of 1989 that had
shaken the capital city. Finally, pre-existing dissident and opposition networks existed primarily in Prague, where there was a
greater access to material resources and the decision to participate
could be taken with greater anonymity than in the regions and
smaller cities. This is evident if we compare (in lesser detail) the activities at Semafor in Prague to the Chamber Theater in Plzeň, the
capital of the region of Western Bohemia; the Theater on a String in

---

[18] For example, 68 percent of the residents of Prague evaluated negatively
the protection of human rights by the old regime, whereas 46 percent of the
residents of Slovakia evaluated the situation positively (Vaněk, 1994: 40).

Brno, the capital of the region of South Moravia; and the Small Theater in České Budějovice, the capital of the region of South Bohemia.

The role of actors from the Chamber Theater in Plzeň highlights the early cooperation among actors, students, and others to organize a previously quiescent population in the absence of an organized democratic opposition.[19] It also demonstrates the mobilization of a highly visible group of workers from the Škoda auto plant. Unlike Prague, in Plzeň the students were not active immediately after November 17 because most of them had returned home for the weekend. The first to respond publicly to the repression of the student demonstration were the actors of the Chamber Theater, who spoke about the events in Prague and the strike at the beginning of their performance on November 18, concluding by singing the national anthem. In spite of the threat by members of the Regional National Council in Plzeň against participation in the strike, the actors joined the strike of theater workers and students on November 19. Civic Forum emerged much more slowly in Plzeň, since attention was focused primarily on developments in Prague. The few members of independent initiatives (such as Charter 77 and Democratic Initiative) began to cooperate with actors and students, after realizing that they would not receive any detailed instructions from the coordinating center in Prague. The civil society framing strategy is evident in the first proclamation on November 22, which announced that Civic Forum Plzeň was "in principle open to all who support the founding proclamation of Forum in Prague. We will cooperate with all citizens, representatives of factories and institutions in Plzeň, independent initiatives and also above all individual members of the state enterprise Skoda Plzeň" (Vaněk, 1993: 102). As across the country, students and actors sought to gain entrance to factories in Plzeň to gather support from the workers. The atmosphere was far less free than in Prague, as enterprise administrators in the Skoda plant threatened those workers collecting signa-

---

[19] For a description of events in Plzeň in November 1989, I draw upon Miroslav Vaněk's 1993 article.

tures on the petition calling for a general strike. At this time, theaters and students substituted for the official media by providing uncensored information about developments in Prague. An information service, complete with night service, began in the Chamber Theater. Local activists, actors, and students organized demonstrations in Republic Square, which grew on November 20 from about thirty people to November 27, when almost fifty thousand attended in support of the general strike.

As noted earlier, actors from Theater on a String and HaTheater in Brno had been in Prague on November 17, performing a piece entitled "Rozrazil 1/89," which contained a section written by Václav Havel. Following the police intervention of the student demonstration, a student from Brno had come to the theater where they were performing and interrupted the show to report what had happened. This interruption was the beginning of the strike for Theater on a String, which participated in the discussions leading to the decision to strike. Its dramaturg, Petr Oslzlý, read the proclamation announcing the strike on November 18. In Brno, the theater extended its performances of "Rozrazil," creating a new edition for every night.[20] As at Semafor in Prague, the evenings began with the television news. Each evening afterward was dedicated to a theme, such as the biography of Václav Havel, who was largely unknown outside of the campaign of disinformation against him by the regime. Because of time pressures, these evenings were improvised, containing songs, sketches, and jokes.

Using a report about the activities of the strike committee at the Small Theater in České Budějovice sent to the Theater Institute in Prague,[21] we can see the pressures upon movement activists outside Prague, in the conflicts between the theaters and the local authorities. The morning after a visit by a member of the Union of Dra-

[20] Interview with Petr Oslzlý, November 24, 1993.

[21] "Informace o činnosti stavkového výboru Malého divadla v českých Budějovicích od 20.11 do 2.12.1989 [Information about the activities of the strike committee of the Small Theater in České Budějovice from November 11 to December 12, 1989]," Theater Institute archive.

matic Artists on November 19, informing them of the student and theater strikes, the company of the Small Theater held a meeting to discuss what to do. At this meeting members of the local regional party authorities (the South Bohemia Regional National Committee) and the acting director for economic matters attempted to persuade the company not to strike, arguing that other theaters were still performing as usual. The company unanimously refused and went on strike, although of the other employees of the theater, no one came out in support of the company, and two came out against it. The local authorities began a campaign against the actors, spreading pamphlets to local factories with the salaries of leading artists and, in so doing, hoping to discredit them. By November 22, the theater club had been transformed into a workroom for the strike committee and a local branch of Civic Forum that coordinated contacts with students and smaller towns nearby. In České Budějovice, the actors participated in organizing demonstrations on the main square in the town. By December 2, the Small Theater had collected twenty-three thousand signatures on the Civic Forum proclamation.

The General Strike

In this chapter, I have argued that at least three real and potential alternative outcomes were possible after state breakdown in November 1989: socialism with a human face led by Alexander Dubček, immediate elections led by the Democratic Initiative, and ethnic secession led by counterfactual Slovak nationalists. I argued that the key to the eventual agreement on the Government of National Understanding was Civic Forum's successful mobilization for the general strike on November 27, 1989, which established its authority to speak for the "nation" in negotiations with the state surrounding the outcome.

The size and form of the strike reflect Civic Forum's emphasis on orderly, nonviolent protest and its disavowal of political ambitions. Although it is impossible to measure precisely how many people participated in the general strike, it has been estimated that three-quarters of the population were active in some form or another.[22] From the beginning, Civic Forum declared that the general strike was "a political protest strike [that] has no other aims" (Wheaton and Kavan, 1992: 203). In a demonstration of orderliness, the strike excluded the health, public transportation, and service industries that Civic Forum called upon to manifest "the strike in a suitable way" (ibid.: 204). The strike was not directed by the center in Prague but, consistent with Civic Forum's informal structure, manifested as local strike committees wished. Although the strike began at noon everywhere in the country, its duration could vary according to the decision of the local strike committee so long as it concluded by 2:00 P.M. The National Strike Coordinating Committee of Civic Forum merely asked to be informed of the preparations, launch, and course of the strike. Finally, if a strike committee was not founded in a particular institution, "the employees can join the strike in the way they themselves choose" (ibid.).

The rapid mobilization and diffusion of the movement were accompanied by mass demonstrations in Prague's Wenceslaus Square, culminating with the general strike on November 27, 1989. These demonstrations, initially spontaneous, were the most visible means by which Civic Forum could define itself and its aims as well as demonstrate its strength. They were, in the words of Ivan Havel, "the engine of our power."[23] The civil society framing strategy was prominent in speeches made at the first organized demonstration in Prague on Tuesday, November 21, at 4:00 P.M. Speakers appeared in Wenceslaus Square from the balcony of the building of the newspaper *Svobodné Slovo*, as they would continue to do at the same time every day in the following weeks. In Bratislava, Public Against Violence held similar daily demonstrations with the same purpose

---

[22] Wheaton and Kavan report that 38 percent stopped work for the full two hours, 9 percent for a shorter period, and 24 percent showed support in ways recommended by Civic Forum and Public Against Violence. They add that participation was higher in the Czech Republic than in Slovakia (1992: 95).

[23] Quoted in Otáhal and Sladek, 1990: 577.

on the SNP Square. In Havel's first speech from the *Svobodné Slovo* balcony, he declared:

> I am a writer, not any sort of expert speaker. I will speak only briefly. Civic Forum is thought of as a spontaneous and temporary representation of the critical, thoughtful public. Anyone may spontaneously join who feels that they are a member. It announces that a delegation of Civic Forum met this afternoon with the speaker of the federal government.[24]

At this first demonstration, Civic Forum continued to try to demonstrate its representativeness, its "forum-ness." Havel was followed by the actors Jiří Bartoška, who had attended the meeting that day with Czechoslovak prime minister Adamec, and Petr Burian, who read the proclamation of Civic Forum. Martin Mejstřík spoke for the strike committee of Prague universities, the miner Milan Hruska spoke, and the Catholic priest Václav Malý read the letter of Cardinal Tomášek to the people of Czechoslovakia. At the conclusion, the pop singer Marta Kubišová, who had been banned from performing in public since 1968, sang the national anthem. In the words of Václav Malý, "It was a question for us of getting known faces to appear—actors, sports figures, scientists, so people understood that it was not only the matter of several dissidents but the entire nation."[25] On November 23, 1989, the appearance of Alexander Dubček on the balcony in Wenceslaus Square gave a sure sign that even the most forbidden topics were now public again. The appearance of the workers from the CKD plant at the demonstration in Wenceslaus Square on Friday was a dramatic symbol that the party had lost the support of at least parts of the working class in Prague.

These demonstrations continued each day, culminating in the demonstration on Sunday, November 26, at Letna, at which an estimated 750,000 people attended. This demonstration, broadcast on national television, provides an opportunity to observe the leaders of competing groups try to frame the general strike with a direct

---

[24] Quoted in ibid.: 207.
[25] Quoted in ibid.: 605.

response from the public. The speeches by Havel, Czechoslovak prime minister Adamec, and Dubček provide three contrasting framing strategies that differ in terms of their interpretation of injustice, identity, and agency. The crowd at the demonstration, encouraged by Civic Forum moderator Father Maly, responded loudly to the speakers. However primitive, the responses to the speakers provide a glimpse into the failure of the state to contest the authority of the civic movements. They demonstrate the potential support for Dubček and his attempt to frame events as an opportunity for Gorbachev-like reform. Above all, they demonstrate Civic Forum's successful linking of its claims with the theaters and artists. This would be crucial for the next day's decisive demonstration of Civic Forum's support in the general strike.

Hypothetically, Prime Minister Adamec's speech could have been a turning point for the Leninist regime whereby the Communist Party would cooperate with Civic Forum, with Adamec as the leader of this joint effort. Public opinion polls rated him as one of the most popular politicians at the time. Although greeted with applause as he approached the microphone, however, he ended his speech interrupted by boos and calls for his resignation audible to the entire country watching on television. After thanking Civic Forum for inviting him, Adamec described his meeting with Civic Forum as an attempt to "calm the situation."[26] On the day before the strike, this interpretation of the meeting clashed with Civic Forum's emphasis on injustice and action. Rather than linking his claims to Civic Forum's framing of the strike, he argued that the strike should last only several minutes rather than two hours. "What is the meaning of dialogue?" he asked rhetorically: "that which joins us, to resolve the situation by political means." At that point, boos broke out. Cries of "demise!" are recorded. Adamec appeared unable to break out of the language of the Communist Party, calling for a perestroika-style "improvement of the economic situation."

---

[26] This and subsequent information comes from the Civic Forum document describing the contents of the Czechoslovak television broadcast of the demonstration, Informační komise, Monitor 2, photocopied document.

"It's already too late!" voices called out. He concluded his speech, which called for further meeting, amid cries of "It's already too late! Demise! That's already been done!" Others on the platform attribute the catcalls his speech received to the "apparatchik-like" style in which he spoke.[27]

Dubček was greeted with applause. In contrast to Adamec, he declared, "This is not a calm time, and so there cannot be calm which would halt the great people's movement. . . . Calm would mean the end of this process." The crowd responded, "Dubček to the castle! [meaning, Dubček for president, whose office is in Prague castle]." Yet, he differed from Civic Forum by framing the situation as an opportunity for socialism with a human face: "Twenty-one years ago we went out on the path of linking socialism and democracy. It was expressed by the slogan 'Socialism with a Human Face'" (ibid.: 516–17). He referred to Gorbachev's declaration in the previous day's *Pravda* that "[t]he main aim of the politics of perestroika is to build socialism with a human face." Despite his conclusion that "we are united with the youth!" Dubček's references to socialism allied him with the past rather than the future. As noted earlier, he retained personal prestige as a symbol of the suffering by Czechs and Slovaks under communism, but his call for reform socialism would fall on deaf ears and would be unable to mobilize the potential support of the networks of reform communists from 1968.

Civic Forum, as the organizer of the event, continued to portray itself as the representative of the nation by presenting speakers from all parts of society. Havel declared, "[A]fter forty years, *citizens* are beginning to meet freely. It has happened after what we all called for—dialogue with the powers that be!" (Wheaton and Kavan, 1992: 89, emphasis added). He called for participation in the strike the next day, stressing the nonviolent and legal agency claims of the civil society framing strategy: "We do not want to destroy, on the contrary, we want everything to work better." He called upon them

---

[27] Václav Malý, quoted in Otáhal and Sladek, 1990: 609; and interview with Martin Palouš, April 19, 1994.

to transform themselves into local branches of Civic Forum and "self-administering and independent representatives of the common will throughout the republic." Consistent with its identity as the embodiment of the nation represented by the striking theaters, actors from the National Theater and the Vinohrady theater in Prague spoke. Popular singers Jaroslav Hutka, Jiří Dedeček, and Vladimír Mišik led the audience in song, which Havel would later say was essential to the calming of the crowd. The speakers at the demonstration also included representatives of the students, of the Romany movement, as well as of soccer players. Miloš Zeman, at that time an economist at the Prognostic Institute, spoke about the economic situation. Karel Najemník, a miner from Most, called for all workers to unite and form strike committees. The peaceful aims of Civic Forum were emphasized by Father Václav Malý's concluding invocation of forgiveness of the old regime.

Conclusion

With this demonstration of their ability to mobilize the public, Civic Forum and Public Against Violence entered a new stage of their existence in the form of negotiations with the government about the resolution of the challenge. The focus on political opportunities and framing strategies explains the success of the civic movements as one of competing groups that sought to take advantage of the repression of the student demonstration in the context of the increasing international isolation of the state. It goes beyond an idealized vision of "civil society" and an all-powerful state to explain how a small group of movement activists could mobilize a previously passive population by transforming the network of striking theaters into local branches of the movement.

The argument in this chapter rests upon the claim that, if Civic Forum and Public Against Violence had framed their challenge in another way, events might have turned out differently. An alternative explanation might argue that Czechs and Slovaks did not need to be mobilized (akin to the argument in Chapter 4 that voting for

Solidarity was low-risk behavior). Once it became clear that the state would not use repression to put down the protests, people would have participated in the general strike regardless of how it was framed. Although this argument may seem plausible from the vantage point of Prague, where one could demonstrate relatively anonymously among the hundreds of thousands of people, it is less plausible in the smaller towns and the countryside, where that anonymity does not exist. The arguments in this chapter emphasize the congruency between the framing strategy of Civic Forum and Public Against Violence with the striking theater networks and with the appeal of the purely political, peaceful nature of the strike to Czechs and Slovaks. As the discussion of the trips by actors and students to the countryside illustrates, the question of mobilization was perceived to be of dire importance outside of Prague. The overwhelming organizational advantage created by the theater networks suggests that whichever groups were able to ally their claims with the striking theaters would have had a formidable advantage. The failure of the call for reform communism around Alexander Dubček and the narrow party appeal of the Democratic Initiative suggest that events could have turned out differently had these groups been able to link their claims to the theaters or offered an organizational alternative. Finally, although this chapter has made it clear that Civic Forum and Public Against Violence did not initiate the idea for the strike, the form and success of the strike was influenced by the agency claim of the civil society framing strategy. Public opinion polls at the time suggest that more people participated in the strike to protest against the repression of the student demonstration and show solidarity with the students and actors (98 and 95 percent, respectively) than to express support for Civic Forum (although an overwhelming 86 percent of the participants identified support for Civic Forum as the reason for their participation) (ibid.: 98). At the same time, the challenge of mobilizing workers from the larger industrial enterprises indicates that the success of the strike was influenced significantly by the appeal emphasizing Civic Forum's identity outside of politics and its agency claim for the legal, peaceful, and emphatically nondestructive nature of the strike held in whatever form each locality deemed appropriate.

Further, this account suggests that if the Leninist regime had acted differently, events might also have gone in a different direction. If the regime had announced immediately that it would be willing to hold roundtable negotiations with all major political forces in Czechoslovak society, it is possible that the mass mobilization would have been avoided, leaving the democratic opposition in a weaker position. If the regime had immediately recognized Václav Havel as the leader of Civic Forum at its first meeting on November 21, it is possible that it could have diffused the public mobilization that built up in the week between the repression of the student demonstration and the general strike. Finally, if it had been able to establish meaningful ties between itself and the Obroda group or Dubček to form the Democratic Forum of Communists, it is possible that this group could have acted with new legitimacy in negotiations and been a partner in the Government for National Understanding.

Getting the people into the streets, however, could be only the first step in resolving the reconstruction of the state. In the next chapter, I extend the mobilization framework to the resolution of the challenge by Civic Forum and Public Against Violence by means of negotiations between the Leninist regime and Civic Forum and Public Against Violence.

CHAPTER SIX

Resolution by Capitulation in Czechoslovakia

L ACKING THE BENEFIT OF hindsight, the reconstruction of the state in Czechoslovakia did not appear to those involved to follow necessarily from the successful general strike. The headline of Civic Forum's daily news service on December 2 declared: "Remember: Beijing!" It continued with a stark reminder that successful mobilization does not always lead to peaceful resolution:

> These days it will be a half-year since the horrible news flew to the world about the massacre of the students in Beijing's Tiananmen Square. . . . I think that no one in Czechoslovakia was surprised that our party leaders supported the murderers in China. . . . We are in full solidarity with the Chinese students in their fight against primitive thinking and gross violence. Their task is also our task![1]

Despite the resignation of the Central Committee, Czechoslovakia still had a communist prime minister and president, and the leaders of the Communist Party maintained control over the army and police. The civil society framing strategy defined Civic Forum's identity outside of the regime, which it pressured to fulfill its demands. The puzzle is that when Prime Minister Adamec resigned, Civic Forum and Public Against Violence did not simply assume power as might be expected when the state has broken down. The movements were not forced to concede guarantees to the old regime, yet they requested that a member of the former politburo resurrect the side

---

[1] Informační Servis no. 14, photocopy.

of the regime in the negotiating process and form a new Government of National Understanding. In this chapter, I examine the agenda-setting influence of the civil society framing strategy upon the reconstruction of the state. It explains the curiously legalistic and partial nature of the resolution culminating in the election of a playwright, Václav Havel, for president in December 1989.

I focus here on (1) the opportunities for negotiations with the regime after the general strike; (2) the limits of the civil society framing strategy and the "15: 5" government; (3) Prime Minister Adamec's resignation and the roundtable negotiations for the Government of National Understanding; and (4) competition over the presidency as guarantee.

Political Opportunities for Negotiating with the Regime

In contrast to Poland, where the regime initiated talks with Solidarity before the mobilization in the elections, the decision by the regime to negotiate with the opposition in Czechoslovakia took place only after mass mobilization in the general strike. The isolation of the regime after the fall of neighboring Leninist regimes and the removal of the threat of repression (with Prime Minister Adamec's announcement on November 22) created new incentives for challengers by changing the perceptions of the likelihood of success. With the successful mobilization in the general strike, the bargaining power of Civic Forum and Public Against Violence was strengthened, and they could demand direct negotiations. Without any precedent for such talks (again, unlike in Poland), the decision by the regime to negotiate was an opening of the political opportunity structure that indicated state breakdown. Below, I examine attempts by the regime to define the terms of the political agenda, which I defined in Chapter 1 as contestation over the purpose of talks, the identity of participants, the range of solutions considered, and the perception of the desirability of particular solutions. For example, until the mass demonstrations established the authority of

Civic Forum, the regime still sought to exclude Václav Havel from participating in negotiations.

Before the student demonstration on November 17, attempts to establish contacts with the regime had been met with indifference, as demonstrated by the unanswered call for dialogue in the "Several Sentences" petition in the summer of 1989. The effort that eventually established a link between Civic Forum and Prime Minister Adamec was composed of two members of the cultural community who called themselves MOST (or "bridge," in Czech): the rock singer Michal Kocab, and the journalist Michal Horáček. Horáček's memoirs, *Jak pukaly ledy [How the Ice Burst]* (1990), provide information on the establishment of contacts between the regime and opposition that culminated in the meeting on November 26, 1989, headed by Prime Minister Adamec and Václav Havel. MOST had been formed in August 1989 because its founders felt it was necessary to create a platform that would be accessible to all. One of the principal difficulties in doing so, they argued, was the absence of any contact between the regime and the opposition that could provide a personal foundation for discussion. Horáček explains that he and Kocab felt the biggest obstacle was the lack of personal contact between the two sides, which perpetuated the images each had of the other: "Perhaps Adamec thought Havel was a gorilla who only spat blood—and so the independents thought about them, about everything: that they are thieves, bandits, Mafia, who do not deserve to be met with. When however people met with people, everything was always a little different" (Otáhal and Sladek, 1990: 581).

In contrast to Poland, where the Catholic Church acted as a mediator between the regime and Solidarity, the solution in Czechoslovakia, Horáček and Kocab felt, was through the cultural community, who "have access to the underground, as well as spokespersons from political life" (Horáček, 1990: 11). They met with members of Charter 77 and with Oskar Krejčí, advisor to Prime Minister Adamec. Until November, however, nothing came of these meetings. After the repression of the student demonstration, on November 19, Krejčí called Horáček, who responded that in these new conditions he would meet only with the prime minister. As noted earlier, a meeting had taken place on Tuesday, November 21, between Adamec and spokespersons for the student, artistic, and civic circles of the Prague public, at which Adamec refused to meet with Havel. As in the roundtable in Poland, this was an attempt by the regime to challenge the authority of the civic movements to represent society by including other groups in the negotiations. Similarly, the opposition sought to "square the roundtable" by defining the negotiations between an "us" representing a broad spectrum of society and a "them," representing the repressive state.

The success of the mass demonstrations shifted the energies of Civic Forum from organizing demonstrations in the public squares to negotiating with the regime about a new government, even though daily demonstrations continued to be held as evidence of Civic Forum's ability to represent the will of the nation. Four days after Prime Minister Adamec's refusal to meet with Havel, there was no question with whom Adamec would have to meet and who would lead the delegation of Civic Forum.

The Limits of the Civil Society Framing Strategy and the "15: 5" Government

With the shift from mobilization in the squares to setting the agenda for the reconstruction of the state, the civil society framing strategy began to strain. The initially modest demands made by Civic Forum began to appear insufficient in light of the successful strike. Analysis of agenda-setting processes illustrates that, under the urgent and uncertain conditions of daily demonstrations, the institutional framework of negotiations as well as the identity of the participants were not fixed, but contested by both sides. As noted in the analysis in Chapter 3 of the Polish roundtable, framing strategies constrain the choices made in negotiations because the public support they mobilize is conditional. In such situations, the perceived limits to maintaining that support constrained the range of outcomes that the participants in negotiations would accept. Civic

Forum and Public Against Violence insisted (at times awkwardly) that they represented the will of the people but would not make demands or put pressure or give ultimatums to the regime, which was responsible for making the necessary changes. With the increased perception of its authority following the general strike, the movements sought to escalate their demands without altering their identity outside of politics, a position that would prove impossible to maintain. On the other side of the negotiating table, representatives of the regime resurrected the fiction of the distinction between the state and the party, arguing that they had limited authority to make decisions involving the party and would have to consult with the party before they could agree to any demands. In this section, I demonstrate the constraints imposed by the civil society framing strategy upon the demands made by Civic Forum and their reception of Prime Minister Adamec's attempts to resolve the situation. Transcripts of these negotiations have been published by Havel's aide, Vladimir Hanzel, and serve as the source of information for these developments.[2]

At the first meeting, on November 26, on one side of the negotiating table sat the government, led by Czechoslovak prime minister Adamec. Despite the opening of some of the satellite party newspapers (such as the Socialist Party's *Svobodné Slovo*) to uncensored information, the government coalition remained largely intact in the form of the so-called National Front, whose spokesperson, Bohuslav Kučera, opened the meeting on November 26. At the beginning of these negotiations, the regime framed its aim as a "political solution" to the current situation,[3] which accepted that violence would not be used but left unclear the nature of the solution. On the other side sat Civic Forum and Public Against Violence, movements created six days earlier that claimed to represent the spectrum of Czechoslovak society—or the "public," as Havel often referred to Civic Forum's base. Consistent with the civil society frame, it

[2] Hanzel, 1991.
[3] Kučera, in his opening speech of the first meeting on November 26, 1989. In ibid.: 13.

claimed that it did not seek political power but rather to create effective pressure upon the regime to change itself. Civic Forum had demonstrated its ability to speak for the public by its preparation of the daily program of the demonstrations in Wenceslaus Square and the increasing size of the crowds that attended them in Prague and in smaller cities. At the first meeting with Adamec, it was clear that the members of the Civic Forum delegation did not know each other well, nor were they experienced in the skills of negotiation.[4]

Opening the first meeting, Adamec dramatized the lack of contacts between them by commenting to Havel, "[We] still don't know each other, do we?" They introduced themselves politely and shook hands across the table, to the applause of all present (Hanzel, 1991: 12). At Havel's invitation, Adamec made the first presentation, in which he attempted to define the aims of the negotiations by explaining that it was not possible to make sudden, radical changes, even though they would try to reach the greatest possible agreement. In turn, Havel, speaking as "empowered by Civic Forum," presented four demands similar to those in the founding proclamation: the resignation of compromised individuals as per the proclamation of Civic Forum, the formation of a parliamentary commission to investigate the November 17 massacre, the release of political prisoners, and respect for freedom of the press and information. His lack of preparation was evident when he forgot and had to be reminded of the third demand and when he got the dates of the proposed general strike wrong. He invited Adamec to speak at that afternoon's demonstration at Letna, to which Adamec agreed. When Adamec insisted that Civic Forum not pressure him to do anything beyond his competence as prime minister, Havel responded by drawing upon the civil society frame, that Civic Forum was not pressuring him to do anything: "[We] are only stating that it is in the interests of the nation to speed up a little work on all structures" (ibid.: 27). To this Adamec laughed, commenting that Havel was a

[4] A memorable moment occurs in the first meeting as Václav Havel introduces the Civic Forum delegation and misintroduces Václav Klaus (eventual prime minister of the Czech Republic) as "Dr. Volf," in ibid.: 13.

writer and perhaps had a better word for it, that he would drop the phrase "pressure" when describing the demands of Civic Forum. In this first exchange, it was clear that Civic Forum would attempt to bolster its authority to make demands by framing itself as the true spokesperson for the country, the "nation," the "public," or even "society."

The four meetings between the regime and Civic Forum illustrate the limits to the civil society framing strategy. After the success of the general strike changed the perception of the likelihood of support, Civic Forum attempted to go beyond its original four demands (calling for removal of the clause from the Constitution guaranteeing the leading role of the Communist Party) but not its identity as a broad movement pressuring the regime to make the necessary changes. These meetings culminated in the rejection of Adamec's attempt to resolve the situation by meeting Civic Forum's demand to form a new government. At the meeting two days later, on November 28, Adamec began by arguing that he had fulfilled the original demands of Civic Forum: the resignation of certain individuals; the formation of a parliamentary commission into the events of November 17; speaking to President Husák about the release of political prisoners; and promising sixty minutes of time on television, having named a new director of national television, who was present at the meeting. Havel, in turn, altered the agenda by presenting new demands that reflected the changing perception of Civic Forum's authority after the general strike. He began for Civic Forum by apologizing for his inability to speak fully about certain topics, saying that there was a scramble and that their work was "marked by a certain improvisation" (ibid.: 44). To illustrate the delegation's authority to speak for both the Czech Republic and Slovakia, he introduced Jan Čarnogurský as the representation of Public Against Violence. Noting the "horrible" working conditions of Civic Forum in the Magic Lantern theater, Havel requested a building with more phone lines. He called for President Husák to resign; for the deletion of Article 4, which guaranteed the leading role of the Communist Party in political life, from the Constitution; and for the formation of a new government that would meet the demands of Civic Forum and Public Against Violence.

Throughout the negotiations, Civic Forum disavowed self-interested political aims, claiming to pressure the regime to undertake political reforms. When Adamec threatened to resign if pressured, Havel insisted that their demands were not an ultimatum. Consistent with the civil society framing strategy, he declared that if they did not press for resignation, Civic Forum would lose credit in the eyes of the public, and "they would say they are there somehow above and conspired with the government" (ibid.: 53). Whether Adamec's threat to resign was strategic or genuine, the members of their delegation constantly sought to mollify his anger, suggesting that Civic Forum believed that he would play an important role in the resolution of the challenge. After one outburst, Havel attempted to restore good faith by recommending that if they were to agree, they should laugh to calm themselves and then continue. In a small bit of merriness, the transcripts read "everyone laughs," and then the discussion continued (ibid.: 67).

At the conclusion of every meeting, the constraints of the civil society framing strategy upon the decisions made were apparent when both sides had to agree upon a public statement for the press. Civic Forum's main constraint was that the outcome of negotiations be consistent with the claims of the civil society framing strategy to avoid losing the conditional support of the public. Havel repeatedly insisted that they had to use everyday formulations understandable by the public, such as resignation and demise. The regime, on the other hand, sought to limit the public perception of its weakness by blurring the identity of the two participants and speaking in vague terms about the results of the meetings. In a meeting between the Czech prime minister Pitra and Civic Forum, led by Havel, most of the negotiation hinged upon acceptance of the word "demise" by the government. Havel emphasized that the communiqué for the meeting must be concrete and that uncertainties such as "reconstruction" or "changes in composition" would not be used. In a curious moment, Havel advised the Czech prime minister, who appeared not to know what to do:

> [T]he word "demise" will calm the public, your speech will gain you support, and the next day you will be the new premier, forming a new government. That is of course—I am originally a dramaturg and so I think dramatically from your perspective, but it is something for you to decide. . . . I am only telling you what would be best from a dramatic point of view to say. (ibid.: 109)

When a member of the government side objected once again to the use of the word "demise," even as they were writing the communiqué, Havel replied that history wanted it, the secret god of history. While writing the communiqué, Havel added, "[C]orrect me if I say it ridiculously" (ibid.: 143).

THE FAILED "15: 5" GOVERNMENT

The limits of the civil society framing strategy became clear on November 28, when Adamec demanded to know whom Havel recommended for a new government to be formed by the following Sunday. He asked whether they were an independent political party and not just independent citizens, since he had eighteen independent political groups that wished to negotiate with him. His challenge was met by Petr Miller, a worker from the CKD plant in Prague on the Civic Forum side, who responded that they were the most correct spokespersons because they had everyone, workers, even communists. When the exasperated Adamec demanded to know why Civic Forum would not make recommendations for the new government, Miller answered that Civic Forum was a meeting of broad opinions and to be otherwise would be to act as a political party. He and others told Adamec that they understood what a difficult situation he was in and that they supported him for the new prime minister. Havel rejected Adamec's challenge in the name of Civic Forum's fragile support, declaring that it was not an organized party and could not create the impression that several usurpers conspired with Adamec against the "nation." The apparently mollified Adamec responded that he took them to represent the people, which was why he was meeting with them (ibid.: 74).

Representatives of the Leninist regime also invoked the constraints of their supporters to resist demands made by the civic movements. The success of the regime's claims illustrates the overestimation of the strength of the Leninist regime by the participants in the negotiations, a perception that would prove crucial to the outcome. The challenge to Civic Forum's ability to speak for the public was repeated in meetings with the general secretary of the Communist Party and the minister of defense. At a December 6 meeting with General Secretary Urbánek, Havel began by telling him that Civic Forum felt itself to be a speaker for the general will and that it was acting as such only so that the government would have some sort of partner for discussion, because it would be difficult for them to meet in the public squares. In response, Urbánek replied that the problem was that the regional party secretaries didn't understand, they thought that they had the support of the people. He told Havel that when he recommended to one that he resign, the secretary answered that he had 140 letters from basic organizations of the party telling him not to do so (ibid.: 220). Similarly, Minister of Defense Vacek, in an otherwise courteous meeting on December 7, warned Civic Forum, "[D]on't think you have united support on everything; people are beginning not to like a certain pressure which they are not fans of" (ibid.: 271). In both cases, Civic Forum was led to strike a more conciliatory tone and explained that they did not intend to threaten public order.

On December 3, 1989, Prime Minister Adamec presented his fulfillment of the demands of Civic Forum in a new government, composed of fifteen members of the Communist Party and five nonparty members (hence known as the 15: 5 government). The proposal in which nonparty members would hold a minority position in the government is strikingly similar to the initial electoral agreement in Poland. Unlike in Poland, however, the international isolation of the regime after the fall of neighboring Leninist regimes and removal of the threat of repression limited the regime's ability to enforce its decisions unilaterally. Adamec's government was immediately dismissed as "a mockery of our demands" by the students, who promised to hold another general strike on December 11 (Wheaton and Kavan, 1992: 104). Civic Forum and Public Against Violence expressed their dismay in the selection of communists for the ministers of defense and interior, declaring that "the federal government that was created today is not a new government."[5] The next day, eleven of the ministers resigned, and Adamec flew to Moscow, where he met with Gorbachev. He claimed to have received Gorbachev's backing for a perestroika-style government, although that was no longer a source of authority in the negotiations. (Later, his advisor Krejčí would claim that this was false, that in fact Gorbachev had made it clear that he did not have his support [Draper, 1993a: 17].)

Adamec's Resignation and the Roundtable

On December 5, Adamec announced to a stunned Civic Forum that he would resign. His resignation dramatically altered the opportunities for reconstruction of the state and created great uncertainty surrounding the outcome. As the subsequent prime minister in the Government of National Understanding later observed, when Adamec resigned:

> the situation all at once lost its clear contours . . . [T]his meant the loss of the concept of a negotiation. The opposition simply had a strategy of pressure, but now they had nothing to apply it to. . . . But now? The 15: 5 government had been refused, the opposition sat in Laterna Magika, Parliament in parliament, the Central Committee on the bank. How to transfer power? Come by car to drive the office holders out of the building and sit down in their offices? Suddenly there was no mechanism at hand for the transferal of power. It wasn't possible to attack the Winter Palace. Therefore the opposition asked me to begin again a situation in which they would have a partner for negotiation. (Calfa, 1994: 1)

The most striking thing is Civic Forum's refusal to assume power, even though the regime had capitulated. The movements were not

[5] Informační Servis no. 17, December 3, 1989.

forced to accept the regime's agenda for negotiations, but they requested that a member of the former politburo resurrect the side of the regime in the negotiating process and form a new government that conceded guarantees to the old regime. The emphasis on legality and continuity in the reconstruction of the state should be explained not by strategic power-seeking behavior of the civic movements but by the conditional nature of Civic Forum's support for its claim to be pressuring the government to make necessary changes. Below, I examine the influence of the civil society framing strategy upon Civic Forum's response to Adamec's resignation, renegotiating the civil society framing strategy, and the formation of the roundtable.

If Adamec had not resigned, Civic Forum appears to have expected him to lead the new government as president, heading toward a Polish-style resolution in which a prominent member of the Leninist regime would maintain authority in the name of continuity. After the rejection of his 15: 5 government, Adamec declared on December 5 that the government was not a club of volunteers nor a discussion club, that he would not direct the national economy with such a government, and he proposed a new candidate for prime minister. The surprise with which his announcement was received suggests that, despite the dramatic changes in the political opportunity structure, Civic Forum had not imagined that the regime would willingly give up its power or that it might have to form a government itself. Havel and others from Civic Forum asked repeatedly if they could change Adamec's mind, saying that they had expected him to be the new prime minister.

Close reading of the transcripts of the negotiations suggests that Adamec's announcement may have been a strategic move, intended to pressure concessions from Civic Forum, but that Civic Forum failed to perceive it as such. After Adamec's claim that he could not work with amateurs, Havel abruptly announced that time was flying and that they had to act. He told Adamec that they should go to the castle and meet with the president. After a pause, Adamec asked him whether this meant that Havel did not accept his earlier proposed candidate for prime minister. Havel responded that this would be a waste of time, that if Adamec brushed them aside as Civic Forum then there would be no partner for any meeting with the regime. Strikes would break out and God knows what would happen. Just then, Adamec's advisor Krejčí interjected, "[Y]ou don't want to meet, just the two of you?" to which Havel exclaimed, "[W]hat?! Can we?" And they left the room for five minutes. When they returned, it appeared that they had agreed that Adamec would resign as prime minister, and, again, Krejčí interjected an attempt to prevent this, saying, "[H]old on, let's begin again." Having apparently had his bluff called, Adamec however insisted he would not form a government under pressure from Civic Forum. To this, Havel halted the discussion, saying:

> I should explain. I had the impression that it was truly unacceptable for you and that you had actually given us your resignation. And in the last few days when I have been in high politics, I have found that it is necessary to act quickly so as not to stir up the nation. It seemed to me that you were serious and that we had asked two or three times to which you had answered, so that I thought it was in the interest of the nation to meet quickly. That's why I said, Let's go to the castle. It appears that that's no longer true. . . . I'm sorry if you took it personally, but I took it seriously when you said that. (Hanzel, 1991: 186)

Havel proposed that Civic Forum name a new prime minister and that Adamec consider becoming the new president. Drawing upon the civil society framing strategy of the opposition, Adamec insisted, "[T]he nation would rather someone else do it" (ibid.: 189). The meeting concluded with Adamec's proposal of Marian Čalfa, previous minister without a portfolio, to become the new prime minister because he was Slovak, which would bring together the Slovaks. They agreed to meet again the next day after Adamec had considered their proposals, at which point it remained unclear whether Adamec's resignation would take place. At a meeting of the crisis crew of Civic Forum the next day, Petr Pithart reported Adamec's comment that he would be willing to rescind his resignation, "as you wish."[6] On December 7, however, Adamec announced his resignation on Czechoslovak television, saying he could not work with a knife held to his throat, and he did not participate in any further negotiations.

FROM CIVIL SOCIETY TO COMPROMISE

After Adamec's resignation, three possible strategies were identified at a meeting of the Civic Forum action group dated December 7: (1) to continue in the politics and tactics of obstruction; (2) the opposite—to pass the decision to form a government to someone with a mandate; and (3) compromise—to secure closer relations to the government.[7] The participants in the meeting concluded that the first two scenarios had been rejected by the public and that Civic Forum should adopt the third. This compromise would be acceptable only if Civic Forum perceived itself able to maintain its public support based in its identity as a broad movement distinct from the regime that sought not power but orderly, democratic change.

Efforts at maintaining Civic Forum's identity apart from politics can be found throughout the negotiations and proclamations at this time. At a meeting with the minister of defense on the day Adamec resigned, Havel introduced himself not as the representative of Civic Forum per se but of the "Prague Coordinating Center of Civic Forum." He attempted to refute Adamec's claim that Civic Forum was making ultimatums and insisted that "we want quiet and all that we are doing is directed toward bringing the country toward a peaceful path to bring the country to free elections" (ibid.: 255). The day after the general strike, on November 28, Civic Forum published a proclamation, consistent with the civil society framing strategy's rejection of traditional politics, that defined its internal organization and the relationship between the national coordinating center in Prague and local branches (Wheaton and Kavan, 1992: 213–14). It began by declaring that Civic Forum was:

---

[6] "Extended meeting of the crisis crew of Civic Forum," *Rudé Pravo* (Sept. 11, 1991): 6.

[7] "From the action group, 12.7.1989, 11 am," unpublished photocopy.

a spontaneously emerging movement of citizens united in their efforts to find a way out of the crisis in our society. Nobody is excluded from this movement who agrees with the principles and program of Civic Forum published on November 26, 1989, and who, above all, rejects the maintenance of the political system of only one governing force.

A similar proclamation of internal organization was announced by Public Against Violence on November 29, using nearly identical language.[8] The coordinating center in Prague was to serve two functions: the facilitation of information among local branches, all of which "work completely independently," and the representation of Civic Forum in negotiations with central, state, and international institutions and, above all, on the basis of the suggestions and recommendations of the local Civic Forums. For these purposes there was a three-tiered structure to the coordinating center: the crisis crew, composed of Václav Havel, Jiří Križan, and Saša Vondra, which met every morning at 8:00 A.M. and made basic decisions that were discussed with the action group of approximately twenty people; later these decisions would be presented to the plenum of around 150 people, which was the final opportunity for discussion before the daily press conference (Otáhal and Sladek, 1990: 577). In explicit contrast to the hierarchical structure of the Communist Party and consistent with the civil society collective action frame, Civic Forum defined its structure as decentralized and local: "It is possible to found local Civic Forums anywhere on the basis of region or working or interest groups with citizens, but not with institutions." It was to have no hierarchy whatsoever but rather to be "a horizontal network, with all local Civic Forums joined to one coordinating center." These local branches:

(a) should help clarify attitudes of citizens in a broadly based democratic discussion. This debate should lead to political differentiation.

(b) can concern themselves only with local solutions that have

---

[8] "Internal organization of VPN," November 29, 1989, unpublished photocopy.

not been satisfactorily dealt with by existing political structures.

(c) can organize strikes, demonstrations, or other actions in support of their demands or, alternatively, for the whole of Civic Forum if these actions are essential. Local Civic Forums are a continuation of the strike committees until the period when all the demands of Civic Forum have been met.

(d) will support all citizens where, in contact with the existing undemocratic structures, civil rights broadly defined are being interfered with. Local Civic Forums are hence the means of citizens' self-defense.

This created a dynamic organizational structure that was able to respond quickly in an uncertain situation, which stood in direct contrast to the rigidity and paralysis of the structures of the communist government.

THE ROUNDTABLE

Drawing upon the notion of a roundtable that had emerged in Poland, Civic Forum agreed to hold a meeting of all political forces to decide upon a resolution to the crisis. The need to establish or agree upon a new agenda for negotiations was the first order of business at the meeting on December 8. Havel opened the first part of the meeting by suggesting that the participants somehow agree upon a "self-identification" of the meeting. Kučera, the speaker of the national front, suggested it should be seen as a meeting to create a "government of national understanding" (Hanzel, 1991: 304). Rather than use the opportunity to form a new government of its own, Civic Forum requested that Adamec's candidate for prime minister, Marian Čalfa, propose a new temporary government that would serve until free elections the following year. At the recommendation of one of the leaders of the Socialist Union of Youth, the participants agreed to focus on four topics: character of the government, prime minister, formation of the government, and other posts to fill. Despite agreement on both sides that Civic Forum was considered the most representative expression of the will of the broadest layer of citizens, half of the members of the new government would be nominated by Civic Forum and half would be from the parties of the National Front. Havel argued that "in the interest of some sort of continuity," Civic Forum would support Čalfa with two conditions: that the president was Czech (respecting the existing constitutional principles guaranteeing equal representation of Czechs and Slovaks) and that Civic Forum's conditions for the cabinet would be met (ibid.: 308).

Stressing democratic means and legality, which was part of the civil society framing strategy, Havel insisted that "none of us wishes to create a constitutional crisis" (ibid.: 316). He emphasized that the president should resign with the formation of the new government, "from the point of view of further peaceful development, from the point of view of stability of state power and its continuity, from the point of view of calm in society" (ibid.: 323). At the next day's meeting with the National Front, the speaker gave Havel a virtual lesson in constitutionalism, explaining the legal procedures by which a new government can be formed following the resignation of the president. Because of its novelty and his lack of experience in politics, Havel agreed that he would rely on Kučera's help, since he "knows how it goes."[9]

The tension that participation in the government brought into Civic Forum's strategy is evident in Havel's presentation of the four categories to be used for evaluating proposed candidates for the new government at the meeting with Čalfa on December 9:

> [We] are not a political party which delegates its candidates into your government and which fights for the chalk. We have become, as history wanted, something strange, which isn't an organization nor a member of the National Front, nor a political party, but which has its own particular weight, as is shown. Through some means it has tried to represent the spontaneous will of the people which we can see on all streets, on television, in meetings, to be their speakers in these meetings with the highest levels. Our position is a little different than meeting with a normal political party. (ibid.: 388)

[9] "The meeting between Kučera and Havel," *Rudé Pravo* (Oct. 23, 1991): 5.

He announced that Civic Forum would neither delegate nor pressure anyone but would either recommend, support, take into consideration, or reject proposed candidates. At one point, a member of the Communist Party asked, What if we don't succeed in forming a new government? Havel responded, "[We] will announce to the public that unfortunately we did not succeed. What else can we do?" (ibid.: 368). To this implicit threat of chaos, the questioner hastily added that he was just asking from a practical point of view.

Agreement on the composition of the Government of National Understanding was secured at the December 9, 1989, meeting between Čalfa and Civic Forum and Public Against Violence. Although Civic Forum claimed not to pressure the decisions, it objected in each case to Čalfa's proposed changes. At one point, Čalfa proposed including Čestmír Cisář (a former communist from the 1968 government), saying he had spoken to the Obroda group, which had demanded three places in the government. Havel responded that, from the standpoint of the new government, it would be extremely "unclever" because these people look backward: Cisář is a symbol of '68 and today he represents those who should have been rehabilitated (ibid.: 434). Havel added that while Obroda had participated in some meetings of Civic Forum, at the same time they were going somewhere else with their own politics (ibid.: 436). Other representatives of Civic Forum explained to Čalfa that they didn't understand why he worried about Obroda, saying they were a small group of people, only the nomenklatura removed from their positions after '68. Čalfa responded that this meant 500,000 people, but he removed the issue from the table.

The ability of the civic movements to bolster their claims by means of mobilizing public support was starkly obvious at one point with the objection to the nomination of a non-Public Against Violence candidate for the Ministry of Information. Jan Čarnogurský declared:

> The clear spokespersons for the public in Slovakia is Public Against Violence. Public Against Violence is capable of organizing demonstrations, simply because Public Against Violence has 100,000 Slovak citizens who are willing to go into the square and express their opin-

ions, but some perhaps nonparty group from the radio, who recommends Mr. Roth, probably does not have these 100,000 willing to go into the square. Maybe it seems cynical but it's the reality. (ibid.: 443)

The final composition of the Government of National Understanding was seven nonparty ministers (each Civic Forum candidates), two Czech socialist ministers, two People's Party ministers, and ten communist ministers (although three of them—including Čalfa, Dlouhý, and Komárek—resigned from the party within a month). In the conclusion of the meeting, it was almost poignantly obvious how little both sides knew each other, when Čalfa asked Havel, Do you have the feeling that we will be able to work together in this collectivity? Havel responded:

> Personally, I hadn't met you, and I met you at two or three discussions with Adamec. . . . I only know that you were in the government for two years . . . and that in this time you did not profile yourself significantly. . . . What you did behind closed doors or in the preparation of the constitution or somewhere else, of course I don't know because the public doesn't know anything. . . . But I will say, after today's meeting, I have the feeling that you will take us to the elections [he laughs]. (ibid.: 482–83)

In the televised announcement of the new government, Havel concluded that Civic Forum and Public Against Violence would hold a one-hour gathering the next day at Wenceslaus Square, "a gathering of joy and merriness." On December 10, 1989, President Gustav Husák presented the new government and then, fulfilling one of the demands of Civic Forum, resigned from his office.

The Presidency as Guarantee

Although the formation of the Government of National Understanding represented the decisive end to the forty-year monopoly of the Communist Party, Havel's nomination as president came to be seen as a guarantee that the direction of political change begun by the civic movements would not be turned back by former members of the Leninist regime. After the announcement of the new government, the presidency remained vacant and the members of the National Assembly, who according to the Constitution nominated the president, remained unchanged. The theaters had called off their strike, although pointedly not their readiness to strike, while the students decided to continue to strike until the situation became more stable.

Havel had been proposed by Civic Forum as their candidate for president with the announcement of the formation of the Government of National Understanding, yet in the beginning of December his candidacy remained uncertain. The resignation of Gustav Husák as president initially appeared to offer the reform communists another opportunity to influence the outcome by proposing their own, better-known, candidates. A survey reported at the December 7 meeting of the Civic Forum action group indicated that although 80 percent of the public was undecided, the largest support went to Dubček with 10 percent, followed by Komárek from the Democratic Forum of Communists with 7 percent, while Havel was named by only 1 percent of respondents.[10]

The first question was how the president would be elected. To the surprise of many, the Communist Party in the National Assembly proposed a national referendum, arguing that this would be the most democratic solution (also perhaps believing that Havel would not be sufficiently known throughout the country to secure his election). Although Civic Forum and Public Against Violence had been able to mobilize the country in the general strike, there were fears expressed (as seen earlier in the negotiation with Defense Minister Vacek) that they would replace the monopoly of the Communist Party with their own. Public opinion polls in December suggested that Civic Forum and Public Against Violence had the confidence of 47 percent of the sample, but that about 33 percent thought they wanted power only for themselves (Wheaton and Kavan, 1992: 109). In a proclamation entitled "Why We Don't Want a Referendum Today," Civic Forum insisted that the conditions for a real democratic referendum did not exist in Czechoslovakia: normal

---

[10] "From the action group, 12.7.1989, 11 am," photocopy.

political parties did not exist, nor was there an independent and impartial media available to all, and the old power apparatus was still very strong behind the scenes. Finally, "[If] today we called for a referendum, we would help unleash a hysterical campaign which would not be about the person of the president but about destabilizing the state and threatening national understanding."[11]

Being better known, it initially appeared possible that the post of the presidency might be filled by a candidate who supported reform socialism, namely Alexander Dubček, Čestmír Cisář, or Ladislav Adamec himself. Competing groups outside of Civic Forum began to mobilize in support of various candidates, such as the demonstration held in front of the building of the Central Committee by the Democratic Forum of Communists on December 14. In response to the uncertainty, students from the entire republic held a demonstration on December 19 in front of the Federal Assembly in support of Havel for president. The National Student Strike Committee called for the president to be elected by parliament, but only from among candidates whose "moral profile was a guarantee of the further democratic development of Czechoslovak society and who have never been members of any political party" (ibid.).

On Czechoslovak television, Havel announced on December 16, 1989, that he would run for president on two conditions: first, that he would be an interim president until free elections next year would nominate a candidate for a five-year term; and second, that this take place side by side with the nomination of Alexander Dubček to a government position. Havel insisted, "I will not allow any dark force to succeed in driving a wedge between him and me, and in so doing, between our two nations."[12] By December 22 the other candidates had withdrawn from running for the presidency. At talks that day between Civic Forum and Public Against Violence and the communists, the participants agreed that Havel would be

[11] "Why we don't want a referendum today," December 13, 1989, photocopy.
[12] Václav Havel, speech on Czechoslovak television, December 16, 1989, unpublished photocopy.

nominated as president and Dubček as chairman of the National Assembly. In fulfillment of Civic Forum's demands, twenty-four members of the old parliament had resigned by that point, including those most notable for their role in normalization after 1968 (such as Bil'ak and Indra) and recent party leaders (such as Jakeš and Štěpan). By means of co-optation, members of Civic Forum and Public Against Violence filled twenty-one of the vacant seats, and one seat was filled by a student representative. In a curious gesture that suggests either the continued overestimation of the strength of the old regime or the unpreparedness of the civic movements, the opposition coalition offered the communists two of the twenty-four seats (Čalda, 1996: 164).

On December 28, Alexander Dubček was named chairman of the National Assembly, and on December 29, Havel was unanimously elected president by the parliament, their last act taken with the customary unanimity for which they were known. This was the revolution Havel characterized as the "triumph of truth over lies, cleanliness over dirtiness, of the human heart over violence."[13]

Conclusion

Analysis of the formation of the Government of National Understanding highlights the process by which successful mobilization emboldened the civic movements to go beyond initially modest demands to calls for broader political change. With the international isolation of the Czechoslovak state due to the fall of neighboring Leninist regimes, the demonstration that new political actors existed with the ability to disrupt routine patterns of state authority through strikes altered the previously rigid pattern of state repression. As demonstrated in the previous chapter, in November 1989 the new civic movements in Czechoslovakia sought to disrupt the political order by mobilizing the nation on behalf of a general strike

---

[13] Speech on Czechoslovak television, December 16, 1989, unpublished photocopy.

and thereby to alter the ability of the old regime to control the conditions under which it would leave power.

Uncertainty surrounding the reconstruction of the state in Czechoslovakia may seem naive in retrospect. At the time, however, the civic movements were aware of their tenuous authority, lacking a prior history and democratic expression of support. This is confirmed by public opinion polls that indicate at the time that although Civic Forum and Public Against Violence together had the confidence of 47 percent of respondents, another 33 percent declared that the civic movements merely wanted power for themselves (Wheaton and Kavan, 1992: 109). The record of the negotiations indicates the caution of the military regarding support for Civic Forum and repeated attempts by the Communist Party to limit the authority with which the movements could claim to speak for the nation without provoking a backlash by the communist nomenklatura.

Throughout the negotiations, the institutional framework as well as the identity of the participants were contested, rather than fixed, due to their novel and unique nature. The negotiations took place under the pressure of daily demonstrations and uncertainty surrounding the aim and limitations to such talks. The records of the negotiations suggest that if Prime Minister Adamec had not resigned, he might have become Civic Forum's candidate for the new president. Like General Jaruzelski in Poland, he could have served as a means of continuity with the Leninist regime and a protector of the interests of the nomenklatura. Even when Adamec resigned and thereby removed the foundation for all talks, the roundtable negotiations remained focused on replacing personnel in the state, rather than on broader or systemic political changes (with the exception of the demand to eliminate the constitutional clause guaranteeing the leading role of the Communist Party). The civil society explanation might emphasize the ability of a strong society to overwhelm illegitimate states. The twenty days that passed between the founding of the Government of National Understanding and the naming of a new minister of interior, however, suggests that the movements were not so powerful, nor the regime so overwhelmed. Some have argued that this lapse gave the secret service the chance to destroy or alter incriminating files or information (Weiss, 1990b). Contrary to the state-pact explanation, which would identify this lapse as evidence of an agreement between communist and opposition elites, Milos Čalda has argued that Civic Forum and Public Against Violence overestimated the party's power and, as a result, "acceded to a far greater number of Communists in the Čalfa government than was warranted by the Party's real power" (1996: 163).

CHAPTER SEVEN

Conclusion

[George Konrad's antipolitics] argument seemed right to me
when I first read his book. Looking back, after the collapse of
communist regimes in Hungary and elsewhere, it is easy to see
how much it was a product of its time—and how short a time
that was!
                                                    —Michael Walzer[1]

THE FALL OF formerly authoritarian regimes across the
world in the latter part of the twentieth century prompted
some to declare the "end of history," in which a global consensus on
liberal democratic governance had emerged (Fukuyama, 1992). In
that light, the demise of military dictatorships in Southern Europe
and Latin America in the 1970s seemed to have been followed by
the fall of communist regimes in Eastern Europe in 1989 and by the
collapse of the Soviet Union in 1991. Even the vicious apartheid regime in South Africa agreed to free elections that resulted in a new
government led by the African National Congress in 1994. In many
cases, the outcomes were influenced by peaceful negotiations between the old regime and representatives of broad-based societal
coalitions invoking the language of human rights and allied with
cultural institutions such as the Catholic Church. Closer attention
to these changes, however, reveals vast differences in both the way
this has taken place and the kinds of governments that have
emerged. As others have observed, "[A]lthough the new national
political regimes in Latin America, Africa, Asia and the former
communist world share important attributes of democracy, many
of them differ profoundly both from each other and from the de-

---

[1] 1992: 102.

mocracies in advanced industrialized countries" (Collier and Levit-sky, 1997: 430). These differences compel us to revisit the trans-formations in light of the ways authoritarian regimes fell and their consequences for sustainable democracies. By contrasting paths of change in Poland and Czechoslovakia, this book has shown that—even among countries that might have seemed similar by virtue of the ideological nature of the Leninist regimes—differences in the way communism fell created different opportunities for the emer-gence of democratic governments.

The arguments in this book are premised on the rejection of a preordained path of democratization, as well as of the notion of a "blank slate" created by the fall of authoritarian regimes onto which democratic governments can relatively freely be inscribed. The chapters have stressed contingency, analyzing bargaining and mobilization among competing challengers seeking to influence the outcome of regime breakdown. They have been guided by the prin-ciple that outcomes were uncertain, that the form of democratic re-construction in each country was only one of many possible out-comes. This may seem controversial in light of the nearly simulta-neous collapse of Leninist regimes across Eastern Europe, and even more so in the context of the dominant Polish national discourse emphasizing protest against communism (symbolized powerfully in the monument at the former Lenin Shipyard in Gdańsk, inscribed with the dates of workers' struggles—1956, 1968, 1970, 1976, 1980—with additional space left for future struggle). Yet this book emphasizes differences across countries and argues that these con-tingent outcomes had consequences in the short and medium term, namely for the creation of new political institutions and structuring of political competition. Bargaining determined which issues were resolved and which remained on the agenda of future governments, and mobilization influenced the organization of groups with vary-ing resources seeking to influence the state.

This chapter extends the analyses of the preceding chapters into the early 1990s. Comparison of the initial postcommunist govern-ments in Poland and Czechoslovakia demonstrates the influence of the path of transformation upon the development of stable democ-racies. To be clear, this does not suggest that pacted or mass mobili-zation paths of transformation *determine* what follows, but they make certain possibilities more likely, while excluding others. Be-cause there is no blank slate, we must understand where the new democratic governments started in order to explain where they eventually go, along continuous degrees of democratization. This approach highlights that free elections—while necessary—are not a sufficient condition for sustainable democracy. While the civil soci-ety master frame was critical for the successful mobilization against the old regime, this chapter will show that it had negative conse-quences for the development of democratic politics, rendering both countries vulnerable to populist and nationalist challengers. In Po-land, political competition to unravel the pacted government after 1989 created an unstable parliament with four prime ministers in three years; the civic movements that had so rapidly emerged in Czechoslovakia, by contrast, formed a stable government that served its full term but split the country after failing to resolve the constitutional relationship between the republics. Below, I return to the concept of civil society and contrast the development of democ-racy across countries.

Eastern Europe in the Early 1990s

In the wake of the fall of communism, many observers hoped that the concept of civil society—prominent in the mobilizing claims by the Citizens' Committees in Poland, and Civic Forum and Public Against Violence in Czechoslovakia—would become a political blue-print for the future of postcommunist countries. For example, Asch-erson declared that the revolutions of Eastern Europe introduced "a new gene . . . about self-managing societies, about the decline of state authority, about a new kind of power-sharing deal between the wealthy and the producers of wealth, about the rise of nationali-ties and the fall of nation-states" (1991: 121; see also Ost, 1990). Václav Havel, as the new president of Czechoslovakia, suggested to

German chancellor Helmut Kohl in an especially heady moment soon after the fall of communism that perhaps a new Europe would be formed around a range of independent civic initiatives, rather than traditional political parties. Yet many of the same observers found themselves dismayed by the apparent lack of civic and social activity after 1989, wondering "how a civil society strong enough to precipitate the collapse of a communist regime could now have become weak" (Bernhard, 1996: 310).[2]

In this book I have argued that the concept of civil society (as a sphere of self-organizing activity outside of and autonomous from the state) cannot explain the fall of communism in Eastern Europe nor the prospects for future democratization. When reconceptualized as a mobilizing frame, however, it explains how the civic movements, lacking organizational resources under repressive regimes, transformed pre-existing networks to mobilize popular support against the Leninist regimes. After 1989, however, the attempts by postcommunist governments to govern in the name of a united society, rather than revitalizing democratic politics, actually obstructed the development of competing political interests within democratic institutions. This failure rendered new governments vulnerable to populism, or the rejection of representative rule in favor of plebiscitarian solutions to the problems of building democratic institutions. Linz and Stepan argue that the "path to democratic transition via ethical civil society inevitably created discourses and practices that, until they can be transformed, will generate systemic problems for the creation of a democratic political society" (1996: 272). Others have observed that the "*'terrible simplicateurs'* benefited from the ideological vacuum which the idea of civil society was not able to fill" (Von Beyme, 1996: 34). Similarly, Kennedy suggests that the rise of nationalism "might be attributed to the weakness of civil society and the absence of serious rival ideologies

[2] See also Arato, 1993; Keane, 1988a, 1988b; Kennedy, 1992, 1994. For theoretical debates on the meaning of civil society, see Cohen and Arato, 1992; Putnam et al., 1993; Seligman, 1992; Von Beyme, 1996.

and rival institutions" (1994: 7; see also Beissinger, 1996; Brubaker, 1996; Laitin, 1998).

If we consider the notion of framing as claims of injustice, identity, and agency, we may see how the civil society master frame failed to foster democratic governance. After 1989, injustice claims concerning the violation of human rights by illegitimate regimes no longer made sense with new governments that renounced the old regime's use of force and declared their commitments to abide by international treaties. In contrast to the emphasis on "truth" in the writings of Havel, postcommunist politicians grappled with disagreement over complicated political, economic, and legal reforms that were difficult to make sense of in such terms. Identity claims on the basis of the unity of society offered little guidance for how to resolve conflicts within democratic institutions. In parliamentary democracies, the "nation" is not represented (in all but extreme circumstances) by a united society, but by a range of groups representing different interests. In fact, the similarity between claims to represent a united society by both civil society and populism highlight its incompatibility with democratic governance. As Hirst observed, "'Civil society' as a homogeneous *political* force is an idea at variance with modern pluralist democracy, which relies on the *divisions* of civil society expressed in political competition contained within the party system to ensure social and political order" (1991: 234, italics in original). Lastly, after the distaste with which Solidarity viewed its "compromise" in 1989, Polish politicians would need to accept compromise as the basis for nearly all agreements within democratic institutions. Agency claims rejecting politics (combined with the mistrust of political parties that was one of the legacies of communism) turned social groups away from their potential role as watchdogs upon the state, which, as Walzer observes, "can never be what it appears to be in liberal theory, a mere framework for civil society" (1992: 105).

Given its strategic nature deriving from opposition to communism, civil society could not be a program for the future because "it had not yet developed into a new consensus in which a new political system could be built. It was actually the other way around: the new political system had to develop step by step the new democratic consensus and civil society in a rather conventional way" (Von Beyme, 1996: 41). Indeed, for some, the fall of communism offered "a restatement of the value of what we already have, of old truths and tested models, of the three essentials of liberal democracy and the European Community as the one and only real existing Common European Home" (Ash, 1991: 122).

After 1989, the diminished potential for mobilization meant that political actors framing their claims in terms of civil society could no longer presume the support of networks associated with the birth of the nation that had been so crucial earlier, namely the Catholic Church in Poland and the theaters in Czechoslovakia. Contrary to the mass media images of thousands of supporters in the streets, Solidarity and Civic Forum and Public Against Violence found themselves institutionally weaker than one might predict. This was especially true when the communist and former communist parties largely retained their national administrative networks. Without the cultural institutions that served as their founding networks, the movements had to create new organizational structures for future elections. While theaters returned to the business of presenting plays in Czechoslovakia, the support of the Catholic Church in Poland seemed to contain implicit promises of support for religious policies favorable to the Church in the postcommunist period. As a result, one observed in Poland "the tendency of almost all political parties, including at one point even the liberals, to seek legitimacy through the Church" (Król, 1996: 282).

The influence of the civil society master frame upon new democracies, however, can be understood only in light of paths of democratization that established the institutional framework in which political actors operated. While Poland and Czechoslovakia both held free elections in the early 1990s, political competition within the rule of law on the basis of competing interests emerged along different dynamics. In Poland, one saw the legendary unity of Solidarity

destroyed almost immediately after 1989, followed by a fragmentary parliament and a series of unstable governments. Lech
Wałęsa's "war on the top" represented a populist challenge to the
gradualist approach of the new government and succeeded in
thwarting the emergence of political consensus in the short term in
Poland. By contrast, while the new government served its full two-
year term in Czechoslovakia, the impact of the collapse of the old
regime differed across republics. In the Czech Republic, market reformers triumphed over the former democratic opposition that
sought to maintain the unity of civil society, whereas in Slovakia,
fragmentation of Public Against Violence combined with the inability of both republics to agree upon a new constitution to create
opportunities for populist challengers such as Vladimir Mečiar,
polarizing the 1992 elections that led to the breakup of the country.
Closer examination of these cases highlights the constraining and
enabling influence of the paths of transformation upon new governments.

POLAND: AN UNSTABLE PARLIAMENT CREATED THROUGH INTENSE COMPETITION

As noted in Chapter 4, international developments made Poland's ground-breaking roundtable agreement obsolete and increasingly problematic. The attempt by the new government to
maintain the unity of Solidarity while implementing radical economic reform complicated the emergence of a new political consensus. While communist governments fell across Eastern Europe in
1989, General Jaruzelski remained president, and the parliament
was still based on the roundtable contract; further, many prominent
leaders of the Solidarity movement (such as Wałęsa, Bujak, and Frasyniuk) were outside the political sphere, having expected that, after
the relegalization of Solidarity, the trade union would become the
focus of democratic action. The legacy of reconstruction was not
only the institutional arrangement with the old regime but also the
economic crisis that had been the basis for the anticrisis pact. The
new government introduced in December 1989 an economic plan

for rapid reform known as "shock therapy" to solve the economic crisis and create a market economy in Poland within a year (see Sachs, 1993).

Wałęsa's decision to remain outside of politics as the representative of the will of the people proved to be one of the most consequential results of the pacted path of democratization, immediately threatening the legitimacy of the new government. Indeed, in early 1990, Wałęsa declared a populist challenge to the Solidarity government in the name of a "war on the top" against the persistence of communists such as Jaruzelski in the presidency, and calling for the "acceleration" of economic reform by the government. As president of the Solidarity trade union, he challenged the government's ability to speak for Solidarity and declared on April 10 that he would run for president. This challenge shattered the myth of Solidarity's representing the Polish nation, united as a trade union, democratic opposition, and movement for national renewal. As argued previously, Solidarity in 1989 was no longer a trade union with ten million members united against the state, as in 1980, but a political movement based in the Citizens' Committees that mobilized support in the partially free elections. Further, Solidarity was not the minority opposition voice in parliament which Wałęsa had expected to defend after the partially free elections, but the unexpected leader of a coalition government responsible for the economic and political transformations. In this light, disagreements surfaced, asking how a government acting in the name of trade unions and farmers could implement policies that would cause economic difficulties for the people on whose behalf it claimed to act. One analyst observed:

> Solidarity began its post-communist life as a very strange interest group indeed: arguing that the interests of its members were best served by accepting deep sacrifices on behalf of a class that did not even exist, in return for benefits that it was hoped—and only hoped—would accrue in the future. In the 1940s the communists had justified their own policies in exactly the same way. (Ost, 1993: 465)

Similarly, Staniszkis argued that the Solidarity government could claim to represent only "theoretical" rather than "real" economic interests, citing the declaration by a candidate for minister of industry who referred to a prospective middle class of businessmen: "I represent subjects that do not yet exist" (1992: 184). Others demanded to know why Solidarity didn't "put into operation its own manifesto from 1981 for a 'self-governing republic'" or the Positions Concerning Social and Economic Policy in the Roundtable Accords instead of the Balcerowicz plan (Kowalik, 1994a: 134).

In October 1990, General Jaruzelski agreed to resign, and new presidential elections were called by parliament. Notably, in the resulting campaign both Wałęsa and Mazowiecki sought the mantle of Solidarity and to unify society or the nation behind them, while differing in their claims about the primary problems facing Poland as well as the proper means to resolve them. As Ost declared, the "transformation of Solidarity is the story of the transmutation of the category of civil society, and particularly its central component, the citizen" (1989: 71). This created an immediate division between those advocating a "procedural" concept of democracy and those stressing "substantivist" outcomes: between the new government committed to maintaining the honorable compromise framing strategy and observing the legal path of evolution set out by the roundtable and those outside the government led by Wałęsa who declared that changing conditions meant the roundtable agreement should be nullified (Ekiert, 1992). Below, I contrast the electoral campaigns of Wałęsa's Center Alliance (*Porozumienie Centrum*) and Mazowiecki's Civic Movement-Democratic Action (*Ruch Obywatelsky Akcja Demokratyczna*, hereafter referred to by its Polish acronym, ROAD).

The creation of the Center Alliance in May 1990 to support Wałęsa represented the shift of Solidarity's most prominent leader away from the forces identified with the roundtable in 1989. The injustice component of the Center Alliance's framing strategy can be identified in its claim that the most important problem facing Poland was not the economic crisis but the persisting communist bureaucracy in persons such as President Jaruzelski: "[T]here can be no political or moral excuse for maintaining or supporting the position of the postcommunist nomenklatura" (Maziarski, 1990: 7; all following quotations are from the same source). Rejecting the honorable compromise framing strategy analyzed in Chapter 3, it declared, "[T]he acceptable limits of compromise with Poland's former owners have been transgressed." The identity claim by the Center Alliance however was not a specific economic or political constituency, but "ordinary Polish citizens, attached to national and Christian values and opting for a market economy." Seeking to maintain the unity of society, one of the Center Alliance's organizers declared that the program and activities of the party:

> follow from the fundamental tradition of Solidarity, identified neither with the Polish Left (which borders on social democracy and recruits its adherents from among scientists, journalists, artists, et al.) nor the Polish Right. The Center Alliance is trying to prevent a head-on collision of left- and right-wing tendencies by establishing a solid political majority located between the two extremes.

Wałęsa's war on the top was based in his call for "acceleration," in which the roundtable pact would be rapidly eliminated without regard for legal means of change such as scheduled parliamentary elections. Wałęsa's political speeches and interviews are notoriously ambiguous and contradictory, yet as he declared in a speech to the Citizens' Committees in May 1990:

> Poland has no stomach for politics, for political parties. This is the honest truth! We have a beautiful victory; we have tremendous understanding for this government and its great effort. But there is no consummation, my dear people! . . . When you have a revolution—and we have a revolution—then you have to rule by decree! What's going on today? We are so very sentimental. We are so understanding to those who tyrannized us, to those who murdered us, who tried to stifle us by showing us graves! Until today. We are so humanitarian! And what are they doing? Six months has passed and this government still can't resolve the problems at the shipyard! Meanwhile, twenty private companies [founded by former communists] are doing just fine![3]

[3] Quoted in Kurski, 1993: 91–92.

This prodded Michnik to declare that the "same behavior that used to destabilize a totalitarian order must now lead to the destruction of the political culture of the young democracy" (1998: 164–65). As a Polish journalist observed about Wałęsa: "When he says that Solidarity is neither left-wing nor right-wing, he speaks primarily about himself. He is not interested in formulas or concepts. . . . He is interested in society's mood, of which he is an unerring register. He knows that if he failed to stay in touch with the attitudes and feelings of the common people, he'd be nobody" (Wierżbicki, 1990: 31).

In response, members of the Civic Parliamentary Club, led by spokesperson Bronislaw Geremek, created the so-called Civic Movement-Democratic Action (or ROAD) and nominated Prime Minister Mazowiecki as their candidate for president. Consistent with the anticrisis pact that formed the basis for the roundtable, ROAD argued that the primary challenge facing Poland was the economic crisis that necessitated unity during the transition period. As early as Prime Minister Mazowiecki's first speech to parliament, he had rejected vengeance toward the Communist Party, vowing "to forsake revenge and the settling of accounts" (1989: 10). In its use of the words "civic movement" in its name, ROAD drew upon the identity component of the civil society framing strategy and sought to maintain the "Solidarity ethos" that argued against dividing into political parties. Geremek later remarked:

> After the elections of 1989, I was among those who tried to preserve the unity of Solidarity in public life. . . . Like citizens of most other postcommunist countries, many Poles viewed the whole phenomenon of political parties with profound unease. The idea of civil society naturally suggested an effort to maintain the national unity and civic spirit of Solidarity. (1992: 9)

As he admitted, however, "[W]hen the common enemy of totalitarianism disappears, the reason for being of such a community begins to evaporate. . . . It is significantly more difficult to meet the need for unity—a need that is especially visible in all of the postcommunist countries during these difficult times—in the context of an open society" (ibid.: 10). The agency claim made by ROAD emphasized evolution, or a proceduralist view of politics that contradicted Wałęsa's challenge to the existing government. Bujak declared that ROAD was "for the rule of law and parliament, for judicial independence, etc., against any methods which might threaten our democratic achievements. . . . One cannot disentangle oneself from totalitarianism by applying undemocratic methods" (1990: 10–11).

In the first round of voting on November 25, 1990, Wałęsa gained 40 percent of the vote, while an outsider candidate, Stanislaw Tymiński, stunned most observers by gaining more votes than Prime Minister Mazowiecki. The voting results indicate that the Solidarity government had far less public support than the 1989 elections might have suggested. In the second round, Wałęsa won with nearly 75 percent of the vote, but Tymiński still garnered 25 percent of the votes, primarily from small towns and urban areas such as Katowice, which were threatened by the Balcerowicz economic plan. The failure of Prime Minister Mazowiecki can be traced in part to the attempt to maintain the united claims of the civil society master frame. Kamiński argues that the emphasis on unity within the Solidarity movement "amounted in the long run to a forceful repression of group and individual interests and reduced the accountability of the ruling elite" (1991: 184). Similarly, Staniszkis (1984) argued that the "anti-political mentality of Solidarity" in the 1980s impeded the formation of political parties based on legitimate differences. She argued that this created an orientation in which all differences in aims, tactics, and opinions are regarded as illegitimate, every compromise is perceived by the movement's members as very painful because to compromise is not merely tactical defeat but the defeat of some basic values, and the democratic process is perceived as the triumph of a majority who share the truth over devious "others" (ibid.: 140–44).

Yet Wałęsa's success did not lay the groundwork for political consensus that could lead to stable government. One of the founders of the Center Alliance observed that it "laid waste to the plans for the creation of a single party, but it deepened the conflict."[4] His success lay not merely in the resonance of his claims with Polish citizens' dissatisfaction over the persistence of communist leaders in political life but in his successful battle for the legacy of Solidarity, especially his ability to prevent Mazowiecki from mobilizing the network of Citizens' Committees. After their successful reconstitution for the local elections in May 1990, the Citizens' Committees became "the main political prize and the victim" of Wałęsa's run for president (Grabowski, 1996: 237–38). On June 1, Wałęsa fired longtime Solidarity activist Henryk Wujec as secretary of the Citizens' Committees, arguing that the Citizens' Committee had become too involved in supporting political parties and should limit their activities to the local level. In an additional challenge to the former democratic opposition to represent Solidarity, he ordered the newspaper *Gazeta Wyborcza* to remove the Solidarity logo from its front page. By contrast, the leaders of ROAD declared that the Citizens' Committees should remain united by the "ethos of Solidarity" and organized at the national level.

In summer 1990, both Wałęsa (as head of the Solidarity trade union) and Bujak (head of the Warsaw Citizens' Committee) called national meetings of the committees to resolve the status of the committees in the presidential election. The competing appeals created confusion among the local members about whom to support. Members of the Citizens' Committees were themselves divided as to whether they should retain their status above parties or join Wałęsa in his challenge to the Mazowiecki government. The Committee in Gorzow revealed its confusion over the battle, declaring, "Mr. Chairman! Mr. Prime Minister! You fought communism together. Together, you can and must build a democratic and independent Poland."[5] Tellingly, thirteen provinces endorsed both the Mazowiecki government *and* Wałęsa's program for acceleration. At the September 1990 conference, the committees decided not to support either ROAD or the Center Alliance and declared that they would

[4] Leszek Kaczyński in ibid.: 90.
[5] Quoted in Grabowski, 1996: 245.

retain their broad national unity with local, autonomous organization. This formulation, however, could no longer work: the Citizens' Committees could not substitute for popular opinion, and the unity that they sought to maintain in the name of Solidarity no longer corresponded to the political forces at the national level.

The last remnant of the roundtable agreement, the guarantee of 65 percent of the seats of the *Sejm* for the Communist Party and its former allies, was eliminated by parliamentary elections in 1991 in which sixty-nine parties competed. After its defeat in the presidential elections, the democratic opposition element of ROAD reconstituted itself as the Democratic Union (*Unia Demokratyczna*), while the Polish United Workers' Party dissolved itself, and reformers led by Aleksander Kwaśniewski formed a new social democratic party, the Alliance of the Democratic Left (Orenstein, 1998). By the time of the October parliamentary elections in 1991, however, the former opposition had lost its previous organizational base, since "the [Citizens'] Committees had disappeared almost without a trace" (Grabowski, 1996: 247). Aided by an electoral law that guaranteed proportional representation and set a very low electoral threshold, at 3 percent,[6] twenty-nine political parties were elected to the *Sejm* and thirteen parties to the Senate, with additional independent candidates in both houses. The Democratic Union won the highest percentage of the vote, but with only 12.3 percent, with the Alliance of the Democratic Left close behind in second place with only 0.33 percent less.

As a result, in a situation described as "approaching a state of anarchy," at least five parties were needed to form a majority government (Ekiert, 1992: 16). Between January 1991 and July 1992, the divided parliament nominated three prime ministers, finally electing Hana Suchocka of the Democratic Union, whose government also fell to a vote of no confidence after eleven months. Stokes refers to this succinctly as the "negative political price Poland paid

[6] Stokes (1993: 214) observes that even if the electoral law had used a 4 percent cutoff for entry to parliament, the nine largest parties would still have entered the *Sejm*.

TABLE 4

1991 Polish Parliamentary Election Results, Lower House

Party	Pct. of the vote	Seats won
Democratic Union	12.31	62
Democratic Left Alliance	11.98	60
Catholic Election Action	8.73	49
Center Democratic Accord	8.71	44
Peasant Party-Programmatic Alliance	8.67	48
Confederation for Independent Poland	7.50	46
Liberal Democratic Congress	7.48	37
Peasant Accord	5.46	28
Solidarity	5.05	27
Polish Friends of Beer	3.27	16
Germany Minority	1.17	7
Christian Democracy	2.36	5
Polish Western Union	0.23	4
Party of Christian Democrats	1.11	4
Labor Solidarity	2.05	4
Union of Political Realism	2.25	3
Party X	0.47	3
Movement for Silesian Autonomy	0.35	2
Democratic-Social Movement	0.46	1
Union of Great Poles		1
Peasant Unity		1
Great Poland and Poland		1
Solidarity 80		1
Piast Peasant Election Alliance		1
Electoral Committee of Orthodox Believers		1
Cracow Coalition of Solidarity with the President		1
Union of Podhale		1
Alliance of Women Against Life's Hardships		1

SOURCE: Millard, 1992: 846.

in the early 1990s for the positive virtues of the Solidarity movement of the 1980s" (1993: 214). Linz and Stepan go so far as to declare that the:

antipolitical style of Solidarity seems to have directly contributed to its fragmentation into many small parties, its waning power as a political force in 1990–92, to the surprisingly strong victory of the former communists and their Peasant Party allies in the September 1993 parliamentary elections, and to the election of a former Communist, Aleksander Kwaśniewski, as President in 1995. (1996: 273)

This book suggests that it was the combination of the civil society master frame with the competition created by the pacted path of democratization that accounts for the fragility of democracy in Poland after 1989 (although, as noted, this book cannot account, for example, for the difficulties in resolving and defining the new presidential powers or a new constitution). Attention to the way that the pacted path of democratization structured political conflict highlights the impact of the civil society master frame and decisions made at the roundtable upon the learning process by new political actors; the electorate itself negotiated and accepted democratic institutions as the legitimate means for resolving political differences.

CZECHOSLOVAKIA: A STABLE GOVERNMENT UNABLE TO FRAME KEY CONSTITUTIONAL QUESTIONS

In Czechoslovakia, the consequences of the capitulation by the old regime initially seemed manageable. The civic movements won an absolute majority in 1990 elections and formed stable governments that lasted their full term (see Table 5 for complete election results). Yet the attempt by many leaders of Civic Forum and Public Against Violence to maintain their authority as representing society above politics prevented them from addressing differences within their broad coalitions, as well as between republics. Their decisions were structured by bargaining at the roundtable with the resurrected regime in 1989, namely concerning the persistence of former and current communists in positions of authority and the reliance upon the existing Constitution, which guaranteed veto power to a parliamentary minority in one house. Ultimately, this government proved unable to resolve the problem of statehood, dissolving Czechoslovakia into two new states in the absence of public opinion supporting independence.

The impact of the civil society master frame rejecting self-interested claims for political power can be seen in Civic Forum's decision to opt for proportional rather than majority representation in the 1990 elections (whereby seats in parliament would be distrib-

TABLE 5

1990 Czechoslovak Parliamentary Election Results

Party	House of People		House of Nations	
	Pct. of the vote	Seats won	Pct. of the vote	Seats won
CZECH REPUBLIC				
Civic Forum	53.15	68	49.96	50
Communist Party CS	13.48	15	13.80	12
Christian-Democratic Union	8.69	9	8.75	6
Moravian-Silesian Association	7.89	9	9.10	7
Parties below 5% threshold	16.79	—	18.39	—
Total:		101		75
SLOVAKIA				
Public Against Violence	32.54	19	37.28	33
Christian Democratic Movement	18.98	11	16.66	14
Communist Party CS	13.81	8	13.43	12
Slovak National Party	10.96	6	11.44	9
Hungarian ethnic party	8.58	5	8.49	7
Parties below 5% threshold	15.13	—	12.70	—
Total:		49		75
Total for both republics:		150		150

SOURCE: Krejčí, 1995: 340–41.

uted among groups by the overall proportion of the vote received, instead of allocated to the winner of the greatest number of votes in each district). While the latter would have likely guaranteed a clean sweep for the civic movements, the former guaranteed the survival of the communists. Even though the civic movements had everything to gain and the authority to impose majoritarian voting, Havel and leaders of Civic Forum opted for a proportional system with the belief that this would not privilege political parties over independent candidates. That, as well as the decision to limit the term for the first assembly to two years, "did not represent the strategic interests of any of the involved individuals, groups or constituencies" (Elster et al., 1998: 57). As one advisor to president Havel observed soberly: "[T]his decision will be seen either as the glory or the weakness of the November revolution: we were winners that accepted a degree of self-limitation."[7] Notably, however, a 5 percent electoral threshold prevented the parliamentary fragmentation in Poland.

Critically, the civic movements failed to resolve constitutional mechanisms for decision-making regarding the relationship between the two republics of the federation. The existing Constitution, written during the "normalization" period after 1968, gave veto powers to the Slovak Republic, whereby "a Slovak group of 31 representatives in the upper house—representing one-fifth of that house and two-fifteenths of the population in the country as a whole—could block any constitutional change" (Elster, 1995: 111). This was the result of a constitutional structure whereby qualified majorities were needed for constitutional change in both houses of parliament, while the upper house was constituted by equal numbers of Czechs and Slovaks. The risks in the potential for representatives of the old regime to obstruct the process of reconstruction were clear when the first proposal of the law on co-optation by which members of the old parliament would be replaced failed to receive the necessary three-fifths of the Slovak vote (Čalda, 1996: 164). Similarly, Linz and Stepan argue that holding the 1990 elections within the framework of the old Constitution and its veto power for a small minority "constrained severely the manner in which the stateness problem of Czechoslovakia could be handled" (1996: 331).

Despite their revolutionary unity and apparent electoral success, the identities of the civic movements as nonhierarchical movements representing "society" quickly gave way to internal differences. Political competition among successors to the civic movements across republics turned around the relationship between the two republics, entailing stances toward the old regime and the proper course of economic reform, as well as repeated incidents of brinksmanship. The breakup of movements into parties took different directions across republics, with market reformers dominating the Czech political scene and populists garnering the greatest popular support in

[7] Quoted in Elster, 1995: 114.

Slovakia on the basis of ambiguously nationalist claims. In both republics, the former opposition sought to maintain its unity as civil society and consequently failed to reach the electoral threshold in the 1992 parliamentary elections. Unlike the unreformed Communist Party of Bohemia and Moravia in the Czech Republic, the Slovak Communist Party dissolved and reformed itself as the Party of the Democratic Left (*Strana Demokratickej L'avici,* or SDL) (Grzymala-Busse, 1998). To contrast differences in the influence of the path of democratization across republics (and lessen confusion over the multiplication of party names and leaders), I analyze each republic separately, focusing on the successors to Civic Forum in the Czech Republic and Public Against Violence in Slovakia.

In the Czech Republic, the debate over the future of Civic Forum crystallized around competition for chairmanship of Civic Forum between the former dissidents led by Martin Palouš and new political figures led by Václav Klaus, culminating with Klaus's election as chairman in October 1990. On the one hand, Palouš argued that Civic Forum should continue to be governed during the transition period by the "consensus-oriented politics" that were the legacy of Charter 77.[8] Similarly, Jiří Dienstbier, the foreign minister and former spokesman for Charter 77, argued that Klaus's attempts to introduce hierarchical qualities into Civic Forum were unnecessary and "inhumane."[9] On the other hand, finance minister Klaus argued that the nonhierarchical nature of Civic Forum had begun to impede its ability to implement political and economic reform. Contrary to Civic Forum's electoral program in the 1990 elections, Klaus declared the need to create formal membership structures that would enable the building of an effective party and link the regions in hierarchical party structures for effective coordination. Under Klaus's chairmanship, a proposal to change the official standpoints of Civic Forum passed on January 1, 1991, declaring that "Civic Forum is a political party, whose members must be citizens older than 18 years, who agree with its political program, are

[8] Interview with the author, April 19, 1994.
[9] Quoted in DeCandole, 1991: 21.

willing to support their fulfillment, are registered with the membership section of Civic Forum and are not members of any other political party or political movement."[10] It announced the creation of a membership fee and declared that the basic organizational unit of Civic Forum would be the local branches, which had to have at least ten registered members. Over differences between these two groupings on the appropriate form of the movement, Civic Forum dissolved itself in February 1991 into the Civic Democratic Party (*Občanská Demokratická Strana*, or ODS), led by Finance Minister Klaus, and Civic Movement (*Občanské Hnutí*, or OH), led by Foreign Minister Dienstbier.

In its founding program, ODS argued that many of the most serious problems facing Czechoslovakia had "arisen due to the hesitant policies pursued by Civic Forum throughout 1990. Little action was taken against many surviving totalitarian structures. The Civic Democratic Party finds it intolerable that many important posts are still held by communists."[11] In December 1990, Klaus, as chairman of Civic Forum, had declared his constituency to be young people, Christians, and entrepreneurs, and not artists and intellectuals, among whom "trends toward leftism originate."[12] Strikingly, such a constituency did not reflect pre-existing social cleavages, nor even a clearly defined social group. At that time, entrepreneurs, when privatization of formerly state-owned companies had not yet taken place, can hardly have been said to exist as a social group with concrete interests. Rather, ODS's constituency was defined in political terms that sought to marginalize the former dissidents that had created and led Civic Forum during the revolution.

Consistent with its claims that the greatest problems facing the country concerned its relationship to the past, ODS supported the screening (or "lustration") law, which banned former communist

---

[10] "Pracovni navrh na zmenu Stanov Obcanskeho fora (schvaleny Radou OF dne 11.1.1991) [Working proposal on changing the standpoints of Civic Forum (passed by the Civic Forum Council on January 11, 1991)]," photocopy.

[11] Quoted in *East European Reporter* 4, no. 4 (1991): 48.

[12] Quoted in DeCandole, 1991: 22.

functionaries and secret police collaborators from elected or appointed public or professional positions in state organizations and joint-stock companies in which the state held a majority interest (Welsh, 1994). Although the law was condemned by the European Union as unconstitutional, the Civic Democratic Party incorporated the same principles into its founding statues, which declared, "I am not a member of any political party and I have never been a member of the People's Militia, StB [secret police], nor a collaborator for them." The eventual law on lustration, passed in October 1991, was led by and publicly supported by parliamentarians from ODS. Klaus repeated antileft discourse throughout the 1992 election campaign, when he described OH as a "left-wing party, using the term 'liberal' in the American sense, not in the European sense, to my regret" (1992: 22). In a claim that would be repeated in the 1992 elections, ODS linked its support for its market reforms with support for democracy and the federal state. Rather than unequivocal support for Czechoslovakia, the party's program declared that the party "wishes to retain the existing Czechoslovak Federation, if the federal state proves to be viable and does not hinder further social change. However, there must be unified defence and foreign policies and financial and tax policies throughout the whole country."[13] This program was accompanied by the implementation of institutional party structures across the country that provided ODS with an organized network with which to conduct the 1992 electoral campaign. That provided ODS with an organized network with which to conduct the 1992 electoral campaign. With this network, it also raised greater income (with forty-three million crowns in 1991) than the Civic Movement (with eighteen million crowns) (Mlynář, 1992). Opinion polls immediately indicated that the right-oriented ODS garnered higher support (20 percent by late January 1992) than the dissident-based OH (with only 4 percent) (Wheaton and Kavan, 1992: 233–34).

By contrast, OH declared its alliance to the principles of Civic Forum as set out in its original 1989 founding document and its in-

---

[13] Quoted in *East European Reporter* 4, no. 4 (1991): 49.

tention to fulfill the 1990 election program, "which has not as yet been implemented."[14] Consistent with its origins, it sought to maintain the unity of society. In contrast to ODS's identification of its supporters as a specific set of potential voters, the OH program called for "dialogue and cooperation with the democratic right and the democratic left." It argued for a "radical but not ruthless" reform of the economy and held the lustration law to be unacceptable from an ethical and legal standpoint. OH's most prominent leader, Foreign Minister Jiří Dienstbier, repeatedly criticized the law and, in an ironic twist of fate, voted with the Communist Party to oppose it in parliament. In contrast to ODS's conditional support for the federation as long as it could be "viable," OH argued that there should be even greater autonomy for ethnic groups: "We believe that the Czechoslovak Federation should be retained. But the new Constitution must make it possible for Moravia and Silesia also to enjoy autonomy; whether as self-contained lands within the Czech republic, or as members of a tripartite federation of Bohemia, Moravia, and Slovakia."[15] In the postcommunist context, OH's similar call for united economic and foreign policies appeared strained at best.

In Slovakia, political competition took a different direction from that of the Czech Republic and proved to have negative consequences for democracy. After 1989, current and former communists retained greater influence than in the Czech Republic. The Slovak communists were not compromised by the repression of the student demonstration in Prague in November 1989, nor were they as repressive in general as their Czech counterparts. The Slovak opposition that formed Public Against Violence was also not as large, nor prepared to create a new government. Indeed, Public Against Violence's highest representatives in the federal government were recent or former communists (Prime Minister Čalfa and Speaker of Parliament Dubček), as was the case in the Slovak government (Prime Minister Čič).

---

[14] Quoted in ibid.: 50.
[15] Quoted in ibid.: 51.

Public Against Violence (*Verejnost' proti nasiliu*, or VPN, to use the Slovak acronym) divided almost immediately in 1990 when its sole representative in the new federal government formed the Christian Democratic Movement (*Krest'anské Democratické Hnutie*, or KDH). In the June 1990 elections, when faced with its weakness in public opinion polls, the movement's leaders deliberately chose to include the popular former communist politicians and saw a corresponding rise in its political fortunes (Antalová, 1998). In 1991, the movement divided again surrounding a leadership struggle for the movement, although the formation of new parties took a less democratic route. After Slovak prime minister Vladimir Mečiar failed to win the chairmanship of the movement in February 1991, his close associate, the Slovak foreign minister, appeared on television and declared that the leadership of VPN had attempted to censor Mečiar's weekly television speech (a claim that was later disavowed). Based on the popular perception that he was a victim of communist-style politics, Mečiar's popularity soared. Subsequently the Presidium of the Slovak National Council (controlled by the VPN leadership) called for Mečiar's resignation, leading him to form the Movement for a Democratic Slovakia (*Hnutie za Demokratické Slovensko*, or HZDS), while the remainder of Public Against Violence merged itself into the Civic Democratic Union (*Občianská Democratická Unia*, or ODU). In April 1991, Mečiar was officially replaced as prime minister not by a representative of the weakened ODU but by the leader of the Christian Democratic Party, Ján Čarnogurský. Opinion polls at that time indicated that although ODU and KDH continued to control the cabinet, HZDS polled support from about 27 percent of the electorate. With the support of the parties on the left (such as the former Slovak Communist Party), Mečiar's party could count on over 50 percent of the electorate, while ODU and KDH together could count on only about 30 percent (ibid.).

Just as ODS in the Czech Republic sought to link the issue of the federation to acceptance of Finance Minister Klaus's economic reforms, new political parties in Slovakia also tied the relations between the republics to claims about the proper speed or direction of economic reform. Because heavy industry dating from the communist period was located primarily in Slovakia, many argued that market reform had to take a different path than in the Czech Republic. Further, the emphasis in the Czech Republic on the lustration of all officials who had been Communist Party members was perceived as a threat in Slovakia, where many prominent former communists (including Mečiar and the speaker of the federal parliament, Alexander Dubček) remained active in politics.

The question of the proper relationship between the republics remained unclear during the election campaign of most Slovak parties, creating uncertainty as to the consequences of electoral victory for one party or another. Given that the Slovak Nationalist Party claimed to advocate outright separation, Mečiar's HZDS took an ambiguous stand, emphasizing Slovak "sovereignty" and "autonomy" but without specifying his intentions for the future of the republic. This enabled him to "take sovereignty onto his agenda but in such a way that left Slovakia's potential legal status completely ambiguous" (Innes, 1997: 420). Draper refers to Mečiar's advocacy of "confederation" as "a code word for loosening the bonds without breaking them" (1993b: 22). While Slovak prime minister Čarnogurský from the Christian Democratic Movement declared his support for the federation, he at the same time identified his goal as "a star for Slovakia in the European flag" (Čarnogurský, 1992). That is, Slovakia would remain part of the Czech and Slovak federation until entry into the European Union, when each republic would enter as a sovereign nation. Only the marginal Slovak National Party, which received low support in public opinion polls, called outright for an independent state, while the successor to Public Against Violence, ODU, declared in its founding program: "We favour the maintenance of a stable, democratic Czech and Slovak Federative Republic based on equal rights for all citizens and nationalities."[16] Although positive toward the federation, this state-

---

[16] Quoted in *East European Reporter* 5 (Jan.–Feb. 1992): 66.

ment avoided answering the constitutional question about how relations would be institutionalized. Lacking a model for resolving differences within existing political institutions, the consequences of election rhetoric concerning a "viable federation" or "confederation" remained unclear until the 1992 elections. President Havel addressed this ambiguity by proclaiming, "[It] is impossible to live in and outside a common state at the same time; to have and not to have simultaneously a common army, foreign policy and currency, to acknowledge and at the same time oppose the validity of common laws."[17]

This chapter can address only part of the complex political dynamics in the Czech Republic and Slovakia after 1989, yet attention to the impact of the civil society master frame and the constraints of political institutions highlight their consequences for the emergence of stable democracy. The June 1992 elections witnessed an 85 percent voter turnout and the success of new political parties that had broken away from the dissident base of the original opposition movements. The Civic Democratic Party led by Finance Minister Klaus and Movement for Democratic Slovakia led by Vladimir Mečiar each won approximately 33 percent of the vote for the Federal Parliament, while the communists placed second with 14 percent (see Table 6 for complete election results). After Klaus's and Mečiar's electoral victories, President Havel called upon them as the leaders of the majority parties to form a government, but both party leaders quickly decided that it was impossible without agreement on the nature of the Czechoslovak state. Klaus proclaimed that the success of his Civic Democratic Party in the Czech Republic:

> was the final blow to those who advocated the ideas of "unpolitical politics," to those who saw the future as a world full of civic movements and temporary initiatives without party structures or clearly defined organizational rules, to those who wanted a world based on brave and innovative ideas implemented directly by enlightened intellectuals who tried to stay above the complicated world of politics. (Klaus, 1997: 110)

[17] Quoted in Draper, 1993b: 24.

TABLE 6

1992 National Election Results in Czechoslovakia

Party	Federal Assembly		Czech Parliament	
	Pct. of the vote	Seats won	Pct. of the vote	Seats won
CZECH REPUBLIC				
Civic Democratic Party	34	85	30	76
Left Bloc (Communists)	14	19	14	35
Social Democrats	8	16	6	16
Republican Party	6	14	6	14
Christian Democrats	6	13	6	15
Liberal Social Union	6	12	7	16
Civic Democratic Alliance	—	—	6	14
Moravia/Silesia Association	—	—	6	14
Parties below the threshold	26	—	19	—
SLOVAKIA				
Movement for Democratic Slovakia	34	57	37	74
Democratic Left	14	23	15	29
Slovak Nationalists	9	15	8	15
Christian Democratic Movement	9	14	9	18
Hungarian ethnic party	7	12	7	14
Slovak Social Democrats	6	5	—	—
Parties below the threshold	21	—	24	—

SOURCE: Olson, 1993: 310.

He declared that the "maimed federation was not capable of guaranteeing a continuation of economic reform" (Žák, 1995: 262). Mečiar announced that he had a mandate that included the independence of Slovakia, a Slovak constitution, and international recognition of a sovereign Slovakia. In the absence of widespread public outcry or mobilization, the two political leaders declared their intention to divide the country into independent states, which took place peacefully on January 1, 1993.

Thus, rather than reflecting public sentiments to divide the country, the dominant successor parties in the Czech Republic and Slovakia sought to mobilize votes in the *absence* of public support for separation by linking their claims for economic reform with the appropriate relationship between republics. Contrary to the argument that new parties in Czechoslovakia reflected pre-existing regional, religious, and ethnic cleavages, the new parties in the Czech Republic and Slovakia successfully mobilized electoral support on the basis of new political cleavages by blurring key issues related to the transformation process. This is not to minimize the very real economic differences in each republic due to different experiences of industrialization under communism. Rather it is to argue that the polarization of the new political parties and breakup of the country was not the unavoidable result of ancient ethnic differences nor economic forces but the *political* outcome of leaders of new parties competing for electoral support in uncertain conditions, both constrained and enabled by the failure to reform political institutions after 1989 and the legacy of the civil society master frame upon political competition.

Democratization in Other Settings, Other Times

The sketches of new democracies in Poland, the Czech Republic, and Slovakia in the 1990s should not be seen as the final contribution of this book. Rather, they embody the conceptual framework I have developed to compare a dynamic, ongoing set of processes of political change. In writing this work, I have been motivated by a desire to address those familiar with political change in Eastern Europe, as well as scholars of contentious politics and democratization who may be unfamiliar with the region. While I hope that the former might benefit from the comparative framework analyzing paths of democratization across countries, I also hope that the latter will benefit from my proposals to adapt concepts developed for parliamentary democracies for nondemocratic and democratizing regimes. From the approach of this book, it should be clear that the question is not whether the precise circumstances that enabled the particular paths of democratization in Poland and Czechoslovakia could or should be repeated elsewhere. But rather, the question is whether these cases provide insight into common causal processes of democratization at work in different historical contexts.

The framework offered here, I believe, has several implications for understanding democratization in other times and settings. First, the ability to compare different *forms* of movement outcomes offers the potential for more nuanced analysis of the outcome of social movement challenges, paths of democratization, and revolutions. In this way, the argument goes beyond overgeneralized concepts of "waves" or "transitions" to democracy (Huntington, 1991; Przeworski, 1991), as well as simplistic characterizations of outcomes in terms of success or failure. Attention to broad similarities of outcome (such as cases of revolution or democratization) can be complemented with analysis of differences across similar outcomes (such as pacted or mass mobilization forms of revolution or democratization). For example, each of the alternative outcomes analyzed in this book might be described broadly as instances of democratization, but differences in the impact upon the path of change in each case could have been considerable. Had the regime in Poland not responded to the August 1988 strikes with an offer to hold roundtable negotiations (or chosen to repress the striking workers as they did in May), the negotiated path might have been impossible in the face of national protest. Both sides at the roundtable feared such a possibility and the violence they anticipated it could have entailed. Further, had the Polish regime not adopted a decentralized election strategy with multiple candidates for each seat, it might have limited Solidarity's gains in parliament to the anticipated minority voice and thereby maintained control over the transformation of new political and economic policies. Had Wałęsa chosen to participate in the June elections, the populist challenge that destroyed the unity of the Solidarity movement might have been prevented and governmental instability avoided. By contrast, if the Czechoslovak regime had imitated the Polish model by holding open negotiations with all interested forces (and not repressed protesters at the national anniversaries in January, October, and November 1989), it seems highly unlikely that mass mobilization like the general strike would have occurred in the absence of previous widespread dissent. Even after the repression of the students in November 1989, if Dubček had not allied himself with the model of socialism with a human face but had sought to mobilize those former communists who had been purged after 1968, it seems likely that representatives of the Communist Party would have maintained greater authority in a subsequent new government.

Second, attention to competing challengers seeking to mobilize popular support highlights the key role of nonpolitical networks associated with the birth of the nation. Because repressive regimes prevented challengers from mobilizing organizational resources *ex ante*, competing challengers sought to mobilize popular support by linking their claims with external political opportunities and to networks of support. In particular, I focused on the articulation between the claims of the civic movements and pre-existing networks, such as the Catholic Church in Poland and theater networks in Czechoslovakia, which were transformed into local branches of the movements. Attention to the role of churches and theaters linked them to the literature on "free spaces" or "havens of opposition" that provide networks on which social movements often draw in the early stages of emergence (Fantasia and Hirsch, 1995; Gamson, 1996; Polletta, 1999). In East Germany the Lutheran Church was critical to organizing the "Monday marches" begun in Leipzig that became forums for demonstrating opposition to the German Democratic Republic. Even in Romania, popular vigils preceding the violent struggle for power in 1989 were centered around the attempt to remove a popular priest from his parish in Timoşoara. Others have observed the tendency in Eastern Europe "to treat enclaves of local languages or dialects—in the theater, the press, parish churches, or in more fortunate cases in the schools and belleslettres—as the true location of national homes" (Bauman, 1992: 168). Similar roles for ostensibly nonpolitical networks and spaces have been noted throughout the history of popular struggle, including neighborhood associations in the Paris Commune (Gould, 1995), the black Baptist churches in the U.S. civil rights movement (McAdam, 1982; Morris, 1984), and mosques in the Iranian revolution (Skocpol, 1994). Notably, the arguments in this book orient attention not to the presence or absence of such networks but to their transformation on behalf of claims by competing challengers. This articulation, especially in terms of identity and agency, provides insight into the mechanism by which individuals are mobilized to act on behalf of one set of claims from the range of real and potential challengers.

Further, the case studies go beyond assertions that particular collective actors are important to democratization by specifying *how* such actors can influence elite negotiations. This provides an analytic foundation from which evidence can be marshaled to evaluate alternative explanations for the dynamic process of democratization in which collective actors can alter elite agendas for change by introducing new issues and limiting the outcomes considered. Although both paths contrasted in this book have aspects of elite reform and popular pressure, this approach specifies the nature of the interaction between elites seeking to control political change and collective actors articulating demands. This directs attention to an underexamined arena of political contestation: the process of agenda-setting. As Schattschneider has argued, the definition of alternatives in political conflict can be "the supreme instrument of power" (1961: 68). This book suggests that, in the absence of formal channels by which collective actors can gain institutional legitimacy, democratization may proceed slowly because of the uncertainty surrounding outcomes and the conditional nature of popular support. In Poland the favorable electoral agreement at the roundtable was premised on the expectation that the regime would maintain control over the new government as the guarantor of change, in light of the international context and the risk of isolation within the Warsaw bloc. Regime negotiator (and subsequent postcommunist president of Poland) Aleksander Kwaśniewski later declared: "This illusion saved us from the Romanian experience. If the Party leadership realized how weak it was, there would never have been the roundtable talks and peaceful change."[18] As argued, the terms of the election package—such as the absence of provisions for

[18] Quoted in Osiatyński, 1996: 26.

the division of seats in parliament among the government coalition partners and for the replacement of defeated candidates on the National List—suggest that neither side predicted Solidarity's sweep of the election. This would prove critical to the outcome, since the new Solidarity government relied upon the unforeseen defection of the satellite parties in the government coalition.

Similarly, others have argued that uncertainty surrounding the old regime led Civic Forum and Public Against Violence in Czechoslovakia to overestimate the party's power and to concede a far greater number of seats in the new cabinet to Communists than was necessary to prevent a potential backlash (Čalda, 1996: 163). Even after prime minister Adamec had resigned and thereby removed the constraints upon talks, the roundtable negotiations remained focused on replacing personnel in the state rather than broader or systemic political changes (with the exception of the demand to eliminate the constitutional clause guaranteeing the leading role of the Communist Party). The records of the negotiations suggest that if Prime Minister Adamec had not resigned, he might have become Civic Forum's candidate for the new president. Like General Jaruzelski in Poland, he could have served as a means of continuity with the Leninist state and a protector of the interests of the nomenklatura. A retrospective portrait of popular support for the civic movements might overemphasize the strength of the movements and their ability to overwhelm illegitimate states. The lapse of twenty days between the founding of the Government of National Understanding and the naming of a new minister of interior, however, suggests that the movements were not so powerful, nor the state so overwhelmed.

Attention to other instances of democratization suggests that competition over the agenda is not necessarily a matter between the old regime and challengers but also among multiple, competing challengers themselves. The case of Hungary provides a striking instance where multiple challengers emerged in the late 1980s to compete for the authority to speak for "society." When the newly formed Hungarian Democratic Forum sought to implement roundtable agreements for direct presidential elections in September 1989, other challengers (including the Alliance for Free Democrats and Alliance of Young Democrats) forced a successful referendum that drew public support away from the Forum. The first parliamentary elections, delayed until March 1990, were free from electoral restrictions (avoiding the complications created by the Polish roundtable agreements) and contested by multiple democratic challengers, rather than a unified opposition (see Stark and Bruszt, 1998; Tokes, 1996). In this way, Hungary avoided the legacy of initially undemocratic parliamentary institutions and the subsequent populist pressures to do away with them.

Further elaboration of the relationship between the form of mobilization and democratization might suggest the conditions under which challengers are likely to emerge and influence the state. For example, in the late 1980s in Russia a wide range of new groups emerged in response to perestroika, taking different forms and mobilization strategies. The transformation of Boris Yeltsin from a member of the Soviet politburo into leader of the democratic opposition highlights the potential shifts from within the old elite, while different types of challengers emerged from outside the state: while a mass movement called the Democratic Union responded to relaxed political control by holding disruptive public rallies, a party-like movement called the Leningrad People's Front sought to capitalize upon new electoral opportunities (Zdravomyslova, 1996). Others have observed that the dissolution of the Soviet Union created opportunities for ethnic mobilization along citizenship categories that had been established under the old regime (see Beissinger, 1996; Brubaker, 1996). Mobilization strategies that had emerged in the process of struggle against the old regime persisted into the postcommunist period across Eastern Europe with sometimes puzzling results, slowly becoming routinized within institutions (see Ekiert and Kubik, forthcoming).

Although the examples given thus far have been formerly communist states, mobilization and bargaining are clearly not without precedent nor subsequent imitators.[19] Adam Michnik observed in the 1980s that one of Poland's choices was what he referred to as the Spanish model, by which he meant a peacefully negotiated regime transformation of the sort that Spain had undertaken in the 1970s. Negotiations between the old regime and democratic challengers were central to the end of authoritarian regimes in Latin America and Brazil. After 1989, representatives of the white apartheid regime and African National Congress agreed to negotiate for the holding of free elections in South Africa that served as the mechanism to a new democratic government. Semidemocratic states such as Indonesia in the late 1990s have seen student strikes calling for political change, including both street protests and negotiations with the regime. Even in a theocratic state such as Iran, in 1999, President Khatami called repeatedly for the building of "civil society" while protesting students demand liberalization and countermobilized street rallies defend the regime. Among Western democracies, elected governments in Ireland and Spain sought to negotiate with domestic factions rejecting their authority in the hope of convincing them to participate within existing democratic institutions. And increasingly, transnational networks of activists using the language of human rights have sought to pressure governments around the world to improve their treatment of minorities and political prisoners. Regrettably, not all challenges to nondemocratic governments end peacefully, as the violence in the former Yugoslavia and Caucasus reminds us.

Finally, this book stresses comparative analysis, by which outcomes can be analyzed in terms of competing challengers seeking to influence the path taken once the state has broken down. Through structured comparison, alternative explanations can be adjudicated, and cases can be analyzed as historical concatenations of common causal processes (Ragin, 1987; Tilly, 1995). In its focus on

[19] Each of the examples that follow have substantial literatures, of which I cannot here cite more than a few examples. For Spain, see Perez-Dias, 1994; on Latin America, see O'Donnell and Schmitter, 1986; on South Africa, see Gastrow, 1995; on transnational activists, see Keck and Sikkink, 1997.

competing challengers, this approach directs attention not merely to the outcome as it occurred, but to the multiple equilibria that might have succeeded state breakdown. By emphasizing competition, I have explained why challengers can fail, as well as why they succeed. Such analysis is naturally complicated by the reality that movements rarely compete with equal material or organizational resources so that we can explain success simply by one feature or another. In hindsight, successful challengers often reinterpret events so as to make their success seem inevitable, and history is not kind to failed challengers—so that often less is known about these attempts. In this way, this book directs attention to areas that have traditionally received less attention in studies of movement outcomes.

While case studies will always remain necessary for scholars to ground their analysis in historical contexts, comparative analysis, I believe, must reassert its central place in analyses of democratization and social movements. When considering the long-term consequences of the way communism fell for the founding of democratic states, it would be easy to recall the response attributed to the Chinese ambassador Chou En-Lai when asked in the 1970s what he thought of the French revolution: "[I]t's too early to tell." Yet by specifying and comparing paths of change across countries, I have highlighted the constraining and enabling influence of the way communism fell for new democracies in the 1990s. Only in the light of attention to similarities and differences will we be able to understand the apparent spread of democracy and its promise for the future.

Chronology of Major Events, 1968-1993

1968

January–March: Polish student strikes around the banning of the play "Forefathers' Eve" suppressed.

August 21: Warsaw Pact invasion of Czechoslovakia, imposition of "normalization."

1970

December 15–18: Workers' strikes in Baltic coast end with military attacks upon striking workers.

1971

Gustav Husák replaces Alexander Dubček as general secretary in Czechoslovakia.

1975

May: Husák becomes president of Czechoslovakia.

Summer: Helsinki Agreements signed, containing "basket three," committing signatories to respect human rights.

1976

June: Workers strikes repressed in Urusus and Radom, Poland.

September: Committee for the Defense of Workers (KOR) founded in Poland.

1977

January 1: Charter 77 established in Czechoslovakia.

Fall: Underground "flying university" begins in Poland.

1978

October 16: Karol Wotyła, cardinal of Cracow, named Pope John Paul II.

1979

June: Pope John Paul II's first visit to Poland.

1980

July 10: Lublin strike in automotive repair works in Poland.

July 15: Lublin strike settled with wage increases.

August 14: Lenin Shipyard strike begins in Gdańsk.

August 16: Agreement for higher wages and reinstatement of Wałęsa and Walentinowicz; workers vote to end strike; Alina Pieńkowska urges workers not to go home; Interfactory Strike Committee formed with demand for free trade unions as number one.

August 24: Commission of Experts formed to advise striking workers in Poland.

August 31: Gdańsk Accords signed in Poland, initiating legal period of Solidarity's existence.

1981

October 30: Jaruzelski, after becoming first secretary of the party, calls for the formation of a Front of National Accord.

November 4: Summit between Wałęsa, Jaruzelski, and Glemp, which Wałęsa calls a dead end.

November 24: Ryszard Reiff, member of Council of State, proposes formation of "Grand Coalition" published in December 13 issue of party Catholic weekly.

November 27–28: VI Plenum of PZPR held, where Jaruzelski announces that tensions created by Solidarity are threatening the entire Polish state, asks *Sejm* to grant him special emergency powers.

December 2: Government settles strike in Warsaw Firefighters Academy by using the army and helicopters to storm the building.

December 11–12: Final meeting of Solidarity National Council in Gdańsk.

December 13: Martial law declared in Poland.

1982

April 22: Temporary Coordinating Commission of Solidarity founded, headed by Solidarity leader Zbigniew Bujak.

September: Solidarity activists Kuroń, Michnik, Lityński, Lipski, and Wujec formally arrested on charges of trying to overthrow the state by force.

November 10: Solidarity Temporary Coordinating Committee calls for strike, which fails.

December: Arrest of seven more Solidarity leaders, including Wałęsa's rivals for union president (Andrzej Gwiazda, Marian Jurczyk, and Jan Rulewski—along with Karol Modzelewski of Wrocław, Seweryn Ja-

worski of Warsaw, Grzegorz Pałka from Łódź, and Andrzej Roz-
plochowski from Katowice).
Late: Patriotic Front for National Renewal (PRON) created by Jaruzelski.

1983
June: Second papal visit to Poland.
July 31: Martial law lifted in Poland.

1984
October 20: Polish priest, Father Jerzy Popiełuszko disappears, his body
found ten days later.

1985
Trial of the four policemen who abducted and killed Popiełuszko broadcast
on national television.
March 10: Mikhail Gorbachev named general secretary of Communist
Party in the Soviet Union.
November 5: General Jaruzelski resigns as prime minister in Poland;
Zbigniew Messner, an economist, becomes prime minister and forms a
government largely of technicians.

1986
May: Solidarity leader Bujak arrested in Poland.
July 17: Limited amnesty declared in Poland; Michnik and Lis released.
September 1: Polish interior minister Kiszczak declares general amnesty,
releasing 225 political prisoners including Bujak.
September 11: Wałęsa creates the Solidarity Provisional Council above-
ground, while Temporary Provisional Council continued underground
activity with anonymous leadership.
Polish Club of Catholic Intelligentsia meets in Cracow to discuss General
Jaruzelski's proposal for a Social Consultative Council that would advise and inform the president of society's views on political, economic,
and social issues. The club decides against participation, although
Chairman Święcicki decides to join as a private citizen, resigning his
chairmanship.
December: First meeting of Consultative Council in Poland.

1987
Gorbachev visits Prague, refers to evaluation of Prague Spring as "above all
a matter for the Czechoslovak comrades themselves" (quoted in Wheaton and Kavan, 1992: 18).
June 9–14: Third papal visit to Poland.
July: Polish politburo member Jozef Czyrek initiates contact with the opposition.

October 13: Polish Communist Party announces it is holding talks with oppositionists.

October 25: Both Solidarity underground Temporary Coordinating Council and aboveground Temporary Provisional Council dissolved; National Executive Commission is formed, consisting of ten regional representatives and headed by Wałęsa.

November 29: Polish party-sponsored referendum asking if voters support "radical economic reform" and favor "deep democratization"; Solidarity National Executive Commission advises voters to ignore it.

November 30: Although 68 percent of the Polish electorate vote and almost two-thirds of them vote yes, the government announces that it had lost because it fell 5 percent short of approval by a majority of voters.

December: Czechoslovak party leadership changes: Miloš Jakeš replaces Husák as general secretary, Ladislav Adamec becomes Czechoslovak prime minister.

1988

January 16: Publication in *Polityka* of "Open Letter to Wojciech Jaruzelski and Lech Wałęsa" calling on leaders to make historic pact.

February: Bronisław Geremek proposes "anticrisis pact" in February issue of *Konfrontacje*.

March: Cardinal Tomášek's petition in Czechoslovakia, "Suggestions of Catholics for the Solution of the Position of the Faithful," begins, signed by 600,000 people.

March 25: 5,000–15,000 demonstrate on feast day of Lord's Annunciation in Bratislava; it is broken up, underground Church leader Frantiśek Mikloško arrested.

April–May: Strike at Lenin Shipyard, not coordinated by Solidarity, ends on May 10 when striking workers are unable to bring anyone else out in their support.

August: Strikes in Poland end August 31 when Wałęsa enters into direct political negotiations with Interior Minister Czeslaw Kiszczak, who offers to discuss the legalization of Solidarity if Wałęsa ends the strike.

August 21: 10,000 demonstrate in Prague on anniversary of Warsaw Pact invasion; broken up by security police.

October 17: Mieczysław Rakowski replaces Messner as prime minister in Poland.

November 30: Wałęsa television debate with Politburo member Alfred Miodowicz.

December 18: Formation of first Solidarity Citizens' Committee with Wałęsa as chair.

December: First half of tenth party plenum in Poland; hard-liners removed by Jaruzelski.

1989

January 15–20: Anniversary of suicide of Jan Palach in Czechoslovakia; international conference in Helsinki; demonstrations in Prague broken up.

January 16–18: Second half of tenth party plenum in Poland. General Jaruzelski announces, after his threat to resign, that he is willing to see the legalization of Solidarity.

January 17: Arrest of Václav Havel in Czechoslovakia, sentenced on February 21 to nine months in jail.

February 6–April 5: Roundtable talks held in Poland, culminating in agreement for partially free elections on April 5.

March 31: Eleventh party plenum in Poland approves Roundtable Accords.

April 7: Polish lower house of parliament approves Roundtable Accords.

April 17–20: Solidarity and Rural Solidarity formally legalized in Poland.

May 8: First issue of *Gazeta Wyborcza* in Poland.

May 17: Havel released from prison in Czechoslovakia.

June 4: Partially free elections held (62 percent voter turnout) in Poland; Solidarity wins all but one of the possible seats. Chinese military brutally suppresses months of protests in Beijing.

June 6: General Jaruzelski invites Solidarity to join grand coalition.

Summer: Circulation of the petition "Several Sentences" begins in Czechoslovakia; by September 40,000 signatures have been collected.

July: Leaders of Movement for Democratic Freedoms, including Ján Čarnogurský and Miroslav Kusý, jailed in Czechoslovakia.

July 19: General Jaruzelski elected president by the new lower house of parliament in Poland.

August 7: Wałęsa announces Solidarity will not support Kiszczak for prime minister, but would be ready to form a coalition with the satellite parties that would produce a parliamentary majority for an opposition cabinet.

August 21: Demonstration on anniversary of Warsaw Pact invasion in 1968 broken up in Prague.

August 22: Gorbachev telephones Polish prime minister Rakowski, indicating that only if Solidarity specifically turns against the Soviet Union will its policy toward Poland change.

August 24: Tadeusz Mazowiecki becomes prime minister in Poland, forms coalition government with Solidarity plus United Peasant Party and Democratic Party, with General Jaruzelski as president.

September 10: East Germans begin exodus through Hungary and Czechoslovakia.

September 12: Mazowiecki government confirmed by parliament in Poland.

October 26: Announcement of the Sinatra doctrine by Soviet spokesperson Gerrasimov.

October 28: Letter sent to Czechoslovak Federal Government by independent initiative MOST, led by rock musician Michal Kocab and journalist Michal Horáček; protests commemorating the seventy-first anniversary of Czechoslovakia broken up in Prague.

November 9: Berlin Wall falls.

November 10: Resignation of General Secretary Zhivkov announced in Bulgaria.

November 17: Anniversary of the Nazi murder of the student Jan Opletal in Czechoslovakia; student demonstration brutally broken up.

November 19: Civic Forum founded in Prague.

November 20: Public Against Violence founded in Bratislava.

November 21: Czechoslovak prime minister Adamec holds meeting with "spokespersons from the student, artistic, and civic circles of the Prague public"; Havel not invited. Leaders of MOST, Kocab with Horáček, Martin Mejstřík, Jan Ruml, and Jiří Bartośka participate.

November 24: Czechoslovak general secretary Jakeš, presidium, and secretariat of Central Committee resign.

November 26: Prime Minister Adamec and Civic Forum with Havel hold first meeting in Czechoslovakia; Letna demonstration in Prague, 750,000 people attend.

November 27: Two-hour general strike in Czechoslovakia.

November 29: "Leading role of party" constitutional clause abolished in Czechoslovakia.

December 3: Replacement government 15: 5 named by Prime Minister Adamec, rejected by OF/VPN; Adamec and party general secretary Urbánek travel to Moscow.

December 10: Government of National Understanding announced in Czechoslovakia.

December 29: Havel elected president in Czechoslovakia.

1990

January 27: Dissolution of Polish United Workers Party at its eleventh congress; Social Democracy of the Polish Republic Party founded by Aleksander Kwaśniewski.

February: Christian Democratic Movement created by Ján Čarnogurský, who leaves Public Against Violence in Slovakia.

April: Second Solidarity Congress re-elects as chairman Wałęsa, who declines to run for president.

May: Wałęsa's Center Alliance formed in Poland.

May 27: Local elections in Poland.

June 8–9: National elections in Czechoslovakia held, civic movements win a parliamentary majority with Petr Pithart as Czech prime minister, Vladimir Mečiar as Slovak prime minister, and Marian Čalfa remains Czechoslovak prime minister.

June 22: Mazowiecki's Civic Movement-Democratic Action formed in Poland.

June 27: New federal government formed in Czechoslovakia, based on coalition between Civic Forum, Public Against Violence, and Christian Democratic Movement.

July 1: Citizens' Committee conference in Poland with debates about their future between Wałęsa and Mazowiecki.

July 5: Havel re-elected president of Czechoslovakia.

September 18: Jaruzelski announces he intends to resign as Polish president.

October 13: Finance Minister Václav Klaus elected chairman of Civic Forum in Czechoslovakia.

October: Mazowiecki announces his candidacy for the Polish presidency; the Solidarity Executive Council backs Wałęsa.

November 24: Local elections in Czechoslovakia; Civic Forum wins in the Czech Republic, Christian Democratic Movement gains more votes than Public Against Violence in Slovakia.

November 25: First round of presidential elections in Poland between Mazowiecki, Wałęsa, and Tymiński. Wałęsa and Tymiński win largest percentage of votes.

December 9: Second round of presidential elections in Poland, Wałęsa wins.

1991

January: Bielecki named prime minister in Poland.

February: Civic Forum splits into Civic Democratic Party and Civic Movement in Czechoslovakia.

April 23: Vladimir Mečiar replaced as prime minister by Čarnogurský in Slovakia.

April 24: Public Against Violence divides into Civic Democratic Union and Movement for a Democratic Slovakia.

June 28: Election law passed by lower house in Poland.

October 27: Parliamentary elections in Poland; Democratic Union wins highest percentage.

December: Jan Olszewski becomes prime minister of minority government in Poland.

1992

June: Czechoslovak parliamentary elections; majority won by Klaus's Civic Democratic Party in the Czech Republic and Mečiar's Movement for a Democratic Slovakia in Slovakia.

June: Olszewski replaced as prime minister by Pawlak, who is unable to form government.

July: Pawlak replaced by Suchocka, who forms seven-party coalition.

1993

January 1: New states of the Czech Republic and Slovakia formally established.

May: Suchocka government falls to vote of no confidence.

September: Polish parliamentary elections; Pawlak becomes prime minister again after Alliance of the Democratic Left and Polish Peasant Party win elections.

Bibliography

ARCHIVES

Citizens' Committees Archive, Polish Senate, Warsaw, Poland
Coordinating Center of Civic Forum Archive, Institute for Contemporary History, Prague, Czech Republic
Coordinating Center of General Strike Archive, Theater Institute, Prague, Czech Republic
Czechoslovak-Polish Solidarity Association Archive, Wroclaw, Poland
Election Archives of Lubomir Brokl, Institute of Sociology, Prague, Czech Republic
Private Papers, Ivan Havel, Prague, Czech Republic
Senate Archives of Republic of Poland, Warsaw, Poland

SOURCES

Adamski, Władysław, et al. 1986. *Raport z badania Polacy '84: Dynamika konfliktu i konsensu* [Report from the Research Poles '84: The Dynamics of the Conflict and Consensus]. Warsaw: University of Warsaw.

———. 1982. *Polacy '81: Postrzeganie kryzysu i konfliktu* [Poles '81: X of the Crisis and Conflict]. Warsaw: Polish Academy of Sciences.

———. 1981. *Polacy '80: Wyniki badan ankietowych* [Poles '80: The Results of Survey Research]. Warsaw: Polish Academy of Sciences.

Adler, Jeremy, 1989. "Rehearsing a merry revolution." *Times Literary Supplement* (Dec. 22): 1412–18.

Agnew, Hugh LeCaine. 1993. *Origins of the Czech National Renaissance.* Pittsburgh: University of Pittsburgh Press.

Alexander, Jeffrey C., and Philip Smith. 1993. "The discourse of American civil society: A new proposal for cultural studies." *Theory and Society* 22: 151–207.

Antalová, Ingrid, ed. 1998. *Verejnost' Proti Nasili 1989–1991: Svedectva a dokumenty* [Public Against Violence 1989–1991: Testimony and Documents]. Bratislava: Milan Simecka Foundation.

Arato, Andrew. 1993. "Interpreting 1989." *Social Research* 60, no. 3: 609–46.

Ascherson, Neal. 1991. "Birds of an East European feather rise above the earthbound west." Pp. 119–21 in *Europe from Below*, Mary Kaldor, ed. London: Verso.

Ash, Timothy Garton. 1991. "Tell me your Europe and I will tell you where you stand." Pp. 122–25 in *Europe from Below*, Mary Kaldor, ed. London: Verso.

———. 1990a. *The Magic Lantern: The Revolution of '89 Witnessed in Warsaw, Budapest, Berlin and Prague*. New York: Random House.

———. 1990b. *The Uses of Adversity: Essays on the Fate of Central Europe*. New York: Vintage.

———. 1990c. "Eastern Europe: After the deluge, nous." *New York Review of Books* (Aug. 16): 52.

———. 1983. *The Polish Revolution: Solidarity 1980–82*. New York: Charles Scribner's Sons.

Bachrach, Peter, and Morton S. Baratz. 1962. "Two faces of power." *American Political Science Review* 56 (Dec.): 947–52

Bacharach, Samuel B., and Edward J. Lawler. 1981. *Bargaining: Power, Tactics, and Outcomes*. San Francisco and London: Jossey-Bass.

Banac, Ivo, ed. 1992. *Eastern Europe in Revolution*. Ithaca: Cornell University Press.

Bauman, Zygmunt. 1992. "The Polish predicament: A model in search of class interests." *Telos*, no. 92: 113–30.

Beetham, David, ed. 1994. *Defining and Measuring Democracy*. London: Sage.

Beissinger, Mark R. 1996. "How nationalisms spread: Eastern Europe adrift on the tides and cycles of nationalist contention." *Social Research* 63, no. 1 (spring): 94–146.

Benda, Václav. 1991. "The parallel polis." Pp. 35–41 in *Civic Freedom in Central Europe: Voices from Czechoslovakia*, H. Gordon Skilling and Paul Wilson, eds. Houndmills, Basingstoke, Hampshire: Macmillan.

———. 1988. "Can Charter 77 influence political changes in Czechoslovakia?" *Uncaptive Minds* (Sept.–Oct.): 11–13.

Bermeo, Nancy. 1990. "Rethinking regime change." *Comparative Politics* 22, no. 3: 359–77.

Bernhard, Michael. 1996. "Civil society after the first transition." *Communist and Post-Communist Studies* 29, no. 3: 309–30.

———. 1993. *The Origins of Democratization in Poland: Workers, In-*

tellectuals, and Oppositional Politics, 1976–1980. New York: Columbia University Press.

Blanchard, Olivier, Rudiger Dornbusch, Paul Krugman, Richard Layard, and Lawrence Summers. 1991. *Reform in Eastern Europe.* Cambridge, Mass.: MIT Press.

Boguszak, Marek, and Vladimir Rak. 1990. *Czechoslovakia—May 1990, Survey Report.* Prague: Association for Independent Social Analysis.

Boni, Michal, ed. 1990. *Plakat wyborczy '89: Voting Poster '89.* Warsaw: NSZZ Solidarnosc Uniwersytetu Warszawskiego.

Borkowski, Tadeusz, and Andrzej Bukowski. 1993. *Komitety Obywatelskie: Powstanie—rozwoj—upadek?* [Citizens' Committees: Creation—Development—Fall?]. Cracow: Universitas Press.

Brown, J. F. 1991. *Surge to Freedom: The End of Communist Regimes in Eastern Europe.* Durham, N.C.: Duke University Press.

Brubaker, Rogers. 1996. *Nationalism Reframed: Nationhood and the National Question in the New Europe.* Cambridge: Cambridge University Press.

Bujak, Zbigniew. 1990. "Interview with Zbigniew Bujak." *East European Reporter* (autumn–winter): 10–11.

Bunce, Valerie. 1999. *Subversive Institutions: The Design and Destruction of Socialism and the State.* Cambridge: Cambridge University Press.

———. 1995. "Should transitologists be grounded?" *Slavic Review* 54, no. 1 (spring): 111–27.

———. 1992. "Two-tiered Stalinism." Pp. 25–46 in *Constructing Capitalism: The Re-emergence of Civil Society and Liberal Economy in the Post-communist World,* Kazimierz Poznanski, ed., Boulder, Colo.: Westview.

Burstein, Paul. 1991. "Legal mobilization as a social movement tactic: The struggle for equal employment opportunity." *American Journal of Sociology* 96: 1201–25.

Burstein, Paul, Rachel L. Einwohner, and Jocelyn A. Hollander. 1995. "The success of political movements: A bargaining perspective." Pp. 275–95 in *The Politics of Social Protest: Comparative Perspectives on States and Social Movements,* J. Craig Jenkins and Bert Klandermans, eds. Minneapolis: University of Minnesota Press.

Butora, Martin, and Zora Butorová. 1999. "Slovakia's democratic awakening." *Journal of Democracy* 10, no. 1: 80–95.

———. 1993. "Slovakia: The identity challenges of the newly born state." *Social Research* 60, no. 4 (winter): 705–36.

Butorová, Zora. 1993. "A deliberate 'yes' to the dissolution of the CSFR?" *Czech Sociological Review* 1, no. 1: 58–72.

CBOS [Centrum Badania Opinii Społecznej]. 1994. *Społeczeństwo i Władza: Lat osiemdziesiątych w badaniach CBOS* [Society and the State: The Eighties in Research by CBOS]. Warsaw: CBOS.

Čalda, Miloš. 1996. "The roundtable talks in Czechoslovakia." Pp. 135–77 in *The Roundtable Talks and the Breakdown of Communism*, Jon Elster, ed. Chicago: University of Chicago Press.

Čalfa, Marian. 1994. "Byl jsem muž 10. prosince [I was a man of the 10th of December]." *Rudě Pravo* (Nov. 17): 1.

Campbell, John L. 1996. "An institutional analysis of fiscal reform in postcommunist Europe." *Theory and Society* 25: 45–84.

Čarnogurský, Ján. 1992. "Politics does not always have to be ethical: An interview." *Uncaptive Minds* (winter): 91–92, 61–68.

Casper, Gretchen, and Michelle Taylor. 1996. *Negotiating Democracy: Transitions from Authoritarian Rule*. Pittsburgh: University of Pittsburgh Press.

Castle, Marjorie. 1995. "A Successfully Failed Pact: The Polish Political Transition of 1989." Unpublished dissertation, Stanford University.

Cecuda, Dariusz. 1989. *Leksykon Opozycji Politycznej 1976–1989* [Lexicon of the Political Opposition 1976–1989]. Warsaw: BIS ZSP and TRUST.

Cerulo, Karen A. 1997. "Identity construction: New issues, new directions." Pp. 385–409 in *Annual Review of Sociology*. Palo Alto: Annual Reviews.

Chan, Kenneth Ka-lok. 1995. "Poland at the crossroads: The 1993 general election." *Europe-Asia Studies* 47, no. 1: 123–45.

Chirot, Daniel, ed. 1990. *The Crisis of Leninism and Decline of the Left*. Seattle: University of Washington Press.

Chruszczewski, Adam. 1993. *Dzieje Kosciola w Polsce: Tablice Chronologiczne* [The History of the Church in Poland: A Chronological Table]. Lublin: Scientific Association of the Catholic University in Lublin.

Chtiguel, Olga F. 1990. "Without theater the Czechoslovak revolution could not have been won." *Drama Review* 34, no. 3: 88–96.

Cobb, Roger, Jennie-Keith Ross, and Marc Howard Ross. 1976. "Agenda building as a comparative political process." *American Political Science Review* 70 (Mar.): 126–38.

Cohen, Jean. L., and Andrew Arato. 1992. *Civil Society and Political Theory*. Cambridge, Mass.: MIT Press.

Collier, David, and Steven Levitsky. 1997. "Democracy with adjectives: Conceptual innovation in comparative research." *World Politics* 49 (Apr.): 430–51.

Collier, Ruth Berins, and James Mahoney. 1997. "Adding collective actors to collective outcomes: Labor and recent democratization in South

America and Southern Europe." *Comparative Politics* 29, no. 3: 285–304.

Connor, Walter, et al., eds. 1992. *The Polish Road from Socialism: The Economics, Sociology and Politics of Transition.* Armonk, N.Y.: Sharpe.

Dahl, Robert A. 1989. *Democracy and Its Critics.* New Haven: Yale University Press.

D'Andrade, Roy G., and Claudia Strauss, eds. 1992. *Human Motives and Cultural Models.* Cambridge: Cambridge University Press.

Dawisha, Karen, and Bruce Parrott, eds. 1997. *The Consolidation of Democracy in East-Central Europe.* Cambridge: Cambridge University Press.

Day, Barbara. 1985. "Theatre on a string." *Index on Censorship* 14, no. 1: 35–36.

Deak, Frantisek. 1990. "A playwright for a president: The story of moral renewal." *Performing Arts Journal* 35/36: 36–44.

DeCandole, James, 1991. "Czechoslovakia: Too velvet a revolution?" *European Security Study,* no. 11. Institute for European Defense and Strategic Studies.

Deyl, Vojtech. 1990. Zprava Komise Prezidenta CSFR pro vysetreni cinnosti CSLA v listopadovych dnech 1989 [Report of the Presidential Commission of the CSFR for the Investigation into the Activities of the Czechoslovak People's Army (CSLA) in November, 1989]. Photocopy.

Diamond, Larry, and Mark Plattner, eds. 1993. *The Global Resurgence of Democracy.* Baltimore: Johns Hopkins University Press.

Diamond, Larry, Mark Plattner, Yun-han Chu, and Hung-mao Tien. 1997. *Consolidating Third Wave Democracies: Themes and Perspectives.* Baltimore: Johns Hopkins University Press.

Diani, Mario. 1996. "Linking mobilization frames and political opportunities: Insights from regional populism in Italy." *American Sociological Review* 61 (Dec.): 1053–69.

Dienstbier, Jiří. 1991. "Central Europe's Security." *Foreign Policy* no. 83: 119–27.

DiPalma, Guiseppe. 1990. *To Craft Democracies.* Berkeley: University of California Press.

Draper, Theodore. 1993a. "A new history of the velvet revolution." *New York Review of Books* (Jan. 14): 14–19.

———. 1993b. "The end of Czechoslovakia." *New York Review of Books* (Jan. 28): 20–26.

Dubiński, Krzysztof. 1990. *Magdalenka Transakcja epoki: Notatki z poufnych sptkan Kiszczak-Walesa* [Magdalenka, the Transaction of an Epoch: Notes from the Secret Meetings of Kiszczak and Walesa]. Warsaw: Sylwa.

Ekiert, Grzegorz. 1997. "Rebellious Poles: Political crises and popular protest under state socialism." *East European Politics and Societies* 11, no. 2: 299–338.

———. 1996. *The State against Society: Political Crises and Their Aftermath in East Central Europe*. Princeton: Princeton University Press.

———. 1992. "Peculiarities of postcommunist politics: The case of Poland." *Studies in Comparative Communism* 25, no. 4: 341–62.

———. 1991. "Democratization processes in East Central Europe: A theoretical reconsideration." *British Journal of Political Science* 21: 285–313.

———. 1990. "Transitions from state-socialism in East Central Europe." *States and Social Structures Newsletter* no. 12 (winter): 1–7.

Ekiert, Grzegorz, and Jan Kubik. Forthcoming. *Rebellious Civil Society: Popular Protest and Democratic Consolidation in Poland*. Ann Arbor: University of Michigan Press.

Elster, Jon. 1995. "Transition, constitution-making and separation in Czechoslovakia." *Archives Europeenes Sociologiques* 35, no. 1: 105–34.

———. 1993. "Constitution-making in Eastern Europe: Rebuilding the boat in the open sea." *Public Administration* 71 (spring–summer): 169–217.

———. 1989a. *Nuts and Bolts for the Social Sciences*. Cambridge: Cambridge University Press.

———. 1989b. *The Cement of Society: A Study in Social Order*. Cambridge: Cambridge University Press.

———. 1988. "Arguments for constitutional choice: Reflections on the transition to socialism." Pp. 303–26 in *Constitutionalism and Democracy*, Jon Elster and Rune Slagstad, eds. Cambridge: Cambridge University Press.

Elster, Jon, ed. 1996. *The Roundtable Talks and the Breakdown of Communism*. Chicago: University of Chicago Press.

Elster, Jon, Claus Offe, Ulrich K. Preuss, et al. 1998. *Institutional Design in Post-communist Societies: Rebuilding the Ship at Sea*. Cambridge: Cambridge University Press.

Emirbayer, Mustafa, and Jeff Goodwin. 1994. "Network analysis, culture, and the problem of agency." *American Journal of Sociology* 99, no. 6 (May): 1411–54.

Fantasia, Rick, and Eric L. Hirsch. 1995. "Culture in rebellion: The appropriation and transformation of the veil in the Algerian revolution." Pp. 144–62 in *Social Movements and Culture*, Hank Johnston and Bert Klandermans, eds. Minneapolis: University of Minnesota Press.

Fearon, James D. 1991. "Counterfactuals and hypothesis testing in political science." *World Politics* 43 (Jan.): 169–95.

Feldek, L'ubomir, ed. 1990. *Ked' sme brali do ruk buducnost'* [When We Took the Future into Our Own Hands]. Bratislava: Archa.

Frič, Pavol. 1992. "Who loves ya Mečiar?" *East European Reporter* (July–Aug.): 79.

Friedman, Debra, and Doug McAdam. 1992. "Collective identity and activism." Pp. 156–73 in *Frontiers in Social Movement Theory*, Aldon D. Morris and Carol McClurg Mueller, eds. New Haven: Yale University Press.

Friszke, Andrzej. 1990. "The Polish political scene (1989)." *East European Politics and Societies* 4, no. 2: 305–41.

Fukuyama, Francis. 1992. *The end of history and the last man*. New York: Free Press.

Gál, Fedor. 1991. *Z prvej ruky [From first hand]*. Bratislava: Archa.

Gamson, William A. 1996. "Safe spaces and social movements." *Perspectives on Social Problems* 8: 27–38.

———. 1992a. *Talking Politics*. Cambridge: Cambridge University Press.

———. 1992b. "The social psychology of collective action." Pp. 53–76 in *Frontiers in Social Movement Theory*, Aldon D. Morris and Carol McClurg Mueller, eds. New Haven: Yale University Press.

———. 1990. *The Strategy of Social Protest*. 2d ed. Belmont, Calif.: Wadsworth.

Gamson, William A., and Davis S. Meyer. 1996. "Framing political opportunity." Pp. 275–90 in *Comparative Perspectives on Social Movements: Political Opportunities, Mobilizing Structures and Cultural Framings*, Doug McAdam, John McCarthy, and Meyer Zald, eds. Cambridge: Cambridge University Press.

Gastrow, Peter. 1995. *Bargaining for Peace: South Africa and the National Peace Accord*. Washington, D.C.: United States Institute of Peace Press.

Gebethner, Stanislaw. 1992. "Political reform in the process of round table negotiations." Pp. 50–68 in *Democratization in Poland, 1988–90: Polish Voices*, George Sanford, ed. New York: St. Martin's.

Gellner, Ernest. 1992–93. "The price of velvet: On Tomas Masaryk and Václav Havel." *Telos*, no. 94: 183–92.

Geremek, Bronislaw. 1992. "Civil society then and now." *Journal of Democracy* 3, no. 2: 3–12.

———. 1990. *Rok 1990: Geremek Opowiada, Zakowski Pyta* [The Year 1990: Geremek Responds, Zakowski Asks]. Warsaw: Plejada.

Giełżyński, Wojciech. 1988. "Notes from the Gdansk Shipyard strike." *Uncaptive Minds* 1, no. 3 (June–July–Aug.): 2–6.

Goldfarb, Jeffrey C. 1982. *On Cultural Freedom: An Exploration of Public Life in Poland and America.* Chicago: University of Chicago Press.

Goldstone, Jack A. 1991. "Ideology, cultural frameworks, and the process of revolution." *Theory and Society* 20: 405–53.

Gomułka, Stanisław, and Antony Polansky, eds. 1990. *Polish Paradoxes.* New York: Routledge.

Goodwyn, Lawrence. 1991. *Breaking the Barrier: The Rise of Solidarity in Poland.* Princeton: Princeton University Press.

Gould, Roger V. 1995. *Insurgent Identities: Class, Community, and Protest in Paris from 1848 to the Commune.* Chicago: University of Chicago Press.

Grabowski, Tomek. 1996. "The party that never was: The rise and fall of the Solidarity Citizens' Committee in Poland." *East European Politics and Societies* 10, no. 2 (spring): 214–54.

Granovetter, Mark. 1973. "The strength of weak ties." *American Journal of Sociology* 78: 1360–80.

Gross, Jan. 1992. "Poland: From civil society to political nation." Pp. 56–71 in *Eastern Europe in Revolution,* Ivo Banac, ed. Ithaca: Cornell University Press.

Grzymala-Busse, Anna. 1998. "Reform efforts in the Czech and Slovak communist parties and their successors." *East European Politics and Societies* 12, no. 3: 442–71.

Guigni, Marco G. 1998. "Was it worth the effort? The outcomes and consequences of social movements." Pp. 371–93 in *Annual Review of Sociology.* Palo Alto: Annual Reviews.

Haggard, Stephan, and Robert R. Kaufman. 1997. "The political economy of democratic transitions." *Comparative Politics* 29, no. 3: 263–84.

Hanak, Jiří, and Jaroslav Veis. 1994. "Konec ruku [The end of the year of footwear]." *Lidové Noviny* (Nov. 12): Section "Nĕdelni," 1, 3.

Hanzel, Vladimír. 1991. *Zrychlený tep dĕjin: Realné drama o deset í jednáních* [The Quickened Pulse of History: The Real Drama of Ten Meetings]. Prague: OK CENTRUM.

Havel, Václav. 1991. *Open Letters: Selected Writings 1965–1990.* Edited by Paul Wilson. New York: Vintage.

———. 1990. *Disturbing the Peace.* New York: Vintage.

———. 1989. "Cards on the table." *East European Reporter* 3, no. 4 (spring/summer): 54–55.

———. 1988a. "My reasons for skepticism and sources of hope." *Uncaptive Minds* 1, no. 3 (June–July–Aug.): 26–28.

———. 1988b. "Where Brezhnev still rules." *The Times* (Aug. 12): 12.

Hedberg, Augustin, 1992. *Faith under Fire and the Revolutions in Eastern Europe.* Princeton: Sturges.

Heyns, Barbara, and Irenusz Bialecki. 1991. "Solidarnosc: Reluctant vanguard or makeshift coalition?" *American Political Science Review* 85, no. 2: 351–70.

Hirst, Paul. 1991. "The state, civil society and the collapse of Soviet communism." *Economy and Society* 20, no. 2 (May): 217–42.

Hlusičková, Ružena, and Blanka Cisarovská, eds. 1994. *Hnutí za Občanskou Svobodou 1988–1989: Sborník documentů* [Movement for Democratic Freedom 1988–1989: A Collection of Documents]. Ustav pro Soudobé Dějiny AV CR. Prague: Maxdorf.

Hlusičková, Ružena, and Milan Otáhal, eds. 1993. *Čas Democratické iniciativy 1987—1990: Sborník dokumentů* [The Time of the Democratic Initiative 1987—1990: A Collection of Documents]. Prague: Nadace Demokratické iniciativy pro kulturu a politku.

Holc, Janine P. 1992. "Solidarity and the Polish state: Competing discursive strategies on the road to power." *East European Politics and Societies* 6, no. 2 (spring): 121–40.

Holý, Ladislav. 1993. "The end of socialism in Czechoslovakia." Pp. 204–17 in *Socialism: Ideals, Ideologies, and Local Practice*, C. M. Hann, ed. ASA Monographs 31.

Holzer, Jerzy. 1987. "Poland: Seven years after August." *East European Reporter* 3, no. 1: 2–6.

Horáček, Michal. 1990. *Jak pukaly ledy* [How the Ice Burst]. Prague: Ex Libris.

Horn, Miriam. 1990. "Campaign carnival: A velvet election?" *New Republic* 203, no. 6: 11–13.

Huntington, Samuel P. 1991. *The Third Wave: Democratization in the Late Twentieth Century*. Norman: University of Oklahoma Press.

Hviždala, Karel. 1990. *Výslech revolucionařů z listopadu 1989* [Interrogation of Revolutionaries from November 1989]. Bestseller 1. Prague: Art-Servis.

Innes, Abby. 1997. "The breakup of Czechoslovakia: The impact of party development on the separation of the state." *East European Politics and Societies* 11, no. 3: 393–435.

Jakeś, Miloś. 1988. "We simply need restructuring." *Time* (Apr. 18): 42–43.

Jan Pawel II. 1987. *Trzecia Pielgrzymka do Polski: Przemowienia Homilie 9 VI 1987–14 VI 1987* [Third Pilgrimage to Poland: Speeches and Homilies June 9, 1987–June 14, 1987]. Cracow: Znak.

Janowski, Karol B. 1992. "From monopoly to death throes: The PZPR in the process of political transformation." Pp. 162–76 in *Democratisation in Poland*, George Sanford, ed. New York: St. Martin's.

Jasiewicz, Krzysztof. 1995. "The Polish voter—Ten years after August

1980." Pp. 143–67 in *From the Polish Underground: Selections from Krytika, 1978–93,* Michael Bernhard and Henryk Szlajfer, eds. University Park: University of Pennsylvania Press.

Jasiewicz, Krzysztof, and Tomasz Zukowski. 1992. "The elections of 1984–89 as a factor in the transformation of the social order in Poland." Pp. 98–126 in *Democratization in Poland,* George Sanford, ed. New York: St. Martin's.

Jenkins, J. Craig. 1983. "Resource mobilization theory and the study of social movements." *Annual Review of Sociology* 9: 527–53.

Jenkins, J. Craig, and Bert Klandermans. 1995. "The politics of social protest." Pp. 3–13 in *The Politics of Social Protest: Comparative Perspectives on States and Social Movements,* J. Craig Jenkins and Bert Klandermans, eds. Minneapolis: University of Minnesota Press.

Jenkins, J. Craig, and Charles Perrow. 1977. "The insurgency of the powerless: Farm worker movements in the U.S." *American Sociological Review* 42: 429–68.

Joppke, Christian. 1994. "Revisionism, dissidence, nationalism: Opposition in Leninist regimes." *British Journal of Sociology* 45, no. 4 (Dec.): 543–61.

Jowitt, Ken. 1998. "Challenging the 'correct' line." *East European Politics and Societies* 12, no. 1: 87–106.

———. 1992. *New World Disorder: The Leninist Extinction.* Berkeley: University of California Press.

———. 1991. "Weber, Trotsky and Holmes on the study of Leninist regimes." *Journal of International Affairs* 45, no. 1: 31–49.

Judt, Tony. 1988. "The dilemmas of dissidence: The politics of opposition in East-Central Europe." *Eastern European Politics and Societies* 2: 185–240.

Kaluza, Roman, ed. 1989. *Polska Wybory '89* [Polish Elections '89]. Warsaw: Andrzej Bonarski.

Kalvoda, Jan. 1992. "The negotiations are a sham: An interview." *Uncaptive Minds* (winter): 69–74.

Kamiński, Bartlomej. 1991. "Systemic underpinnings of the transition in Poland: The shadow of the round-table agreement." *Studies in Comparative Communism* 24, no. 2: 173–90.

Karabel, Jerome. 1993. "Polish intellectuals and the origins of Solidarity: The making of an opposition alliance." *Communist and Post-Communist Studies* 26, no. 1 (Mar.): 25–46.

Karl, Terry Lynn, and Philippe C. Schmitter. 1991. "Modes of transition in Latin America, Southern and Eastern Europe." *International Social Science Journal* 128: 269–84.

Karpiński, Jakub. 1982. *Countdown: The Polish Upheavals of 1956, 1968, 1970, 1976, 1980*. New York: Karz-Cohl.

Keane, John. 1988a. *Democracy and Civil Society*. London: Verso.

———. 1988b. *Civil Society and the State*. London: Verso.

Keck, Margaret E., and Kathryn Sikkink. 1997. *Activists beyond Borders: Advocacy Networks in International Politics*. Ithaca: Cornell University Press.

Kennedy, Michael D. 1994. "An introduction to East European ideology and identity in transformation." Pp. 1–45 in *Envisioning Eastern Europe: Postcommunist Cultural Studies*, Michael D. Kennedy, ed. Ann Arbor: University of Michigan Press.

———. 1992. "The intelligentsia in the constitution of civil societies and post-communist regimes in Hungary and Poland." *Theory and Society* 21: 29–76.

———. 1991. *Professionals, Power and Solidarity in Poland: A Critical Sociology of Soviet-type Society*. Cambridge: Cambridge University Press.

Kingdon, John W. 1995. *Agendas, Alternatives and Public Policies*. 2d ed. New York: Harper Collins.

Kitschelt, Herbert P. 1996. "Formation of party cleavages in post-communist democracies." *Party Politics* 1, no. 4: 447–72.

———. 1993. "Comparative historical research and rational choice theory: The case of transitions to democracy." *Theory and Society* 22, no. 3: 413–28.

———. 1986. "Political opportunity structures and political protest: Antinuclear movements in four democracies." *British Journal of Political Science* 16: 57–85.

Klandermans, Bert. 1992. "The social construction of protest and multiorganizational fields." Pp. 77–103 in *Frontiers in Social Movement Theory*, Aldon D. Morris and Carol McClurg Mueller, eds. New Haven: Yale University Press.

Klandermans, Bert, Hanspeter Kreisi, and Sidney Tarrow, eds. 1988. *From Structure to Action: Comparing Movement Participation across Culture*. Greenwich, Conn.: JAI Press.

Klaus, Václav. 1992. *Dismantling Socialism: A Preliminary Report (A Road to a Market Economy II)*. Prague: Top Agency.

———. 1997. *Renaissance: The rebirth of liberty in the heart of Europe*. Washington, D.C.: Cato Institute.

Klima, Ivan. 1992. Comments as part of the panel on "The Humanities and Culture Heroes." *Partisan Review* 59, no. 4, 740–46.

Kohout, Pavel. 1990. "A failure of the intellect." *Lidové Noviny: Digest of an Independent Czechoslovak Daily*, Prague: 6–8.

Koopmans, Ruud, and Jan Willem Duyvendak. 1995. "The political construction of the nuclear energy issue and its impact on the mobilization of anti-nuclear movements in Western Europe." *Social Problems* 42, no. 2: 235–51.

Koopmans, Ruud, and Paul Statham. 1996. "Ethnic nationalism vs. the political community: The divergent success of the extreme right in Germany and Italy." Unpublished manuscript.

Koordinační centrum OF Praha. 1990. *Kandidat Občanskeho For a* [Candidates of Civic Forum]. Prague: Co-ordinating Center of Civic Forum.

Koseła, Krzysztof. 1990. "The Polish Catholic Church and the elections of 1989." *Religion in Communist Lands* 18, no. 2: 124–37.

Kosicki, Gerald M. 1993. "Problems and opportunities in agenda-setting research." *Journal of Communication* 43, no. 2: 100–127.

Kowalik, Tadeusz. 1994a. "A reply to Maurice Glasman." *New Left Review* no. 206: 133–44.

———. 1994b. "The great transformation and privatization: Three years of Polish experience." Pp. 171–90 in *The New Great Transformation?: Change and Continuity in East-Central Europe*. London: Routledge.

Kowalski, Sergiusz. 1993. "Poland's new political culture: The relevance of the irrelevant." *Economy and Society* 22, no. 2: 233–42.

Krejčí, Oskar. 1995. *History of Elections in Bohemia and Moravia*. New York: Columbia University Press.

Kriseová, Eda. 1993. *Václav Havel: The Authorized Biography*. New York: St. Martin's.

Król, Marcin. 1996. "The Church, the legacy, the transformation." Pp. 279–86 in *Grappling with Democracy: Deliberations on Post-Communist Societies (1990–1995)*, Elżbieta Matynia, ed. Prague: Sociologicke Nakladatelstvi.

———. 1994. "Poland's longing for paternalism." *Journal of Democracy* 5, no. 1: 85–95.

Krtilová, Mariana, ed. 1992. *Poslední Hurá: Stenograticky zaznam z mimoradných zasedáni UV KSC 24. a 26.11.1989* [The Last Hurrah: Stenographic Notes from the Extraordinary Sessions of the Central Committee of the Communist Party of Czechoslovakia on November 24 and 26, 1989]. Prague: Cesty.

Kubik, Jan. 1994. *The Power of Symbols against the Symbols of Power: Cultural Roots of Solidarity*. University Park: Pennsylvania State Press.

Kuran, Timor. 1991. "Now out of never: The element of surprise in the East European revolution of 1989." *World Politics* 44 (Oct.): 7–48.

Kurski, Jaroslaw. 1993. *Lech Walesa: Democrat or Dictator?* Boulder, Colo.: Westview.

Kurzman, Charles. 1996. "Structural opportunity and perceived opportunity in social-movement theory: The Iranian revolution of 1979." *American Sociological Review* 61: 153–70.

Kwiatkowski, Stanislaw. 1992. "Public Opinion in Poland during the 1980s." Pp. 127–35 in *Democratisation in Poland*, George Sanford, ed. New York: St. Martin's.

Laba, Roman. 1991. *The Roots of Solidarity: A Political Sociology of Poland's Working-class Democratization*. Princeton: Princeton University Press.

Laitin, David. 1998. *Identity in Formation: The Russian Speaking Population in the Near Abroad*. Ithaca: Cornell University Press.

———. 1988. "Political culture and political preferences." *American Political Science Review* 82, no. 2: 589–96.

Lane, Ruth. 1992. "Political culture: Residual category or general theory?" *Comparative Political Studies* 25, no. 3: 362–87.

Linz, Juan, and Alfred Stepan. 1996. *Problems in Democratic Transition and Consolidation: Southern Europe, South America and Postcommunist Europe*. Baltimore: Johns Hopkins University Press.

———. 1992. "Political identities and electoral sequences: Spain, the Soviet Union, and Yugoslavia." *Daedalus* 121: 123–39.

Lipski, Jan Josef. 1985. *KOR: A history of the Workers' Defense Committee in Poland, 1976–1981*. Berkeley: University of California Press.

Łopiński, Maciej, Marcin Moskit, and Mariusz Wilk. 1990. *Konspira: Solidarity Underground*. Berkeley: University of California Press.

Mason, David S. 1985. *Public Opinion and Political Change in Poland*. Cambridge: Cambridge University Press.

Maziarski, Jacek. 1990. "The goals of the center alliance." *East European Reporter* (autumn–winter): 7.

Mazowiecki, Tadeusz. 1989. "Prime Minister Mazowiecki's speech to parliament." *Uncaptive Minds* 2 (Nov.–Dec.): 10–14.

McAdam, Doug. 1996. "Conceptual origins, current problems, future directions." Pp. 23–40 in *Comparative Perspectives on Social Movements: Political Opportunities, Mobilizing Structures and Cultural Framings*, Doug McAdam, John McCarthy, and Meyer Zald, eds. New York: Cambridge University Press.

———. 1986. "Recruitment to high-risk activism: The case of freedom summer." *American Journal of Sociology* 92: 64–90.

———. 1982. *Political Process and the Development of the Black Insurgency, 1930–1970*. Chicago: University of Chicago Press.

McAdam, Doug, John McCarthy, and Meyer Zald, eds. 1996. *Comparative Perspectives on Social Movements: Political Opportunities, Mobilizing Structures and Cultural Framings*. New York: Cambridge University Press.

McAdam, Doug, Sidney Tarrow, and Charles Tilly. 1996. "To map contentious politics." *Mobilization* 1, no. 1: 17–34.

McCombs, Maxwell E., and Donald L. Shaw. 1993. "The evolution of agenda-setting research: Twenty-five years in the marketplace of ideas." *Journal of Communication* 43, no. 2: 58–67.

Meyer, David S., and Suzanne Staggenborg. 1996. "Movement, counter movements, and the structure of political opportunity." *American Journal of Sociology* 101: 1628–60.

Michnik, Adam. 1998. *Letters from Freedom: Post–Cold War Realities and Perspectives.* Berkeley: University of California Press.

——. 1993. *The Church and the Left.* Edited and translated by David Ost. Chicago: University of Chicago Press.

——. 1988. "Towards a new democratic compromise: An interview with Adam Michnik." *East European Reporter* 3, no. 2: 24–29.

——. 1985. *Letters from Prison.* Berkeley: University of California Press.

Michnik, Adam, and Josef Tischner. 1995. *Miedzy Panem a Plebanem* [Between God and Man]. Cracow: Znak.

Millard, Frances. 1992. "The Polish Parliamentary Elections of October 1991." *Soviet Studies* 44, no. 5: 837–55.

Misztal, Bronislaw, and J. Craig Jenkins. 1995. "Starting from scratch is not always the same: The politics of protest and the postcommunist transitions in Poland and Hungary." Pp. 324–40 in *The Politics of Social Protest: Comparative Perspectives on States and Social Movements,* J. Craig Jenkins and Bert Klandermans, eds. Minneapolis: University of Minnesota Press.

Mlynař, Vladimír. 1992. "Jak bohatě jsou naše strany [How rich are our parties]." *Respekt,* no. 48 (Nov. 11): 4.

Modzelewski, Karol. 1994. "What happened to Solidarity?" *Uncaptive Minds* 7 (winter–spring): 63–72.

Moore, Barrington. 1966. *Social Origins of Dictatorship and Democracy: Lord and Peasant in the Making of the Modern World.* Boston: Beacon Press.

Morawska, Ewa. 1984. "Civil religion vs. state power in Poland." *Society* 21, no. 4 (May/June): 29–34.

Morris, Aldon D. 1984. *The Origins of the Civil Rights Movement: Black Communities Organizing for Change.* New York: Free Press.

Morris, Aldon D., and Carol McClurg Mueller, eds. 1992. *Frontiers in Social Movement Theory.* New Haven: Yale University Press.

Naple, J. 1999. *Democracy and Democratization: Post-communist Europe in Comparative Perspective.* London: Sage.

Noonan, Rita K. 1995. "Women against the state: Political opportunities and collective action frames in Chile's transition to democracy." *Sociological Forum* 10: 81–111.

Novotný, Jiří Datel, Černý, Karel, Kopačková, Marcela and Petr Pražák. 1990. *Semafor ve stavce [Semafor on strike]*. Prague: Czechoslovak State Pedagogical Publishing House.

Oberschall, Anthony. 1996. "Opportunities and framing in the Eastern European revolts of 1989." Pp. 93–121 in *Comparative Perspectives on Social Movements: Political Opportunities, Mobilizing Structures and Cultural Framings*, Doug McAdam, John McCarthy, and Meyer Zald, eds. Cambridge: Cambridge University Press.

———. 1994. "Protest demonstrations and the end of communist regions in 1989." *Research in Social Movements, Conflicts and Change* 17: 1–24.

O'Donnell, Guillermo, and Philippe C. Schmitter. 1986. *Transitions from Authoritarian Rule: Tentative Conclusions about Uncertain Democracies*. Baltimore: Johns Hopkins University Press.

OECD. 1992. *OECD Economic Surveys, Poland*. Paris: Organisation for Economic Co-operation and Development.

———. 1991. *OECD Economic Surveys, Czech and Slovak Federal Republic*. Paris: Organisation for Economic Co-operation and Development.

Olson, David M. 1993. "Dissolution of the state: Political parties and the 1992 election in Czechoslovakia." *Communist and Post-communist Studies* 26, no. 3: 301–14.

Olson, Mancur. 1965. *The Logic of Collective Action: Public Goods and the Theory of Groups*. Cambridge, Mass.: Harvard University Press.

Orenstein, Mitchell. 1998. "A genealogy of communist successor parties in East-Central Europe and the determinants of their success." *East European Politics and Societies* 12, no. 3: 472–99.

Osa, Maryjane. 1996. "Pastoral mobilization and contention: The religious foundations of the Solidarity movement in Poland." Pp. 67–85 in *Disruptive Religion: The Force of Faith in Social Movement Activism*, Christian Smith, ed. New York: Routledge.

———. 1989. "Resistance, persistence, and change: The transformation of the Catholic Church in Poland." *European Politics and Societies* 3, no. 2: 269–99.

Osiatyński, Wiktor. 1996. "The roundtable talks in Poland." Pp. 21–68 in *The Roundtable Talks and the Breakdown of Communism*, Jon Elster, ed. Chicago: University of Chicago Press.

Oslzlý, Petr. 1990. "On stage with the velvet revolution." *Drama Review* 34, no. 3: 88–96.

Ost, David. 1993. "The politics of interest in post-communist East Europe." *Theory and Society* 22: 453–86.

———. 1990. *Solidarity and the Politics of Anti-Politics: Opposition and Reform in Poland since 1968.* Philadelphia: Temple University Press.

———. 1989. "The transformation of Solidarity and the future of Central Europe." *Telos* no. 79 (spring): 69–94.

Otáhal, Milan, and Zdeněk Sladek, eds. 1990. *Deset pražských dnů (17.–27. listopad 1989) Dokumentace* [Ten Prague Days (November 17–27, 1989) Documentation]. Prague: Academia Praha.

Otáhal, Milan, et al. 1993. *Svedectvi o Duchovním Utlaku 1969/1970* [Evidence of Spiritual Pressure]. Ustav pro Soudobé Dějiny. Prague: Maxdorf.

Palmer, Bryan D. 1990. *Descent into Discourse: The Reification of Language and the Writing of Social History.* Philadelphia: Temple University Press.

Palouś, Martin. 1993. "Poznamky ke generacním sporum v Charte 77 v druhé polovině osmdesátých let [Comments on generational groups in Charter 77 in the second half of the 1980s]." In *Dvě desitiletí před listopadem '89* [Two Decades before November '89], Emmanuel Mandler, ed. Prague: Maxdorf.

———. 1991. "Jan Patočka versus Václav Benda." Pp. 121–30 in *Civic Freedom in Central Europe: Voices from Czechoslovakia*, H. Gordon Skilling and Paul Wilson, eds. Houndmills, Basingstoke, Hampshire: Macmillan.

Patočka, Jan. 1981. "What Charter 77 is and what it is not." Pp. 217–19 in *Charter 77 and Human Rights in Czechoslovakia*, Gordon H. Skilling, ed. London: Allen and Unwin.

Pehe, Jiří. 1992a. "Czechoslovakia's changing political spectrum." *RFE/RL Research Report* 1, no. 5 (Jan. 31): 1–7.

———. 1992b. "Czechoslovakia: Parties register for elections." *RFE/RL Research Report* 1, no. 18 (May 1): 20–25.

Perez-Dias, Victor. 1994. *The Return of Civil Society.* Cambridge: Harvard University Press.

Pernal, Marek, and Jan Skorzynski, 1990. *Kalendarium Solidarnosci: 1980–1989 [Calendar of Solidarity: 1980–1989].* Warszawa: Agencja Omnipress & Zakl. Wydawnicze Versus.

Perzkowski, Stanislaw, ed. 1994. *Tajne Dokumenty Biura Politycznego i Sekretariatu KC Ostatni Rok władzy 1988–1989* [Secret Documents of the Politburo of the Polish Communist Party, the Last Year in Power 1988–1989]. London: Aneks.

Pithart, Petr. 1993. "Intellectuals in politics: Double dissident in the past, double disappointment today." *Social Research* 60, no. 4 (winter): 751–61.

Polletta, Francesca. 1999. "'Free spaces' in collective action." *Theory and Society* 28, no. 1: 1–38.

Popkin, Samuel L. 1994. *The Reasoning Voter: Communication and Persuasion in Presidential Campaigns.* 2d ed. Chicago: University of Chicago Press.

Przeworski, Adam, ed. 1995. *Sustainable Democracy.* Cambridge: Cambridge University Press.

———. 1991. *Democracy and the Market.* Cambridge: Cambridge University Press.

Putnam, Robert. 1995. "Bowling alone." *Journal of Democracy* 6: 65–78.

Putnam, Robert, et al. 1993. *Making Democracy Work: Civic Traditions in Modern Italy.* Princeton: Princeton University Press.

Radio Free Europe Research. 1979. *The Pope in Poland.* Munich: Radio Free Europe.

Ragin, Charles. 1987. *The Comparative Method: Moving beyond Qualitative and Quantitative Strategies.* Berkeley: University of California Press.

Raina, Peter. 1995. *Rozmowy z Władzami PRL: Arcybiskup Dąbrowski, Tom Drugi 1982–1989* [Talks with the Government of the People's Republic of Poland: Archbishop Dabrowski. Vol. 2, 1982–1989]. Warsaw: Ksaizka Polska.

———. 1985a. *Poland 1981: Towards Social Renewal.* London: Allen and Unwin.

———. 1985b. *Kościół w Polsce 1981–1984* [The Church in Poland 1981–1984]. London: Veritas.

———. 1982. *Independent Social Movements in Poland.* London School of Economics and Political Science. London: Orbis.

Ramet, Sabrina Petra. 1991. "The Catholic Church in Czechoslovakia 1948–1991." *Studies in Comparative Communism* 24, no. 4: 377–93.

Research Center for Social Problems. 1990. "Slovak separatism: How strong?" *Uncaptive Minds* 3 (Nov.–Dec.): 41–43.

Reykowski, Janusz. 1993. "Resolving of the large scale political conflict: The case of the round table negotiations in Poland." Pp. 214–32 in *Conflict between People and Groups: Causes, Processes, and Resolutions,* Stephen Worchel and Jeffrey A. Simpson, eds. Nelson Hall.

Robinson, William F., ed. 1980. *August 1980: The Strikes in Poland.* Munich: Radio Free Europe Research.

Rose, Richard. 1995. "Mobilizing demobilized voters in post-communist societies." *Party Politics* 1, no. 4: 549–63.

Ross, Marc Howard. 1997. "Culture and identity in comparative political analysis." Pp. 42–80 in *Comparative Politics*, Mark Lichbach and Alan S. Zuckerman, eds. Cambridge: Cambridge University Press.

Rueschemeyer, Dietrich, Evelyne Huber Stephens, and John D. Stephens. 1992. *Capitalist Development and Democracy*. Chicago: University of Chicago Press.

Ruml, Jan. 1989. "Is the time ripe?" *Uncaptive Minds* 2 (Aug.–Sept.–Oct.): 38.

Rutland, Peter. 1992–93. "Thatcherism Czech-style: Transition to capitalism in the Czech republic." *Telos*, no. 94: 103–29.

Rychard, Andrzej. 1992. "Politics and society after the breakthrough: The sources and threats to political legitimacy in post-communist Poland." Pp. 136–51 in *Democratization in Poland*, George Sanford, ed. New York: St. Martin's.

Sabata, Jaroslav. 1992. "What kind of dream is disappearing in Prague?" *Peace Review* (winter): 5–10.

Sachs, Jeffrey. 1993. *Poland's Leap into the Market Economy*. Cambridge: MIT Press.

Saideman, Stephen M. 1994. "International organizations and secessionist crises: The relevance of agenda setting." *Studies in Conflict and Terrorism* 17: 275–91.

Sanford, George, ed. 1992. *Democratization in Poland*. New York: St. Martin's.

Saxenberg, Stephen. 1999. "A new phase in Czech politics." *Journal of Democracy* 10, no. 1: 96–111.

Schattschneider, E. E. 1961. *The semi-sovereign people*. New York: Holt, Reinhart and Winston.

Seligman, Adam. 1992. *The Idea of Civil Society*. New York: Free Press.

Siedlecki, Marek. 1989. "Time for positive action." *East European Reporter* 3, no. 4 (spring/summer): 35.

Šimečka, Milan. 1991. "Speaking my mind." Pp. 77–81 in *Europe from Below*, Mary Kaldor, ed. London: Verso.

———. 1984. *The Restoration of Order: The Normalization of Czechoslovakia*. London: Verso.

Skilling, H. Gordon. 1989. *Samizdat and an Independent Society in Central and Eastern Europe*. Houndmills, Basingstoke, Hampshire: Macmillan.

———. 1981. *Charter 77 and Human Rights in Czechoslovakia*. London: Allen and Unwin.

Skilling, H. Gordon, and Paul Wilson, eds. 1991. *Civic Freedom in Central Europe: Voices from Czechoslovakia*. Houndmills, Basingstoke, Hampshire: Macmillan.

Skocpol, Theda. 1994. *Social Revolutions in the Modern World*. Cambridge: Cambridge University Press.

———. 1979. *States and Social Revolutions: A Comparative Analysis of France, Russia, and China*. Cambridge: Cambridge University Press.

———, ed. 1984. *Vision and Method in Historical Sociology*. Cambridge: Cambridge University Press.

Skocpol, Theda, and Margaret Somers. 1980. "The uses of comparative history in macrosocial inquiry." *Comparative Studies in Society and History* 22: 174–97.

Smolar, Aleksander. 1994. "The dissolution of Solidarity." *Journal of Democracy* 5, no. 1: 70–84.

Snow, David A., and Robert D. Benford. 1992. "Master frames and cycles of protest." Pp. 133–55 in *Frontiers in Social Movement Theory*, Aldon D. Morris and Carol McClurg Mueller, eds. New Haven: Yale University Press.

———. 1988. "Ideology, frame resonance, and participant mobilization." *International Social Movement Research* 1: 197–217.

Snow, David A., E. Burke Rochford, Steven K. Worden, and Robert D. Benford. 1986. "Frame alignment processes, micromobilization, and movement participation." *American Sociological Review* 51, no. 4: 464–81.

Snyder, Tim, and Milada Vachudova. 1997. "Are transitions transitory? Two types of political change in Eastern Europe since 1989." *East European Politics and Societies* 11, no. 1: 1–35.

Sorenson, Georg. 1993. *Democracy and Democratization: Processes and Prospects in a Changing World*. Boulder, Colo.: Westview.

Staniszkis, Jadwiga. 1992. *The Ontology of Socialism*. Oxford: Clarendon.

———. 1991. *The Dynamics of the Breakthrough in Eastern Europe: The Polish Experience*. Berkeley: University of California Press.

———. 1984. *Poland's Self-Limiting Revolution*. Princeton: Princeton University Press.

Stark, David. 1992. "Path dependence and privatization strategies in East Central Europe." *East European Politics and Societies* 6, no. 1: 17–54.

Stark, David, and Laszlo Bruszt. 1998. *Postsocialist Pathways: Transforming Politics and Property in East Central Europe*. Cambridge: Cambridge University Press.

Stokes, Gale. 1993. *The Walls Came Tumbling Down: The Collapse of Communism in Eastern Europe*. Oxford: Oxford University Press.

Strang, David, and John W. Meyer. 1993. "Institutional conditions for diffusion." *Theory and Society* 22: 487–511.

Swidler, Ann. 1986. "Culture in action: Symbols and strategies." *American Sociological Review* 51: 273–86.

Szacki, Jerzy. 1994. *Liberalism after Communism*. Budapest: Central European University Press.

Szomolányi, Soňa. 1994. "Old elites in the new Slovak state and their current transformations." Pp. 63–82 in *The Slovak Path of Transition to Democracy*, Soňa Szomolányi and Grigorij Mesežnikov, eds. Bratislava: Slovak Political Science Association.

Szomolányi, Soňa, and Grigorij Mesežnikov, eds. 1994. *The Slovak Path of Transition to Democracy*. Bratislava: Slovak Political Science Association.

Szporluk, Roman. 1988. *Communism and Nationalism: Karl Marx versus Friedrich List*. New York: Oxford University Press.

Tabako, Tomas. 1992. *Strajk 88* [Strike '88]. Warsaw: NOWA.

Tajne Dokumenty Państwo—Kościół 1980–1989 [Secret Documents, State-Church Relations in Poland 1980–1989]. 1993. London: Aneks; Warsaw: Polityka.

Taras, Raymond. 1995. *Consolidating Democracy in Poland*. Boulder, Colo.: Westview.

Tarrow, Sidney. 1998. *Power in Movement: Social Movements, Collective Action and Politics*. 2d ed. Cambridge: Cambridge University Press.

———. 1992. "Mentalities, political cultures, and collective action frames." Pp. 174–202 in *Frontiers in Social Movement Theory*, Aldon D. Morris and Carol McClurg Mueller, eds. New Haven: Yale University Press.

———. 1991. "Aiming at a moving target: Social science and the recent rebellions in Eastern Europe." *PS: Political Science & Politics* 24 (Mar.): 12–20.

Terry, Sarah Meiklejohn. 1993. "Thinking about postcommunist transitions: How different are they?" *Slavic Review* 52: 333–37.

Tilly, Charles. 1997. "Means and ends of comparison in macrosociology." *Comparative Social Research* 16: 43–53.

———. 1995. "Contentious repertoires in Great Britain." Pp. 15–42 in *Repertoires and Cycles of Collective Action*, Mark Traugott, ed. Durham: Duke University Press.

———. 1993. *European Revolutions: 1492–1992*. London: Blackwell.

———. 1984. *Big Structures, Large Processes, Huge Comparisons*. New York: Russell Sage.

———. 1978. *From Mobilization to Revolution*. Reading, Mass.: Addison-Wesley.

———, ed. 1996. *Citizenship, Identity and Social History*. Cambridge: Cambridge University Press.

Tismaneanu, Vladimir. 1999. "Reassessing the revolutions of 1989." *Journal of Democracy* 10, no. 1: 69–73.

————. 1992. *Re-inventing Politics*. New York: Free Press.

Tokes, Rudolf L. 1996. *Hungary's Negotiated Revolution: Economic Reform, Social Change, and Political Succession, 1957–1990*. Cambridge: Cambridge University Press.

Touraine, Alain, et al. 1983. *Solidarity: The Analysis of a Social Movement, Poland 1980–81*. Cambridge: Cambridge University Press.

Traynor, Ian. 1989. "Police and workers' militia attack Czechoslovak protestors." *Manchester Guardian* (Aug. 27): 9.

Tuma, Oldrich. 1994. *Zítra zase tady!: protirežimové demonstrace v předlistopadová Praze jako polický a socialní fenomen* [Tomorrow Is Here Again!: Anti-regime Demonstrations in Pre-November Prague as Political and Social Phenomena], Ustav pro Soudobé Dějiny. Prague: Maxdorf.

Turek, Otakar. 1995. *Podíl ekonomiky na padu komunismu v Československu* [The Role of Economics in the Collapse of Communism in Czechoslovakia], Sešity Ustavu pro Soudobé Dějiny. Vol. 23. Prague: Institute for Contemporary History.

Tymicki, Jerzy. 1986. "New dignity: The Polish theater 1970–85." *Drama Review* 30, no. 3: 13–46.

Urban, Jan. 1990. "The crisis of Civic Forum." *Uncaptive Minds* 3 (Aug.–Sept.–Oct.): 36–37.

————. 1988. "To create unsolvable problems." *Uncaptive Minds* 1 (June–July–Aug.): 32–34.

Vaněk, Miroslav. 1994. *Veřejné Mínění o Socialismu před 17. listopadem 1989* [Public Opinion about Socialism before November 17, 1989]. Historia Nova sv. 5, Ustav pro Soudobé Dějiny. Prague: Maxdorf.

————. 1993. "Listopadové události roku 1989 v Plzni [The November events of 1989 in Plzen]." Pp. 93–109 in *Dvé desetilet í před listopadem '89. Sborník* [Two Decades before November, 1989: A Collection], Emmanuel Mandler, ed. Prague: Maxdorf.

Vavroušek, Josef. 1989. "Perspektivy OF [Perspectives for Civic Forum]." February 12, 1989. Unpublished photocopy.

Verdery, Katherine. 1996. *What Was Socialism, and What Comes Next?* Princeton: Princeton University Press.

Vladislav, Jan, and Vilem Prečan, eds. 1990. *Horký Leden 1989 v Československu* [Hot January 1989 in Czechoslovakia]. Ostrava, Czech Republic: Novinar.

Von Beyme, Klaus. 1996. *Transition to Democracy in Eastern Europe*. New York: St. Martin's.

Wade, Larry L., Peter Levelle, and Alexander J. Groth. 1995. "Searching for voting patterns in post-communist Poland's Sejm elections. *Communist and Post-Communist Studies* 28, no. 4: 411–25.

Walaszek, Zdzislawa. 1986. "An open issue of legitimacy: The state and the Church in Poland." *Annals of the American Academy of Political and Social Science*, no. 483: 118–34.

Walder, Andrew G. 1994. "The decline of communist power: Elements of a theory of institutional change." *Theory and Society* 23, no. 2 (Apr.): 297–323.

———, ed. 1995. *The Waning of the Communist State: Economic Origins of the Political Decline in China and Hungary*. Berkeley: University of California Press.

Wałęsa, Lech. 1992. *The Struggle and the Triumph*. New York: Arcade.

Walzer, Michael. 1992. "The civil society argument." Pp. 89–107 in *Dimensions of Radical Democracy: Pluralism, Citizenship, Community*, Chantal Mouffe, ed. London: Verso.

Weber, Max. 1949. "Objective possibility and adequate causation in historical explanation." Pp. 164–88 in *The Methodology of the Social Sciences*. New York: Free Press.

Weigle, Marcia, and Jim Butterfield. 1992. "Civil society in reforming communist regimes: The logic of emergence." *Comparative Politics* 25 (Oct.): 1–23.

Weiss, Martin. 1990a. "Czechoslovak referendum on democracy." *Uncaptive Minds* 3 (May–June–July): 21–23.

———. 1990b. "Aging velvet." *Uncaptive Minds* 3 (Aug.–Sept.–Oct.): 33–35.

Welsh, Helga A. 1994. "Political transition processes in Central and Eastern Europe." *Comparative Politics* 26, no. 4: 379–94.

Weschler, Lawrence. 1989. "A Grand Experiment." *New Yorker* 65 (Nov. 13): 59–60.

Wheaton, Bernard, and Zdeněk Kavan. 1992. *The Velvet Revolution: Czechoslovakia, 1988–91*. Boulder, Colo.: Westview.

Whipple, Tim, ed. 1991. *After the Velvet Revolution: Václav Havel and the New Leaders of Czechoslovakia Speak Out*. New York: Freedom House.

Wickham-Crowley, Timothy P. 1991. *Exploring Revolution: Essays on Latin American Insurgency and Revolutionary Theory*. London: Sharpe.

Wierzbicki, Piotr. 1990. "Lech Walesa: The sphinx from Gdansk." *Uncaptive Minds* 3 (Nov.–Dec.): 27–31.

Wightman, Gordon. 1991. "Czechoslovakia." Pp. 53–69 in *New Political Parties in Eastern Europe and the Soviet Union*, Bogdan Szajkowski, ed. Harlow: Longman.

Wolchik, Sharon. 1991. *Czechoslovakia in Transition*. New York: Pinter.

World Bank. 1990. *Poland: Economic Management for a New Era.* Washington, D.C.: World Bank.

Wuthnow, Robert. 1989. *Communities of Discourse.* Cambridge: Harvard University Press.

Začek, Pavel. 1994. "Proč v listopadu padl komunistický režim? [Why did the communist regime fall in November 1989?]." *Lidové Noviny* (Nov. 18): 9.

Žák, Václav. 1995. "The velvet divorce—Institutional foundations." Pp. 245–68 in *The End of Czechoslovakia*, Jiří Musil, ed. Budapest: Central European University Press.

Zakaria, Fareed. 1997. "The rise of illiberal democracy." *Foreign Affairs* (Nov.–Dec.): 22–43.

Zdravomyslova, Elana. 1996. "Opportunities and framing in the transition to democracy: The case of Russia." Pp. 122–37 in *Comparative Perspectives on Social Movements: Political Opportunities, Mobilizing Structures and Cultural Framings*, Doug McAdam, John McCarthy, and Meyer Zald, eds. Cambridge: Cambridge University Press.

Zubek, Vojtek. 1996. "The phoenix out of the ashes: The rise to power of Poland's post-communist SdRP." *Communist and Post-Communist Studies* 28, no. 3: 275–306.

———. 1994. "The reassertion of the left in post-communist Poland." *Europe-Asia Studies* 46, no. 5: 801–37.

Zuo, Jiping, and Robert D. Benford. 1995. "Mobilization processes and the 1989 Chinese Democracy Movement." *Sociological Quarterly* 36, no. 1: 131–56.

Index

In this index an "f" after a number indicates a separate reference on the next page, and an "ff" indicates separate references on the next two pages. A continuous discussion over two or more pages is indicated by a span of page numbers, e.g., "57–59." *Passim* is used for a cluster of references in close but not consecutive sequence.